The Computer Science of TeX and LaTeX;
based on CS 594, fall 2004, University of Tennessee

Victor Eijkhout
Texas Advanced Computing Center
The University of Texas at Austin

2012

About this book.

These are the lecture notes of a course I taught in the fall of 2004. This was the first time I taught the course, and the first time this course was taught, period. It has also remained the *only* time the course was taught. These lecture notes, therefore, are probably full of inaccuracies, mild fibs, and gross errors. Ok, make that: are *definitely* full of at the least the first two categories, because I know of several errors that time has prevented me from addressing.

My lack of time being what it is, this unfinished book wil now remain as is. The reader is asked to enjoy it, but not to take it for gospel.

Victor Eijkhout
eijkhout@tacc.utexas.edu
Knoxville, TN, december 2004;
Austin, TX, january 2012.

copyright 2012 Victor Eijkhout
ISBN 978-1-105-41591-3

Enjoy!

4

Contents

	About this book 3
1	**TEX and LATEX** 9
	LATEX 10
1.1	Document markup 10
1.2	The absolute basics of LATEX 12
1.3	The TEX conceptual model of typesetting 15
1.4	Text elements 15
1.5	Tables and figures 25
1.6	Math 25
1.7	References 28
1.8	Some TEXnical issues 30
1.9	Customizing LATEX 30
1.10	Extensions to LATEX 34
	TEX programming 38
	TEX visuals 39
	Projects for this chapter 40
2	**Parsing** 41
	Parsing theory 42
2.1	Levels of parsing 42
2.2	Very short introduction 42
	Lexical analysis 45
2.3	Finite state automata and regular languages 45
2.4	Lexical analysis with FSAs 50
	Syntax parsing 52
2.5	Context-free languages 52
2.6	Parsing context-free languages 55
	Lex 67
2.7	Introduction 67
2.8	Structure of a *lex* file 67
2.9	Definitions section 68
2.10	Rules section 69
2.11	Regular expressions 71
2.12	Remarks 72
2.13	Examples 73
	Yacc 77
2.14	Introduction 77
2.15	Structure of a *yacc* file 77
2.16	Motivating example 77
2.17	Definitions section 79
2.18	Lex Yacc interaction 79
2.19	Rules section 81
2.20	Operators; precedence and associativity 82
2.21	Further remarks 83
2.22	Examples 86
	Hashing 93
2.23	Introduction 93
2.24	Hash functions 94
2.25	Collisions 97

2.26	*Other applications of hashing* 102			*Curve plotting with* `gnuplot` *170*
2.27	*Discussion* 103		4.4	*Introduction* 170
	Projects for this chapter 104		4.5	*Plotting* 170
				Raster graphics 172
3	**Breaking things into pieces** 105		4.6	*Vector graphics and raster graphics* 172
	Dynamic Programming 106		4.7	*Basic raster graphics* 172
3.1	*Some examples* 106		4.8	*Rasterizing type* 176
3.2	*Discussion* 114		4.9	*Anti-aliasing* 179
	TeX paragraph breaking 116			Projects for this chapter 183
3.3	*The elements of a paragraph* 116		5	**TeX's macro language – unfinished chapter** 185
3.4	*TeX's line breaking algorithm* 120			
	NP completeness 130			Lambda calculus in TeX 186
3.5	*Introduction* 130		5.1	*Logic with TeX* 186
3.6	*Basics* 132		6	**Character encoding** 199
3.7	*Complexity classes* 133			Input file encoding 200
3.8	*NP-completeness* 135		6.1	*History and context* 200
	Page breaking 138		6.2	*Unicode* 203
3.9	*Introduction* 138		6.3	*More about character sets and encodings* 207
3.10	*TeX's page breaking algorithm* 139			
3.11	*Theory of page breaking* 141		6.4	*Character issues in TeX / LaTeX* 210
	Projects for this chapter 150			Font encoding 212
4	**Fonts** 151		6.5	*Basic terminology* 212
	Bezier curves 152		6.6	*Æsthetics* 215
4.1	*Introduction to curve approximation* 152		6.7	*Font technologies* 216
4.2	*Parametric curves* 157		6.8	*Font handling in TeX and LaTeX* 218
4.3	*Practical use* 167			

	Input and output encoding in LaTeX *221*	7.2	*Knuth's philosophy of program development* *224*
6.9	*The* `fontenc` *package* *221*		Software engineering *225*
	Projects for this chapter *222*	7.3	*Extremely brief history of TeX* *225*
7	**Software engineering** *223*	7.4	*TeX's development* *225*
	Literate programming *224*		Markup *229*
7.1	*The Web system* *224*	7.5	*History* *229*
			Projects for this chapter *231*

TEX – LATEX – CS 594

Chapter 1

TeX and LaTeX

In this chapter we will learn

- The use of LaTeX for document preparation,
- LaTeX style file programming,
- TeX programming.

Handouts and further reading for this chapter

For LaTeX use the 'Not so short introduction to LaTeX' by Oetiker *et al.* For further reading and future reference, it is highly recommended that you get 'Guide to LaTeX' by Kopka and Daly [15]. The original reference is the book by Lamport [16]. While it is a fine book, it has not kept up with developments around LaTeX, such as contributed graphics and other packages. A book that does discuss extensions to LaTeX in great detail is the 'LaTeX Companion' by Mittelbach *et al.* [17].

For the TeX system itself, consult 'TeX by Topic'. The original reference is the book by Knuth [12], and the ultimate reference is the published source [11].

LaTeX.

1.1 Document markup

If you are used to 'wysiwyg' (what you see is what you get) text processors, LaTeX may seem like a strange beast, primitive, and probably out-dated. While it is true that there is a long history behind TeX and LaTeX, and the ideas are indeed based on much more primitive technology than what we have these days, these ideas have regained surprising validity in recent times.

1.1.1 A little bit of history

Document markup dates back to the earliest days of computer typesetting. In those days, terminals were strictly character-based: they could only render mono-spaced built-in fonts. Graphics terminals were very expensive. (Some terminals could switch to a graphical character set, to get at least a semblance of graphics.) As a result, compositors had to key in text on a terminal – or using punched cards in even earlier days – and only saw the result when it would come out of the printer.

Any control of the layout, therefore, also had to be through character sequences. To set text in bold face, you may have had to surround it with `<B>` .. the text .. `</B>`. Doesn't that look like something you still encounter every day?

Such 'control sequences' had a second use: they could serve a template function, expanding to often used bits of text. For instance, you could imagine `$ADAM$` expanding to 'From our correspondent in Amsterdam:'.

LaTeX works exactly the same. There are command control sequences; for instance, you get bold type by specifying `\bf`, et cetera. There are also control sequences that expand to bits of text: you have to type `\LaTeX` to get the characters 'LATEX' plus the control codes for all that shifting up and down and changes in font size.

```
\TeX => T\kern -.1667em\lower .5ex\hbox {E}\kern -.125emX
\LaTeX => L\kern -.36em {\sbox \z@ T\vbox to\ht \z@ {\hbox
   {\check@mathfonts \fontsize \sf@size \z@ \math@fontsfalse
     \selectfont A} \vss }}\kern -.15em\TeX
```

1.1.2 Macro packages

The old typesetting systems were limited in their control sequences: they had a fixed repertoire of commands related to typesetting, and there usually was some mechanism

1.1. DOCUMENT MARKUP

to defining 'macros' with replacement text. Formally, a macro is a piece of the input that gets replaced by its definition text, which can be a combination of literal text and more macros or typesetting commands.

> An important feature of many composition programs is the ability to designate by suitable input instructions the use of specified formats. Previously stored sequences of commands or text replace the instructions, and the expanded input is then processed. In more sophisticated systems, formats may summon other formats, including themselves ["System/360 Text Processor Pagination/360, Application Description Manual," Form No. GE20-0328, IBM Corp., White Plains, New York.].

That was the situation with commercial systems by manufacturers of typesetting equipment such as Linotype. Systems developed by (and for!) computer scientists, such Scribe or nroff/troff, were much more customizable. In fact, they sometimes would have the equivalent of a complete programming language on board. This makes it possible to take the basic language, and design a new language of commands on top of it. Such a repertoire of commands is called a macro package.

In our case, TeX is the basic package with the strange macro programming language, and LaTeX is the macro package[1]. LaTeX was designed for typesetting scientific articles and books: it offers a number of styles, each with slightly different commands (for instance, there are no chapters in the article style) and slightly different layout (books need a title page, articles merely a title on the first page of the text). Styles can also easily be customized. For different purposes (art books with fancy designs) it is often better to write new macros in TeX, rather than to bend the existing LaTeX styles.

However, if you use an existing LaTeX style, the whole of the underlying TeX programming language is still available, so many extensions to LaTeX have been written. The best place to find them is through CTAN `http://wwww.ctan.org/`.

> **Exercise 1.** Discuss the difference between a macro and a function or procedure in a normal programming language. In a procedural language, looping is implemented with `goto` instructions. How would you do that in a macro language? Is there a difference in efficiency?

---

[1]. In this tutorial I will say 'TeX' when a statement applies to the basic system, and 'LaTeX' if it *only* applies to the macro package.

1.1.3 Logical markup

Macro packages are initially motivated as a labour-saving device: a macro abbreviates a commonly used sequence of commands. However, they have another important use: a well designed macro package lets you use commands that indicate the structure of a document rather than the formatting. This means that you would write `\section{Introduction}` and not worry about the layout. The layout would be determined by a statement elsewhere as to what macros to load[2]. In fact, you could take the same input and format it two different ways. This is convenient in cases such as an article being reprinted as part of a collection, or a book being written before the final design is commissioned.

In a well written document, there will be few explicit typesetting commands. Almost all macros should be of the type that indicates the structure, and any typesetting is taken care of in the definition of these. Further control of the layout of the document should be done through global parameter settings in the preamble.

1.2 The absolute basics of LaTeX

Here is the absolute minimum you need to know to use LaTeX.

1.2.1 Different kinds of characters

A TeX input file mostly contains characters that you want to typeset. That is, TeX passes them on from input to output without any action other than placement on the page and font choice. Now, in your text there can be commands of different sorts. So TeX has to know how to recognize commands. It does that by making a number of characters special. In this section you will learn which characters have special meaning.

- Anything that starts with a backslash is a command or 'control sequence'. A control sequence consists of the backslash and the following sequence of letters – no digits, no underscores allowed either – or one single non-letter character.
- Spaces at the beginning and end of a line are ignored. Multiple spaces count as one space.
- Spaces are also ignored after control sequences, so writing `\LaTeX is fun` comes out as 'LaTeXis fun'. To force a space there, write `\LaTeX{} is fun`

---

2. Compare this to the use of CSS versus HTML in web pages.

1.2. THE ABSOLUTE BASICS OF LaTeX

or `\LaTeX\ is fun`. Spaces are *not* ignored after control symbols such as `\$`, but they are again after the 'control space' `\`␣[3].

- A single newline or return in the input file has no meaning, other than giving a space in the input. You can use newlines to improve legibility of the input. Two newlines (leading to one empty line) or more cause a paragraph to end. You can also attain this paragraph end by the `\par` command.
- Braces {,} are mostly used for delimiting the arguments of a control sequence. The other use is for grouping. Above you saw an example of the use of an empty group; similarly `\TeX{}ing is fun` comes out as 'TeXing is fun'.
- Letters, digits, and most punctuation can be typed normally. However, a bunch of characters mean something special to LaTeX: `%$&^_#~{}`. Here are their functions:

  `%` comment: anything to the end of line is ignored.

  `$,_,^` inline math (toggle), subscript, superscript. See section 1.6.

  `&` column separator in tables.

  `~` nonbreaking space. (This is called an 'active character')

  `{}` Macro arguments and grouping.

  In order to type these characters, you need to precede them with a backslash, for instance `\%` to get '%'. This is called a 'control symbol'. Exception: use `$\backslash$` to get '\'.
- Some letters do not exist in all styles. As the most commonly encountered example, angle brackets <> do not exist in the roman text font (note that they are in the typewriter style here, in roman you would get '¡¿'), so you need to write, somewhat laboriously `$\langle$S$\rangle$` to get '⟨S⟩'[4].

Exercise 2. You read in a document 'This happens only in 90rest of the time it works fine.' What happened here? There are articles in print where the word 'From' has an upside down question mark in front of it. Try to think of an explanation.

1.2.2 LaTeX document structure

Every LaTeX document has the following structure:

```
\documentclass[ <class options> ]{ <class name> }
    <preamble>
\begin{document}
    <text>
\end{document}
```

---

3. The funny bucket character here is how we visualize the space character.
4. That's what macros are good for.

Victor Eijkhout

Typical document classes are `article`, `report`, `book`, and `letter`. As you may expect, that last one has rather different commands from the others. The class options are optional; examples would be `a4paper`, `twoside`, or `11pt`.

The preamble is where additional packages get loaded, for instance

`\usepackage{times}`

switches the whole document to the Times Roman typeface. This is also the place to define new commands yourself (section 1.9.2).

1.2.2.1 Title

To list title and author, a document would start with

```
\title{My story}
\author{B.C. Dull}
\date{2004} %leave this line out to get today's date
\maketitle
```

After the title of an article and such, there is often an abstract. This can be specified with

```
\begin{abstract}
... The abstract text ...
\end{abstract}
```

The stretch of input from `\begin` to `\end` is called an 'environment'; see section 1.4.1.2.

1.2.2.2 Sectioning

The document text is usually segmented by calls

```
\section{This}
\subsection{That}
\subsection{The other}
\paragraph{one}
\subparagraph{two}
\chapter{Ho}
\part{Hum}
```

which all get numbered automatically. Chapters only exist in the `report` and `book` styles. Paragraphs and subparagraphs are not numbered. To prevent sections et cetera from being numbered, use `\section*{...}` and such[5].

---

5. This also makes the title not go into the table of contents. See section 1.7.2 on how to remedy that.

1.3. THE TEX CONCEPTUAL MODEL OF TYPESETTING

1.2.2.3 Frontmatter, backmatter

You can use commands `\frontmatter`, `\mainmatter`, `\backmatter` – in `book` class only – to switch page numbering from roman to arabic, and, for the back matter, section numbering from numbers to letters.

1.2.3 Running LaTeX

With the last two sections you should know enough to write a LaTeX document. Now how do you get to see the final output? This takes basically two steps: formatting and viewing.

You need to know that TEX's original output format is slightly unusual. It is called 'DVI' for DeVice Independent. There are viewers for this format, but usually you need another step to print it.

Traditionally, you would run an executable called `latex` (or `tex`), which gives you a `dvi` file, which you then view with a previewer such as `xtex` or `xdvi`. To print this file, you would use

```
dvips -Pcmz foo.dvi -o foo.ps
```

to generate a `ps` file. This can be printed, or converted to `pdf`.

There are version of the `latex` executable that output to other formats, for instance `pdflatex` (there is also a `pdftex`) goes straight to `pdf`, which you can view with the Adobe Acrobat Reader, or `xpdf`. The big advantage of this approach is that you can get hyperlinks in your pdf file; see section 1.10.3.

> **Exercise 3.** Set up a document that will have the answers to your homework exercises of the whole course.

1.3 The TEX conceptual model of typesetting

In TEX, the question 'on what page does this character appear' is hard to answer. That is because TEX typesets all material for a page, sort of on a long scroll, before cutting a page off that scroll. That means that when a piece of text is set, you do not know if it falls before or after a certain page break.

A similar story holds for paragraph breaking, but the question on what line something occurs is not usually interesting.

1.4 Text elements

Here are the main elements that make up a LaTeX document.

1.4.1 Large scale text structure

We already discussed sectioning commands in section 1.2.2.2. Here are more major text elements in a LaTeX document.

1.4.1.1 Input files

Use `\include{<file>}` to input a file beginning on a new page, and `\input` for just plain input. With

`\includeonly{file1,file2}`

you can save processing time – provided the files are `\included` to begin with.

The `.tex` extension can usually be left off; because of the way TeX works, be careful with funny characters in the file name.

On Unix installations, input files can be in other directories, specified by the `TEXINPUTS` environment variable.

1.4.1.2 Environments

If a certain section of text needs to be treated in a different way from the surrounding text, it can be segmented off by

```
\begin{<environment name>}
... text ...
\end{<environment name>}
```

An environment defines a group, so you can have local definitions and changes of parameters.

Some predefined environments are

flushleft (flushright) for text that is left (right) aligned, but not right (left).
center for text that is centered.
quote, quotation for text that needs to be set apart, by indenting both margins. The `quote` environment is for single paragraphs, the `quotation` for multiple.
abstract for the abstract that starts an article, report, or book. In the report and book style it is set on a separate page. In the article style it is set in a smaller type size, and with indented margins.
verbatim see section 1.4.1.3.

1.4. TEXT ELEMENTS

1.4.1.3 Verbatim text

As we have observed already, TeX has a number of special characters, which can be printed by prefixing them with a backslash, but that is a hassle. Good thing that there is a mechanism for printing input completely verbatim. For inline text, use `\verb+&###\text+` to get '`&###\text`'. The essential command here is `\verb`. Unlike with other commands that have arguments, the argument is not delimited by braces, but by two occurrences of a character that does not appear in the verbatim text. A plus sign is a popular choice. The `\verb*` variant makes spaces visible: `\verb*+{ }+` gives '`{␣}`'.

For longer verbatim text there is a `verbatim` environment. The `verbatim*` version prints each space as a ␣ symbol. To input whole files verbatim, use `\verbatiminput{file}`, which is defined in the `verbatim` package.

For TeXnical reasons, verbatim text can not appear in some locations such as footnotes or command definitions.

> **Exercise 4.** Why does the `\verb` command not have its argument in braces?

1.4.1.4 Lists

Lists in LaTeX are a special case of an environment; they are specified by

```
\begin{<list type>}
\item ...
\item ...
\end{<list type>}
```

The three main list types are unnumbered lists, `itemize`, numbered lists, `enumerate`, and definition or description lists, `description`.

In the case of a description list, it is mandatory to give the item label:

```
\begin{description}
\item[Do] A deer, a female deer.
\item[Re] A drop of golden sun.
...
\end{description}
```

You can give item labels in the other list types too.

Putting a list inside a list item will change the style of the item labels and numbers in a way that is dictated by the document class.

You can put a `\label` command after an item to be able to refer to the item number.

```
\begin{enumerate}
\item\label{first:item} One
\item Two comes after \ref{first:item}
\end{enumerate}
```
Output:

    1. One

    2. Two comes after 1

This only makes sense with enumerate environments.

1.4.1.5 Tabbing

The `tabbing` environment is useful for setting pieces of text, such as source code, that use a small number of 'tab stops'. Tab stops (a term deriving from old mechanical typewriters) are locations on the line that one can 'tab to', no matter how much material is currently on the line.

Example:

```
\begin{tabbing}
The first line sets this: \=point;\\
the second jumps\>there
\end{tabbing}
```

Output:

    The first line sets this: point;

    the second jumps   there

The `\=` command in the first line defines a tab stop; in every subsequent line a `\>` command will jump to that position, if it has not been reached yet. There can be multiple tab stops, not necessarily defined in the same line, and tab stops can be redefined.

A more interesting case is where the tab stop is used before the line that defines it. For this case there is the `\kill` command, which prevents a line from being displayed. Example:

```
\begin{tabbing}
while \=\kill
do\>\{\\
\>$i_1\leftarrow{}$\=1\\
\>$\ldots$\>2\\
\>\}\\
while (1)
\end{tabbing}
```

1.4. TEXT ELEMENTS 19

Output:

$$
\begin{array}{ll}
\text{do} & \{ \\
& i_1 \leftarrow 1 \\
& \ldots \quad 2 \\
& \} \\
\text{while } (1) &
\end{array}
$$

1.4.1.6 Tabular material

The `tabular` environment generates a table. Tables are often placed independently of the text, at the top or bottom of the page; see section 1.5 for details. The table itself is generated by

```
\begin{tabular}{<alignment>}
... material ...
\end{tabular}
```

Each line of the table has items separated by characters, and \\ at the end of each line but the last.

In its simplest form, the alignment directions are a combination of the letters l, r, c:

```
\begin{tabular}{rl}
"Philly" Joe & Jones\\ Dizzie & Gillespie\\ Art&Tatum
\end{tabular}
```

Output:

$$
\begin{array}{rl}
\text{"Philly" Joe} & \text{Jones} \\
\text{Dizzie} & \text{Gillespie} \\
\text{Art} & \text{Tatum}
\end{array}
$$

Vertical rules are inserted by placing a | character in the alignment specification; horizontal lines you get from \hline.

```
\begin{tabular}{|r|rl|}
\hline
instrument&name&\\ \hline
drums: &"Philly" Joe & Jones\\
trumpet:& Dizzie & Gillespie\\
piano: &Art&Tatum\\ \hline
\end{tabular}
```

Output:

Victor Eijkhout

instrument	name	
drums:	"Philly" Joe	Jones
trumpet:	Dizzie	Gillespie
piano:	Art	Tatum

Some more tricks:

- In headings you often want to span one item over several columns. Use
  ```
  \begin{tabular}{|r|rl|}
  \hline
  instrument&\multicolumn{2}{|c|}{name}\\ \hline
  drums: &"Philly" Joe & Jones\\
  trumpet:& Dizzie & Gillespie\\
  piano: &Art&Tatum\\ \hline
  \end{tabular}
  ```
  Output:

instrument	name	
drums:	"Philly" Joe	Jones
trumpet:	Dizzie	Gillespie
piano:	Art	Tatum

- LaTeX inserts a standard amount of space between columns. You can override this with `@{<stuff>}`:
  ```
  \begin{tabular}{r@{.}l}
  2&75\\ 800&1
  \end{tabular}
  ```
  gives
  2.75
  800.1

- A column specification of `p{<size>}` (where `<size>` is something like `5.08cm` or `2in`) makes the items in that column formatted as paragraphs with the width as specified.

1.4.1.7 Footnotes

Use the command `\footnote`. The numbering style is determined by the document class. The kinds of footnote to denote affiliation of the author of a paper and such (these often use asterisk symbols and such, even if footnotes are numbered in the rest of the document) are given by the command `\thanks`.

There are two common cases where want more detailed control over footnotes:

- You want to dictate the label yourself, for instance using the same label again (this often happens with author affiliations)
- You want to place a footnote in a table or such; LaTeX has trouble with that.

1.4. TEXT ELEMENTS 21

In such cases you can use `\footnotemark` to place the marker, and `\footnotetext` for the text. You can also set or change the `footnote` counter explicitly with counter functions (section 1.9.4), or use

`\footnote[<label>]{<text>}`

where the label is used instead, and the counter is not increased.

1.4.1.8 Text boxes

Sometimes you want a small amount of text to behave like one or more paragraphs, except not as part of the main page. The main commands for that are

`\parbox[pos]{width}{text}`
`\begin{minipage}[pos]{width}   text   \end{minipage}`

The optional `pos` parameter specifies whether the top (`t`) or bottom (`b`) line of the box should align with surrounding text: top-aligned box of text:

`Chapter 1. \parbox[t]{2in}{\slshape Introduction. First easy lessons. Exercises. More about things to come. Conclusions}`

Output:

> Chapter 1. *Introduction. First easy lessons.*
> *Exercises. More about things to*
> *come. Conclusions*

The default is a vertically centered position.

The `minipage` environment is meant for longer pieces of text; it can also handle other environments in the text.

The `\mbox` command is for text (or other objects) that need to stay on one line.

1.4.2 Minor text issues

1.4.2.1 Text styles

You can switch between roman (the style for this text), *italic* (also called 'cursive'), *slanted* (in some typefaces, italic and slanted may be identical), and **bold** with the commands `\texrm`, `\textit`, `\textsl`, and `\textbf` respectively, used as

`Text is stated \textbf{boldly} or \textsl{with a slant}.`

These combinations are not independent: nesting the commands can give you **bold *slanted*** text.

The above commands are mostly for short bits of text. See section 1.4.2.2 for commands to change font parameters in a more global manner.

Victor Eijkhout

If you are using italics for emphasis, consider using `\emph` instead, which works better, especially if you emphasize something in text that is already italic.

1.4.2.2 Fonts and typefaces

You already saw commands such as `\textrm` and `\textit` for switching from one type style to another. These commands hide a more complicated reality: LaTeX handles its fonts as combination of three parameters. These individual switches can be used inside a group, or as an environment:

```
{\ttfamily This is typewriter text}
\begin{mdseries}
  This text is set in medium weight.
\end{mdseries}
```

Here are the categories and possible values.

family roman, sans serif, typewriter type: `\rmfamily`, `\sffamily`, `\ttfamily`.
series medium and bold: `\mdseries`, `\bfseries`.
shape upright, italic, slanted, and small caps: `\upshape`, `\itshape`, `\slshape`, `\scshape`.

1.4.2.3 Comments

Anything from `%` to the end of line is ignored. For multiline comments, load either

`\usepackage{comment}`

or

`\usepackage{verbatim}`

and in both cases surround text with

```
\begin{comment}
to be ignored
\end{comment}
```

where the closing line *has to be* on a line of its own.

1.4.2.4 Hyphenation

Sometimes TeX has a hard time finding a breakpoint in a word. When you are fixing the final layout of a document, you can help it with `helico\-pter`. If TeX consistently breaks your name wrong, do

`\hyphenation{Eijk-hout}`

1.4. TEXT ELEMENTS

in the preamble.

This is not the mechanism for telling TeX about a new language; see section 1.10.5.

To keep text together, write `\mbox{do not break}`. You could also write this with a non-breaking space as `do~not~break`. (See also section 1.4.2.5.) It is a good idea to write

```
A~note on...
increase by~$1$.
```

to prevent single characters at the beginning of a line (first example), or the end of a line (second example). The second example could even give a line with a single character on it if it were to occur at the end of a paragraph.

1.4.2.5 Tilde

The tilde character has special meaning as a nonbreaking space; see section 1.4.2.4. To get a tilde accent, use `\~`. To get a literal tilde, do `\~{}`, `$\sim$`, or `\char`\~`. If you need a tilde in URLs, consider using the `url` or `hyperref` package; see section 1.10.3.

1.4.2.6 Accents

In basic TeX, accents are formed by putting a control symbol of that accent in front of the letter:

```
Sch\"on b\^et\'e
```

for 'Schön bête'. If you have an occasional foreign word in English text this works fine. However, if your terminal allows you to input accented characters, you can use them in LaTeX with the `inputenc` package.

Standard TeX (or LaTeX) does not understand Unicode encodings such as UTF-8.

1.4.2.7 Line/page breaking

In general, you should leave line and page breaking to TeX, at most adjusting parameters. However, should you really need it, you can use the commands `\linebreak[<num>]` and `\pagebreak[<num>]`, where the number is 1, 2, 3, 4, with 4 the highest urgency. There is also `\nolinebreak` and `\nopagebreak` with a similar urgency parameter.

In this last paragraph there was a \linebreak after 'need it'. You notice that TEX still tried to fill out to the right margin, with ugly consequences. After 'highest' there was a \newline, which really breaks then and there. Similarly, there is \newpage.

There is also \nolinebreak and \nopagebreak, both with optional numerical parameter, to discourage breaking.

1.4.2.8 Manual spacing

Most of the time you should leave spacing decisions to LaTeX, but for custom designs it is good to know the commands.

```
\hspace{1cm} \hspace*{1in} \hspace{\fill}
\vspace{1cm} \vspace*{1in} \vspace{\fill}
```

- The *-variants give space that does not disappear at the beginning or end of a line (for horizontal) or page (vertical).
- A space of size \fill is infinite: this means it will stretch to take up however much space is needed to the end of the line or page.

1.4.2.9 Drawing lines

Let us get one thing out of the way: underlining is a typewriter way of emphasizing text. It looks bad in typeset text, and using italics or slanted text is a much better way. Use \emph.

Lines can be used a typographical decorations, for instance drawn between the regular text and the footnotes on a page, or as part of chapter headings. The command is

```
\rule[lift]{width}{height}
```

Example

```
1\ \rule{2cm}{\fboxrule}\ The title
```

Output:

      1 ⎯⎯⎯⎯⎯⎯⎯⎯ The title

You can draw a whole box around text: \fbox{text} gives ⎕text⎕. The thickness of the line is \fboxrule.

1.4.2.10 Horizontal and vertical mode

TEX is in horizontal or vertical mode while it is processing[6]. In horizontal mode, elements – typically letters – are aligned next to each other; in vertical mode elements

---

6. The story is actually more complicated; for the whole truth see the notes about TEX.

are stacked on top of one another. Most of the time you do not have to worry about that. When TeX sees text, it switches to horizontal mode, and LaTeX environments will briefly switch to vertical mode so that they start on a new line.

In certain cases you want to force vertical mode; for that you can use `\par`. You can force things into a line with `\mbox` (section 1.4.1.8). In rare cases, `\leavevmode`.

1.5 Tables and figures

Tables and figures are objects that typically do not appear in the middle of the text. At the very least they induce a paragraph break, and often they are placed at the top or bottom of a page. Also, some publishers' styles demand that a document have a list of tables and a list of figures. LaTeX deals with this by having environments

```
\begin{<table or figure>}[placement]
... table or figure material ...
\caption{Caption text}\label{tabfig:label}
\end{<table or figure>}
```

In this,

- The 'placement' specifier is a combination of the letters `htbp` for 'here', 'top', 'bottom', and 'page', telling LaTeX where to place the material, if possible. Suppose a placement of `[ht]` is given, then the material is placed 'right here', unless there is not enough space on the page, in which case it will be placed on top of the page (this one or the next).
- Table material is given by a `tabular` environment; see section 1.4.1.6.
- Figure material needs some extra mechanism, typically provided by another package; see section 1.10.4.
- The caption goes into the list of tables/figures.
- The label will refer to the number, which is automatically generated.

The list of tables/figures is generated by the command `\listoftables` or `\listoffigures`.

1.6 Math

TeX was designed by a computer scientist to typeset some books with lots of mathematics. As a result, TeX, and with it LaTeX's, math capabilities are far better than those of other typesetters.

Victor Eijkhout

1.6.1 Math mode

You can not just write formulas in the middle of the text. You have to surround them with `$<formula>$` or `\(<stuff>\)` for inline formulas, or

```
\begin{displaymath} ... \end{displaymath}
\[ ... \]
```

for unnumbered and

```
\begin{equation} ... \end{equation}
```

for numbered displayed equations respectively. You can refer to an equation number by including a `\label` statement.

In math mode, all sorts of rules for text typesetting are changed. For instance, all letters are considered variables, and set italic: `$a$` gives 'a'. Roman text is either for names of functions, for which there are control sequences – `\sin(x)` gives '$\sin(x)$' – or for connecting text, which has to be marked as such:

```
\forall x \in \mathbf{R}
\quad \mathrm{(sufficiently large)} \quad: \qquad x>5
```

Output:
$$\forall x \in \mathbf{R} \quad (\text{sufficientlylarge}) \quad : \quad x > 5 \qquad (1.1)$$

A formula is limited to one line; if you want to break it, or if you need several formulas vertically after one another, you have to do it yourself. The `eqnarray` environment is useful here. It acts as a three-column alignment.

```
\begin{eqnarray}
\sin x&=&x-\frac{x^3}{3!}+\frac{x^5}{5!}- \nonumber \\
      &&{}-\frac{x^7}{7!}+\cdots
\end{eqnarray}
```

Output:

$$\sin x \;=\; x - \frac{x^3}{3!} + \frac{x^5}{5!} -$$
$$- \frac{x^7}{7!} + \cdots \qquad (1.2)$$

Note the use of `\nonumber` here; with the `eqnarray*` all lines would be unnumbered by default.

In AMS LaTeX there is an `align` environment which looks better than `eqnarray`.

1.6. MATH

1.6.2 Super and subscripts

In math mode, the character ^ denotes a superscript, and _ denotes a subscript: x_i^2 is x_i^2. (Outside of math mode these characters give an error.) Sub and superscripts of more than one character have to be grouped.

1.6.3 Grouping

Grouping, in math mode as outside, is done with braces: x_{i-1}^{n^2} looks like $x_{i-1}^{n^2}$.

1.6.4 Display math vs inline

Math looks different when used inline in a paragraph from that used as display math. This is mostly clear for operators with 'limits':

$$\text{text mode:} \sum_{i=1}^{\infty} \quad \text{displaymode}: \sum_{i=1}^{\infty}$$

1.6.5 Delimiters, matrices

Delimiters are () [] \{ \}. You can prefix them with \big, \Big and such, but TeX can resize them automatically:

```
\left( \frac{1}{1-x^2} \right)
\left\{ \begin{array}{ccc}
    \mathrm{(a)}&\Rightarrow&x>0\\
    \mathrm{(b)}&\Rightarrow&x=0\\
    \mathrm{(c)}&\Rightarrow&x<0
        \end{array} \right.
```

Output:

$$\left(\frac{1}{1-x^2} \right) \left\{ \begin{array}{ccc} (a) & \Rightarrow & x > 0 \\ (b) & \Rightarrow & x = 0 \\ (c) & \Rightarrow & x < 0 \end{array} \right. \quad (1.3)$$

Note that with \right. you get a omitted right delimiter.

In the above example you also saw the `array` environment, which can be used for anything tabular in math mode, in particular matrices. Here is a good example of a matrix. Note the different kinds of dots:

```
A = \left( \begin{array}{cccccc}
    a_{11}&0&&\ldots&0&a_{1n}\\
```

Victor Eijkhout

```
            &a_{22}&0&\ldots&0&a_{2n}\\
            &&\ddots&\ddots&\vdots&\vdots\\
            &&&a_{n-2n-2}&0&a_{n-2n}\\
            &\emptyset&&&a_{n-1n-1}&a_{n-1n}\\
            &&&&&a_{nn}
\end{array} \right)
```

Output:

$$A = \left(\begin{array}{cccccc} a_{11} & 0 & & \ldots & 0 & a_{1n} \\ & a_{22} & 0 & \ldots & 0 & a_{2n} \\ & & \ddots & \ddots & \vdots & \vdots \\ & & & a_{n-2n-2} & 0 & a_{n-2n} \\ & \emptyset & & & a_{n-1n-1} & a_{n-1n} \\ & & & & & a_{nn} \end{array} \right) \quad (1.4)$$

1.6.6 There is more

See a good book for the whole repertoire of symbols. If what LaTeX has is not enough, you can also get AMS LaTeX, which has even more fonts and tricky constructs.

1.7 References

1.7.1 Referring to document parts

One of the hard things in traditional typesetting is to keep references such as 'see also section 3' in sync with the text. This is very easy in LaTeX. You write

`\section{Results}\label{section:results}`

after which you can use this as

```
see also section~\ref{section:results}
on page~\pageref{section:results}.
```

The `\label` command can appear after headings, or in general every time some counter has been increased, whether that's a section heading or a formula number.

LaTeX implements this trick by writing the information to an auxiliary file – it has extension `.aux` – and reading it in next run. This means that a LaTeX document usually has to be typeset twice for all references to be both defined and correct. You get a reminder after the first run if a second one is needed, or if there are missing or duplicately defined labels.

1.7. REFERENCES

Exercise 5. A document with references usually takes two passes to get right. Explain why a table of contents can increase this number to three.

1.7.2 Table of contents

Something that typically goes into the front or back matter is the table of contents. This gets inserted automatically by the command `\tableofcontents`. No other actions required. You can add your own material to the contents with `\addcontentsline` or `\addtocontents`.

1.7.3 Bibliography references

Another kind of the reference is that to external bibliographies. This needs a bit more work.

- You write `\cite{Knuth:1978}` where you want the citation.
- At the end of your document you write
  `\bibliographystyle{plain}`
  `\bibliography{cs}`
  to get the bibliography included.
- The bibliography references have to be defined in a file `cs.bib`.
- After running LaTeX once, you need to invoke `bibtex <yourfile>`, which creates another auxiliary file, this time with `.bbl` extension, and run LaTeX once or twice more.

The bibliography files have a syntax of their own, but you can figure that out from looking at some examples.

1.7.4 Index

Finally, a document can have an index. For this you need to have a statement `\usepackage{makeidx}` in the preamble, `\printindex` wherever you want the index, and commands `\index{<some term>}` throughout your document. Additionally, as with `bibtex`, you need to run the program `makeindex` to generate the external `.ind` file.

Further indexing commands: `\index{name!sub}` for subentry; `\index{foo@\textit{foo}}` for sorting under 'foo' but formatted differently.

Victor Eijkhout

1.8 Some TeXnical issues

1.8.1 Commands inside other commands

For deep technical reasons you can get completely incomprehensible error messages by writing things like

`\section{My first section \footnote{and not my last}}`

Remedy that by writing

`\section{My first section \protect\footnote{and not my last}}`

1.8.2 Grouping

Most modern programming languages have a block structure of some sort, where variables can be declared inside a block, and are no longer known after the block ends. TeX has a stronger mechanism, where assignments to a variable made inside a block are reverted at the end of that block.

In LaTeX you notice that only `\newcommand` and `\newenvironment` declarations are local; `\newcounters` are global, as are `\setcounter` assignments. However, `\savebox` assignments are local.

1.9 Customizing LaTeX

LaTeX offers a number of tools (on top of the possibility of doing straight TeX programming) for customizing your document. The easiest customization is to change already defined parameters. However, you can also define new commands and environments of your own.

In fact, several of the customization we will see in this section are not part of standard LaTeX, but have been written by other users. If they do not come with your installation, you can download them from the Central TeX Archive Network; see section 1.10.1.

1.9.1 Page layout

1.9.1.1 Layout parameters

Page layout is controlled by parameters such as `\textheight`, `\textwidth`, `\topmargin` (distance to the running head, not to the first text line), and `\odd/evensidemargin` (distance to the 'spine' of the document). These are set with commands like

```
\setlength{\textwidth}{10in}
\addtolength{\oddsidemargin}{-1cm}
```

1.9. CUSTOMIZING LATEX

Some lengths are 'rubber length'
`\setlength{\parskip}{10pt plus 3pt minus 2pp}`

1.9.1.2 Page styles

Use the commands
`\pagestyle{<style>}`
and
`\thispagestyle{<style>}`
to change the style of all pages or one page. Available styles are `empty` (no page numbers), `plain` (the default), and `headings` (page numbers and running headers). See also section 1.10.2 for many more options.

For two-sided printing, use the `twoside` option for the document class.

> **Exercise 6.** Take a look at the headers and footers in Oetiker's 'Not so short introduction' and 'TEX by Topic' (the LATEX and TEX part of the handout). Can you find a reason to prefer one over the other from a point of usability? In both books, what is the rationale behind the header on the odd pages? See in particular page 35 of the former and 77 of the latter. Do you agree with this design?

1.9.1.3 Running page headers

The `headings` page style (section 1.9.1.2) uses running heads that can change through the document. For instance it would have chapter titles in the left page head and section titles in the right head. You can achieve this effect yourself by using the `myheadings` page style, and using the
`\markright{<right head>}`
`\markboth{<left>}{<right>}`
You have access to these texts as `\rightmark` and `\leftmark`; this is needed in the `fancyhdr` style.

1.9.1.4 Multicolumn text

Load
`\usepackage{multicol}`
and write
`\begin{multicol}{3}`
`text in three column mode`
`\end{multicol}`

Victor Eijkhout

1.9.2 New commands

You can define your own commands in LaTeX. As example of a a simple command, consider an often used piece of text

`\newcommand{\IncrByOne}{increased by~$1$}`

The replacement text can have parameters:

`\newcommand{\IncrDecrBy}[2]{#1creased by~$#2$}`

In this definition, the number of arguments is listed after the command name: `[2]`, and occurrences of the arguments in the replacement text are indicated by `#1`, `#2` etc. Example calls: `\IncrDecrBy{in}{5}`, `\IncrDecrBy{de}{2}`.

The declaration of a new command can specify an optional argument. If we define

`\newcommand{\IncrDecrBy}[2][in]{#1creased by~$#2$}`

the `[in]` specification means that the first argument is optional (only the first argument can ever be optional) with a default value of `in`. Example calls:

`\newcommand{\IncrDecrBy}[2][in]{#1creased by~$#2$}`
`\IncrDecrBy[de]{1}, \IncrDecrBy{5}.`

Output:

> decreased by 1, increased by 5.

To redefine an existing command, use `\renewcommand`.

1.9.3 New environments

It is possible to define environments, by specifying the commands to be used at their start and end:

```
\newenvironment{example}%
  {\begin{quote}\textbf{Example.}}%
  {\end{quote}}
```

which, used as `\begin{example}...\end{example}` gives a `quote` environment that starts with the word 'Example' in bold face. While defining that environment does not save a lot of typing, it is a good idea nevertheless from a point of view of logical markup. Using the example environment throughout ensures a uniform layout, and makes design changes easy if you ever change your mind.

Special case: defining mathematical statements with

```
\newtheorem{majorfact}{Theorem}
\newtheorem{minorfact}[majorfact]{Lemma}
\begin{minorfact}Small fact\end{minorfact}
\begin{majorfact}Big fact\end{majorfact}
```

giving

Lemma 1 *Small fact*

Theorem 2 *Big fact*

The optional argument in the definition of `lemma` makes it use the `theorem` counter.

Exercise 7. Why does this not work:
```
\newenvironment{examplecode}%
  {\textbf{Example code.}\begin{verbatim}}{\end{verbatimm}}
```

Exercise 8. Write macros for homework typesetting; make one master document that will contain all your homework throughout this course.

1. Define an environment `exercise` so that
   ```
   \begin{exercise}
   My answer is...
   \end{exercise}
   ```
   gives

   > **Problem 5.** My answer is...

   The counter should be incremented automatically. List your solution in your answer, and find a way that the listing is guaranteed to be the code you actually use.

2. Write a macro `\Homework` that will go to a new page, and output

   > **Answers to the exercises for chapter 3**

   at the top of the page. The `exercise` environment should now take the question as argument:
   ```
   \begin{exercise}{Here you paraphrase the question that was asked}
   My answer is...
   \end{exercise}
   ```
   and this outputs

   > **Problem 1.8** *Here you paraphrase the question that was asked*
   >   My answer is...

   (Hint: read the section on text boxes. Also be sure to use `\par` to get LaTeX to go to a new line.) Allow for the question to be more than one line long. Unfortunately you can not get verbatim text in the question. Find a way around that.

Victor Eijkhout

1.9.4 Counters

LaTeX has a number of counters defined, for sections and such. You can define your own counters too. Here are the main commands:

create A new counter is created with
>`\newcounter{<name>}[<other counter>]`
>where the name does *not* have a backslash. The optional `other counter` indicates a counter (such as `chapter`) that resets the new counter every time it is increased. (To do this reset for an already existing counter, check out the `chngcntr` package.)

change values A counter can be explicitly set or changed as
>`\setcounter{<name>}{<value>}`
>`\addtocounter{<name>}{<value>}`
>The command `\refstepcounter` also make the new value the target for a `\label` command.

use To get a counter value numerically, use `\value`. To print the value, use
>`\arabic{<name>}`, `\roman{<name>}`, `\Roman{<name>}`
>et cetera.

1.9.5 Lengths

Parameters such as `\textwidth` (section 1.9.1.1) are called 'lengths'. You can define your own with

`\newlength{\mylength}`
`\setlength{\mylength}{5in}`

These lengths can be used in horizontal or vertical space commands (section 1.4.2.8) for your own designs.

1.9.6 The syntax of `\new...` commands

Have you noticed by now that the name you define starts with a backslash in `\newcommand` and `\newlength`, but not in `\newenvironment` or `\newcounter`? Confusing.

1.10 Extensions to LaTeX

LaTeX may be a package on top of TeX, but that doesn't mean that the programming power of TeX is no longer available. Thus, many people have written small or large extensions to be loaded in addition to LaTeX. We will discuss a couple of popular ones here, but first we'll see how you can find them.

1.10. EXTENSIONS TO LaTeX

1.10.1 How to find a package, how to use it

Packages are typically loaded in the file preamble with

`\usepackage{pack1,pack2,...}`

(These course notes load about a dozen packages.)

Many popular packages are already part of the standard LaTeX distribution, but you will have to search to find where they are stored on your computer. Make a document that uses a common package, say `fancyhdr`, and see in the log output on the screen or in the log file where the file is loaded from. A typical location is `/usr/share/texmf/....` With a bit of searching you can also find[7] the documentation, which can be a `dvi`, `ps`, or `pdf` file.

If you have heard of a package and it is not on your system, go to the 'Comprehensive TeX Archive Network' (CTAN for short) and download it from there: `http://www.ctan.org/`.

1.10.2 Fancy page headers and footers

The `fancyhdr`[8] package provides customized headers and footers. The simple interface is

`\lhead{<text>}   \chead{<text>}   \rhead{<text>}`

for specifying text to get left, center, and right in the header. Likewise `\lfoot` and such for the footer.

This is assuming that all pages are the same. If you format for two-sided printing (section 1.9.1.2), you can specify different text for odd and even pages:

`\fancyhead[LE,RO]{<text>}`

for text that is Left on Even and Right on Odd pages. Typically, you specify text for `[LE,RO]` and `[RE,LO]`, for instance

`\fancyhead[EL,OR]{\textsl{\rightmark}}`

(see section 1.9.1.3).

1.10.3 Pdf file generation

Making beautiful pdf documents, complete with hyperlinks and table of contents, from your LaTeX files is simplicity itself. Insert

---

7. For instance using the Unix command '`find`'.
8. This supersedes the `fancyheadings` package.

Victor Eijkhout

`\usepackage[pdftex]{hyperref}`

in the preamble, and format with `pdflatex`. That's it. Do see section 1.10.4.2 about including pictures.

1.10.4 Graphics

Because of TeX's ancient origins – and its desire to be machine-independent – graphics is not standard, and frankly a bit of a hassle. The basic TeX system knows nothing about graphics, it just keeps some space open. An extension mechanism ('specials') then puts information in the output file that the printer driver can use to place graphics. With `pdflatex` this situation has become a bit less messy: now any graphics go straight into the pdf output file.

1.10.4.1 The `picture` environment

There is a way to generate graphics from inside LaTeX, using some graphics fonts rather than a full drawing mode. While primitive and limited, the `picture` environment has two advantages:

- It is easier to get the fonts for labels to be the same as the text font.
- Since it involves explicit drawing instructions, you can automatically draw bar charts and such.

1.10.4.2 Including external graphics

Most of the time, you will have graphics to include that come from some drawing package. Using the `graphicx` package, you write

`\includegraphics[key=value,...]{<file name>}`

where the file name can refer to any format, but if you use pdflatex, Postscript can not be used; if your picture is in Postscript, you can convert it with `ps2pdf`.

Commands such as `\includegraphics`, as well as similar commands in other packages, leave space in your document for the graphic. Now you have to be careful: you can not leave space for a 3 inch picture, an inch from the bottom of the page. Here are two approaches for placing a picture:

- Just place it where you want it, and if it falls on a page break, deal with it later by moving it.
- Put the figure in a floating figure object (section 1.5) and let LaTeX sort out the placement.

You can also have text wrap around a figure, by using the `wrapfig` package.

There is a package `color` for colour output.

1.10.5 Other languages than English

The fact that TeX and LaTeX were written by Americans becomes obvious in a couple of places.

- Various typographical conventions are geared towards American English.
- Words like 'Chapter' are the default in the style files[9].

To address this and make LaTeX easier to use with other languages, there is a package `babel`.

---

9. They used to be hard-wired, so the situation is improved.

TEX programming. No separate handout for this chapter; see the book 'TEX by Topic'.

Exercise 9. Write a macro \intt ('in typewriter type') such that \intt{foo} and \intt{foo_bar} are output as foo and foo_bar, in typewriter type.

Exercise 10. Write a macro that constructs another macro: \tees\three3 should be equivalent to \def\three{TTT}, \tees\five5 equivalent to \def\five{TTTTT} et cetera. In other words, the first argument of \tees is the name of the macro you are defining, the second is the number of letters 'T' the defined macro expands to. To make sure that your solution really expands to that string of 'T's, and not some code that generates it when the macro is called, do \show\five and check the screen output.

Exercise 11. TEX natively has addition, multiplication, and division arithmetic. Write a square root routine in TEX. Hint: Use Newton's method.

Exercise 12. Make this work:
```
\def\LeftDelim{(}\def\RightDelim{)}
\DefineWithDelims{foo}{My argument is '#1'.}
\def\LeftDelim{<}\def\RightDelim{>}
\DefineWithDelims{bar}{But my argument is '#1'.}
\foo(one)\par
\bar<two>
```
Output:

   My argument is 'one'.

   But my argument is 'two'.

In other words, \DefineWithDelims defines a macro – in this case \foo – and this macro has one argument, delimited by custom delimiters. The delimiters can be specified for each macro separately.

Hint: \DefineWithDelims is actually a macro with only one argument. Consider this code snippet:
```
\Define{foo}{ ... #1 ...}
\def\Define#1{
   \expandafter\def\csname #1\endcsname##1}
```

1.10. EXTENSIONS TO LaTeX

TeX visuals.

Exercise 13. Use the `\everypar` command so that the first paragraph after a heading (define your own heading command) will have a bullet ($\bullet$) in the left margin.

Exercise 14. Set TeX up so that every paragraph starts in mediaeval 'initial' style: the first letter of the paragraph is set in a large type size, and takes the first two or three lines. Use the following auxiliary macro:
```
\def\Hang#1{\hbox to 0pt
              {\raise 1.2ex \vbox to 0pt
                 {\hbox{#1}\vss}\hss}}
% small test:
A \Hang{$\bullet$} B \Hang{\Huge B} C. \bigskip
```
Output:

A •B B

Also, set `\parindent=0pt`. The result should look like this. Input:
```
This is an old-fashioned mediaeval paragraph that has lots
of text and...

Also, the second paragraph is an old-fashioned mediaeval
paragraph that...
```
with output:

T his is an old-fashioned mediaeval paragraph that has lots of text and a very long first sentence. The second sentence is also long, and only serves the purpose to make this more than 2 or so lines long. For good measure we throw in a third line which should make this four lines long, if not five with a little luck.

A lso, the second paragraph is an old-fashioned mediaeval paragraph that has lots of text and a very long first sentence. The second sentence is also long, and only serves the purpose to make this more than 2 or so lines long. For good measure we throw in a third line which should make this four lines long, if not five with a little luck.

Victor Eijkhout

Projects for this chapter.

Project 1.1. TeX has a syntax that can to a large extent be altered, dynamically or statically. This has had the effect that macro packages typically use a syntax that is somewhere between ad hoc and plain unsystematic. Explore how it would be possible to set up a macro package with object-oriented syntax and design. It would probably be a good idea to read [3, 4, 5], and to look at macro package such as Lollipop and ConTeXt.

Project 1.2. The web site `http://wwww.cookingforengineers.com` uses a table-like layout for notating recipes. Design an easy syntax for inputting these diagrams, and write a LaTeX package that implements them.

Chapter 2

Parsing

The programming language part of TeX is rather unusual. In this chapter we will learn the basics of language theory and parsing, and apply this to parsing TeX and LaTeX. Although TeX can not be treated like other programming languages, it is interesting to see how far we can get with existing tools.

Handouts and further reading for this chapter

The theory of languages and automata is discussed in any number of books, such as the Hopcroft and Ulman one. For a discussion that is more specific to compilers, see the compilers book by Aho and Ulman or Aho, Seti, and Ulman.

The tutorials on *lex* and *yacc* should suffice you for most applications. The O'Reilly book by Levine, Mason, and Brown is probably the best reference on *lex* and *yacc*. A copy of it is on reserve in the library, *QA76.76.U84M37*.

The definitive reference on hashing is Knuth's volume 3 of The Art of Computer Programming [14], section 6.4. This is on reserve, *QA76.5.K57*.

Parsing theory.

2.1 Levels of parsing

A compiler, or other translation software, has two main tasks: checking the input for validity, and if it is valid, understanding its meaning and transforming it into an executable that realizes this meaning. We will not go into the generation of the executable code here, but focus on the validity check and the analysis of the meaning, both of which are parsing tasks.

A parser needs to look at the input on all sorts of levels:

- Are all characters valid – no 8-bit ascii?
- Are names, or identifiers, well-formed? In most programming languages `a1` is a valid name, but `1a` is not. By contrast, in TeX a name can only have letters, while in certain Lisp dialects `!!important_name!!` is allowed.
- Are expressions well-formed? An arithmetic expression like `5/*6-` does not make sense, nor does `CALL )FOO(` in Fortran.
- If the input is well-formed, are constraints satisfied such as that every name that is used is defined first?

These different levels are best handled by several different software components. In this chapter we will look at the two initial stages of most translators[1].

1. First of all there is the lexical analysis. Here a file of characters is turned into a stream of tokens. The software that performs this task is called a tokenizer, and it can be formalized. The theoretical construct on which the tokenizer is based is called a 'Finite State Automaton'.
2. Next, we need to check if the tokens produced by the tokenizer come in a legal sequence. For instance, opening and closing parentheses need to come in matched pairs. This stage is called the syntactical analysis, and the software doing this is called a parser.

2.2 Very short introduction

A language is a set of words (strings) over an alphabet, that satisfies certain properties. It is also possible to define a language as the output of a certain type of grammar, or as

---

1. I will use the terms 'translating' and 'translator' as informal concepts that cover both compilers and interpreters and all sorts of mixed forms. This is not the place to get philosophical about the differences.

2.2. VERY SHORT INTRODUCTION

the strings accepted by a certain type of automaton. We then need to prove the equivalences of the various formulations. In this section we briefly introduce the relevant concepts.

2.2.1 Languages

A language is a set of words that are constructed from an alphabet. The alphabet is finite in size, and words are finite in length, but languages can have an infinite number of words. The alphabet is often not specified explicitly.

Languages are often described with set notation and regular expressions, for example '$L = \{a^n b^* c^n | n > 0\}$', which says that the language is all strings of equal number of as and cs with an arbitrary number of bs in between.

Regular expressions are built up from the following ingredients:

$\alpha|\beta$ either the expression α or β
$\alpha\beta$ the expression α followed by the expression β
$\alpha*$ zero or more occurrences of α
$\alpha+$ one or more occurrences of α
$\alpha?$ zero or one occurrences of α

We will see more complicated expressions in the *lex* utility.

2.2.2 Automata

A description of a language is not very constructive. To know how to generate a language we need a grammar. A grammar is a set of rules or productions $\alpha \to \beta$ that state that, in deriving a word in the language, the intermediate string α can be replaced by β. These strings can be a combination of

- A start symbol S,
- 'Terminal' symbols, which are letters from the alphabet; these are traditionally rendered with lowercase letters.
- 'Non-terminal' symbols, which are not in the alphabet, and which have to be replaced at some point in the derivation; these are traditionally rendered with uppercase letters.
- The empty symbol ϵ.

Languages can be categorized according to the types of rules in their grammar:

type 0 These are called 'recursive languages', and their grammar rules can be of any form: both the left and right side can have any combination of terminals, non-terminals, and ϵ.

type 1 'Context-sensitive languages' are limited in that ϵ can not appear in the left side of a production. A typical type 1 rule would look like
$$\alpha A \beta \to \gamma$$
which states that A, in the context of $\alpha A \beta$, is replaced by γ. Hence the name of this class of languages.

type 2 'Context-free languages' are limited in that the left side of a production can only consist of single non-terminal, as in $A \to \gamma$. This means that replacement of the non-terminal is done regardless of context; hence the name.

type 3 'Regular languages' can additionally have only a single non-terminal in each right-hand side.

In the context of grammars, we use the notation $\alpha \Rightarrow \beta$ to indicate that the string β as derived from α by a single application of a grammar rule; $\alpha \Rightarrow^* \beta$ indicates multiple rules. For example, $\alpha A \beta \Rightarrow \alpha B \gamma$ indicates that the rhs string was derived from the lhs by replacing $A\beta$ with $B\gamma$.

2.2.3 Automata

Corresponding to these four types of formal languages, there are four types of 'automata': formal machines that can recognize these languages. All these machines have a starting state, they go from one state to another depending on the input symbols they encounter, and if they reach the end state, the string is accepted as being in the language. The difference between the different types of automata lies in the amount of memory they have to store information. Very briefly the classes of automaton are:

for type 3 Finite State Automata. These machines have no memory. They can only make transitions.

for type 2 Pushdown Automata. These machines have a stack where they can store information; only the top of the stack can be inspected.

for type 1 Linear Bounded Automata. These have random-access memory, the size of which is equal to (a linear function of) the size of the input.

for type 0 Turing machines. These have an unbounded tape for storing intermediate calculations.

Lexical analysis.

The lexical analysis phase of program translation takes in a stream of characters and outputs a stream of tokens.

A token is a way of recognizing that certain characters belong together, and form an object that we can classify somehow. In some cases all that is necessary is knowing the class, for instance if the class has only one member. However, in general a token is a pair consisting of *its type and its value*. For instance, in `1/234` the lexical analysis recognizes that `234` is a number, with the value 234. In an assignment `abc = 456`, the characters `abc` are recognized as a variable. In this case the value is not the numeric value, but rather something like the index of where this variable is stored in an internal table.

Lexical analysis is relatively simple; it is performed by software that uses the theory of Finite State Automata and Regular Languages; see section 2.3.

Remark. It might be tempting to consider the input stream to consist of lines, each of which consist of characters, but this does not always make sense. Programming languages such as Fortran do look at the source, one line at a time; C does not. TeX is even more complicated: the interpretation of the line end is programmable.[2]

2.3 Finite state automata and regular languages

Regular languages are the strings accepted by a particularly simple kind of automaton. However, we initially define these languages – non-constructively – by so-called 'regular expressions'.

2.3.1 Definition of regular languages

A regular language over some alphabet can be described by a 'regular expression'.
- ϵ denotes the empty language: the language with no words in it.
- If `a` is a letter in the alphabet, then `a` denotes the language $\{a\}$.
- If α and β are expressions denoting regular languages A and B, then
  - $\alpha\beta$ or $\alpha \cdot \beta$ denotes the language $\{xy | x \in A, y \in B\}$.
  - $\alpha|\beta$ denotes the language $A \cup B$.
  - α^* denotes the language $\cup_{n \geq 0} A^n$.

---

[2]. Ok, if we want to be precise, TeX does look at the input source on a line-by-line basis. There is something of a preprocessor *before* the lexical analysis which throws away the machine-dependent line end, and replaces it with the TeX-defined one.

- Parentheses can be used to indicate grouping: (α) simply denotes the language A.

Any regular expression built up this way describes a regular language.

2.3.2 Non-deterministic automata

A Finite State Automaton is an abstract machine that recognizes ('accepts') words from a language:

- The automaton is initially in a beginning state;
- every letter or 'symbol' from the input word causes unambiguously a transition to the same or to a next state; if no transition is defined for a given combination of current state and input symbol, then the word is not in the language;
- a word is accepted if the last symbol causes a transition to a state that is marked as an accepting state.

Formally, we can define a FSA as the combination of

- A set S of states, with a starting state S_0 and a set of final states.
- A finite input alphabet I.
- A transition diagram $I \times S \to S$ that specifies how the combination of a state and an input symbol effects a transition to a new state.

This kind of automaton is deterministic in the sense that every transition from one state to the next is deterministically made by accepting an input symbol. However, in the context of lexical analysis, the so-called 'non-deterministic FSA' is more convenient. A non-deterministic FSA (also NFA) differs in two ways from the deterministic type:

- An NFA can make spontaneous transitions from one state to another. If an automaton has such a transition, we can say that this is caused by the symbol ϵ, and this is called an ϵ-transition.
- An NFA can be ambiguous in that there can be more than one possible transition for a given state and input symbol.

Exercise 15. Show that the second condition in the definition of an NFA can be reduced to the first. Is a reduction the other way possible?

2.3.3 The NFA of a given language

We now construct a nondeterministic automaton that accepts a regular language.

2.3. FINITE STATE AUTOMATA AND REGULAR LANGUAGES

- The automaton that accepts the expression ϵ has a single transition from the starting state to the accepting state.

- The automaton that accepts the expression a has a single transition from the starting state to the accepting state.

- If **A** and **B** are automata accepting the languages A and B with expressions α and β, then
  - the language AB is accepted by the automaton that has the states and transition of both automata combined, with the initial state of **A** as the new initial state, the accepting state of **B** as the new accepting state, and an ϵ-transition from the accepting state of **A** to the initial state of **B**;

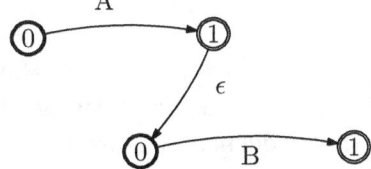

  - the language $A \cup B$ is accepted by an automaton with a new starting state that has ϵ-transitions to the initial states of **A** and **B**;

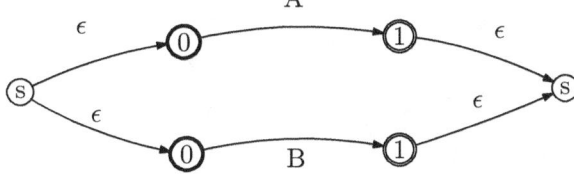

  - the expression α^* is accepted by **A** modified such that the initial state is also the accepting state, or equivalently by adding an ϵ-transition from the starting to the accepting state, and one the other way around.

2.3.4 Examples and characterization

Any language that can be described by the above constructs of repetition, grouping, concatenation, and choice, is a regular language. It is only slightly harder to take a transition diagram and write up the regular expression for the language that it accepts.

An informal way of characterizing regular languages is to say that FSAs 'do not have memory'. That means that any language where parts of words are related, such as $\{a^n b^m | m \geq n\}$, can not be recognized by a FSA. Proof: suppose there is a recognizing

FSA. When it first accepts a b, it can come from only a fixed number of states, so that limits the information it can carry with it.

We can give a slightly more rigorous proof if we first characterize regular languages:

Theorem 1 *Let L be a regular language, then there is an n so that all strings α in L longer than n can be written as $\alpha = uvw$, such that for any k uv^kw is also in the language.*

Using this theorem it is easy to see that the above language can not be regular.

This theorem is proved by observing that in order to accept a sufficiently long string the same state must have been encountered twice. The symbols accepted in between these encounters can then be repeated arbitrarily many times.

2.3.5 Deterministic automata

Non-deterministic automata, as defined above, are easy to define. However, from a practical point of view they do not look very constructive: a string in the language is accepted by the automaton if there is *any* sequence of transitions that accepts it. Fortunately, for every NFSA, there is a DFSA that accepts the same language.

Sometimes it is easy to derive the DFSA. Consider the language $a^*|b^*$ and the automaton

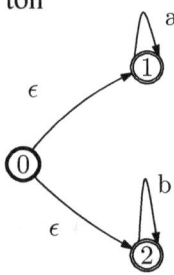

The following automaton is derived by splitting off one a and one b:

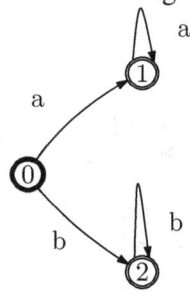

2.3. FINITE STATE AUTOMATA AND REGULAR LANGUAGES

This next example leads up to what happens in the lexical analysis of a compiler:

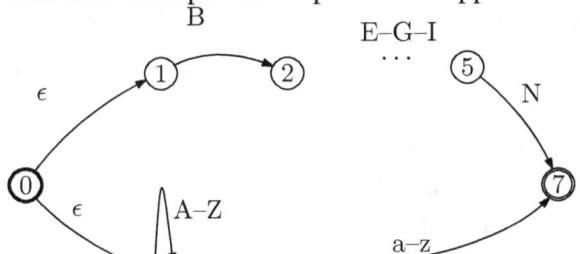

The resulting DFA is a bit more messy:

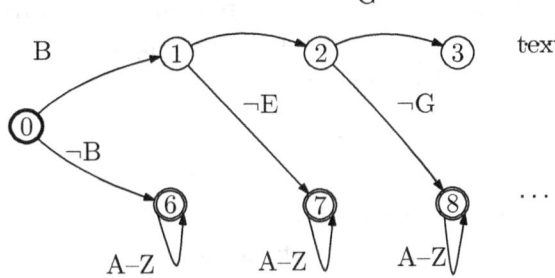

(and we can collapse states 6 ... to one.)

Sketch of the proof: the states of the DFSA are sets of states of the NFSA. The states we are actually interested in are defined inductively, and they satisfy the property that they are closed under ϵ-transitions of the original NFSA. The starting state contains the original starting state plus everything reachable with ϵ-transitions from it. Given a state of the DFSA, we then define more states by considering all transitions from the states contained in this state: if there is a transition based on a symbol x, the next state has all states reachable from this state by accepting x, plus any subsequent ϵ-transitions.

Since the number of subsets of a finite set of states is finite, this will define a finite number of states for the DFSA, and it is not hard to see that an accepting sequence in the one automaton corresponds to an accepting sequence in the other.

2.3.6 Equivalences

Above, we saw how the NFA of a regular language is constructed. Does every NFA correspond to a regular language, and if so, how can that be derived? We make a detour by first talking about the equivalence of automata and grammars.

Let X be a string in the language L of a DFA, and suppose that after t transitions state i is reached. That means we can split $X = X_i(t)Y_i$. This is merely one of the strings that is in state i at time t; let us call the set of all these strings $L_i(t)$. Let us call the set of all strings that, given a state i, bring the automaton to an accepting state R_i. This set is clearly not dependent on t. Defining $L_i = \cup_{t=0}^{\infty} L_i(t)$, we have that $L = \cup_{i=1}^{m} L_i R_i$ where m is the number of states.

This inspires us to tackle the derivation of a grammar by describing the production of the remainder strings R_i. Suppose the automaton is in state i; we will derive the productions $N_i \to \ldots$. If state i is an accepting state, there will be a production $N_i \to \epsilon$; for all other transitions by a symbol x to a state $N_{i'}$ we add a production $N_i \to x N_{i'}$. It is easy to see the equivalence of strings accepted by the DFA and derivations of the grammar thus constructed.

Going the other way, constructing an automaton from a grammar runs into a snag. If there are productions $N_i \to a N_{i'}$ and $N_i \to a N_{i''}$, we can of necessity only construct an NFA. However, we know that these are equivalent to DFAs.

We note that the grammars used and constructed in this – informal – proof are right-recursive, so they generate precisely the regular languages.

> **Exercise 16.** Show how this proof can be modified to use left-recursive grammars, that is, grammars that have productions of the form $N_i \to N_{i'} a$.

2.4 Lexical analysis with FSAs

A FSA will recognize a sequence of language elements. However, it's not enough to simply say 'yes, this was a legal sequence of elements': we need to pass information on to the next stage of the translation. This can be done by having some executable code attached to the accepting state; if that state is reached, the code snippet tells the next stage what kind of element has been recognized, and its value. This value can be a numerical value for numbers recognized, but more generally it will be an index into some table or other.

Formally, we can extend the definition of a FSA (section 2.3.2) by the addition of an output alphabet O and an output table $I \times S \to O$. This models the output of a symbol, possibly ϵ, at each transition.

> **Exercise 17.** One could also define the output with a mapping $S \to O$. Show that the definitions are equivalent.

An FSA is not enough to recognize a whole language, but it can recognize elements from a language. For instance, we can build multiple FSAs for each of the keywords of a language ('begin' or 'void'), or for things like numbers and identifiers. We can

2.4. LEXICAL ANALYSIS WITH FSAS

then make one big FSA for all the language elements by combining the multiple small FSAs into one that has

- a starting state with ε-transitions to the start states of the element automata, and
- from each of the accepting states an ε-transition back to the start state.

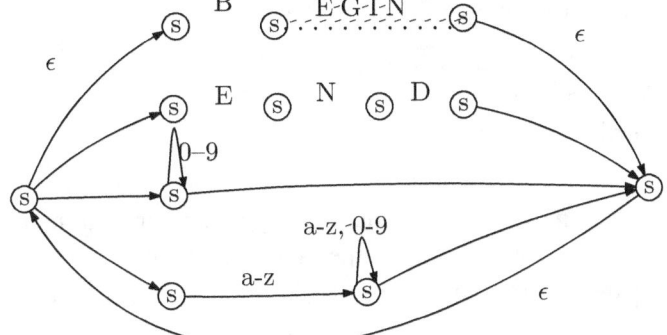

Exercise 18. Write a DFA that can parse Fortran arithmetic expressions. In Fortran, exponentiation is written like 2**n. It is also not allowed to have two operators in a row, so 2×-3 is notated 2*(-3).

There is a problem with the ε-transition from the final state to the initial state in the above NFA. This transition should only be taken if no other transitions can be taken, in other words, if the maximal string is recognized. For instance, most programming languages allow quote characters inside a quoted string by doubling them: '"And then he said ""Boo!"""'. The final state is reached three times in the course of this string; only the last time should the jump back be taken.

However, sometimes finding the maximum matched string is not the right strategy. For instance, in most languages, 4.E3 is a floating point number, but matching the E after the decimal point is not necessarily right. In Fortran, the statement IF (4.EQ.VAR) ... would then be misinterpreted. What is needed here is one token 'look-ahead': the parser needs to see what character follows the E.

At this point it would be a good idea to learn the Unix tool *lex*.

Syntax parsing.

Programming languages have for decades been described using formal grammars. One popular way of notating those grammars is Backus Naur Form, but most formalisms are pretty much interchangable. The essential point is that the grammars are almost invariably of the context-free type. That is, they have rules like

$$\langle \texttt{function call} \rangle \longrightarrow \langle \texttt{function name} \rangle (\langle \texttt{optargs} \rangle)$$
$$\langle \texttt{optargs} \rangle \longrightarrow \text{empty} \mid \langle \texttt{args} \rangle$$
$$\langle \texttt{args} \rangle \longrightarrow \text{word} \mid \text{word}, \langle \texttt{args} \rangle$$

The second and third rule in this example can be generated by a regular grammar, but the first rule is different: when the opening parenthesis is matched, the parser has to wait an unlimited time for the closing parenthesis. This rule is of context-free type**CHECKTHIS**.

It is important to keep some distinctions straight:

- A grammar has a set of rules, each indicating possible replacements during a derivation of a string in the language. Each rule looks like $A \to \alpha$.
- A derivation is a specific sequence of applications of rules; we denote each step in a derivation as $\alpha \Rightarrow \beta$, where β can be derived from α by application of some rule. The derivation of some string α is a sequence of step such that $S \Rightarrow \cdots \Rightarrow \alpha$; we abbreviate this as $S \Rightarrow^* \alpha$.
- Ultimately, we are interested in the reverse of a derivation: we have a string that we suspect is in the language, and we want to reconstruct whether and how it could be derived. This reconstruction process is called 'parsing', and the result often takes the form of a 'parse tree'.

We will first give some properties of context-free languages, then in section 2.6 we will discuss the practical parsing of context-free languages.

2.5 Context-free languages

Context-free languages can be defined as the output of a particular kind of grammar (the left side can only consist of a single nonterminal), or as the set of string accepted by a certain kind of automaton. For languages of this type, we use a Pushdown Automaton (PDA) to recognize them. A PDA is a finite-state automaton, with some scratch memory that takes the form of a stack: one can only push items on it, and inspect or remove the top item. Here we will not give an equivalence proof.

2.5. CONTEXT-FREE LANGUAGES

An example of a language that is context-free but not regular is $\{a^n b^n\}$. To parse this, the automaton pushes as on the stack, then pops them when it finds a b in the input, and the string is accepted if the stack is empty when the input string is fully read.

2.5.1 Pumping lemma

As with regular languages (section 2.3.4), there is a way to characterize the strings of a context-free language.

Theorem 2 *Let L be a context-free language, then there is an n so that all strings α in L longer than n can be written as $\alpha = uvwxy$, such that for any k the string $uv^k wx^k y$ is also in the language.*

The proof is as before: the derivation of a sufficiently long string must have used the same production twice.

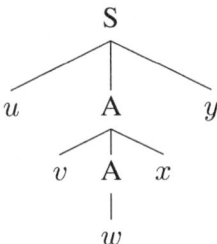

2.5.2 Deterministic and non-deterministic PDAs

As with Finite State Automata, there are deterministic and non-deterministic pushdown automata. However, in this case they are not equivalent. As before, any DPA is also a NPA, so any language accepted by a DPA is also accepted by a NPA. The question is whether there are languages that are accepted by a NPA, and that are not accepted by a DPA.

A similar example to the language $\{a^n b^n\}$ above is the language over an alphabet of at least two symbols $L = \{\alpha \alpha^R\}$, where α^R stands for the reverse of α. To recognize this language, the automaton pushes the string α on the stack, and pops it to match the reverse part. However, the problem is knowing when to start popping the stack.

Let the alphabet have at least three letters, then the language $L_c = \{\alpha c \alpha^R | c \notin \alpha\}$ can deterministically be recognized. However, in absence of the middle symbol, the automaton needs an ϵ-transition to know when to start popping the stack.

Victor Eijkhout

2.5.3 Normal form

Context-free grammars have rules of the form $A \to \alpha$ with A a single nonterminal and α any combination of terminals and nonterminals. However, for purposes of parsing it is convenient to have the rules in a 'normal form'. For context-free grammars that is the form $A \to a\alpha$ where a is a terminal symbol.

One proof that grammars can always be rewritten this way uses 'expression equations'. If **x** and **y** stand for sets of expressions, then $\mathbf{x} + \mathbf{y}$, $\mathbf{xy}$, and $\mathbf{x}^*$ stand for union, concatenation, and repetition respectively.

Consider an example of expression equations. The scalar equation $\mathbf{x} = \mathbf{a} + \mathbf{xb}$ states that **x** contains the expressions in **a**. But then it also contains **ab**, **abb**, et cetera. One can verify that $\mathbf{x} = \mathbf{ab}^*$.

The equation in this example had a regular language as solution; the expression $\mathbf{x} = \mathbf{a} + \mathbf{bxc}$ does not have a regular solution.

Now let **x** be a vector of all non-terminals in the grammar of a context-free language, and let **f** be the vector of righthandsides of rules in the grammar that are of normal form. We can then write the grammar as

$$\mathbf{x}^t = \mathbf{x}^t \mathbf{A} + \mathbf{f}^t$$

where the multiplication with **A** describes all rules not of normal form.

Example:
$$\begin{array}{rcl} S & \to & aSb|XY|c \\ X & \to & YXc|b \\ Y & \to & XS \end{array} \Rightarrow [S,X,Y] = [S,X,Y] \begin{bmatrix} \phi & \phi & \phi \\ Y & \phi & S \\ \phi & Xc & \phi \end{bmatrix} + [aSb+c, b, \phi]$$

The solution to this equation is

$$\mathbf{x}^t = \mathbf{f}^t \mathbf{A}^*$$

which describes rules on normal form. However, we need to find a more explicit expression for $\mathbf{A}^*$.

Noting that $\mathbf{A}^* = \lambda + \mathbf{A}\mathbf{A}^*$ we get

$$\mathbf{x}^t = \mathbf{f}^t + \mathbf{f}^t \mathbf{A}\mathbf{A}^* = \mathbf{f}^t + \mathbf{f}^t \mathbf{B} \tag{2.1}$$

where $\mathbf{B} = \mathbf{A}\mathbf{A}^*$. This is a grammar on normal form. It remains to work out the rules for **B**. We have

$$\mathbf{B} = \mathbf{A}\mathbf{A}^* = \mathbf{A} + \mathbf{A}\mathbf{A}\mathbf{A}^* = \mathbf{A} + \mathbf{A}\mathbf{B}$$

These rules need not be of normal form. However, any elements of **A** that start with a nonterminal, can only start with nonterminals in **x**. Hence we can substitute a rule from equation (2.1).

2.6 Parsing context-free languages

The problem of parsing is this:

> Given a grammar G and a string α, determine whether the string is in the language of G, and through what sequence of rule applications it was derived.

We will discuss the LL and LR type parser, which correspond to a top-down and bottom-up way of parsing respectively, then go into the problem of ambiguity

2.6.1 Top-down parsing: LL

One easy parsing strategy starts from the fact that the expression has to come from the start symbol. Consider the expression $2*5+3$, which is produced by the grammar

$$\text{Expr} \longrightarrow \text{number Tail}$$
$$\text{Tail} \longrightarrow \epsilon \mid + \text{ number Tail} \mid * \text{ number Tail}$$

In the following analysis the stack has its bottom at the right

initial queue:	$2*5+3$	
start symbol on stack:		Expr
replace		number Tail
match	$*5+3$	Tail
replace		* number Tail
match	$5+3$	number Tail
match	$+3$	Tail
replace		+ number Tail
match	3	number Tail
match	ϵ	Tail
match		

The derivation that we constructed here is

$$E \Rightarrow nT \Rightarrow n*nT \Rightarrow n*n+nT \Rightarrow n*n+n$$

that is, we are replacing symbols from the left. Therefore this kind of parsing is called LL parsing: read from left to right, replace from left to right. Because we only need to look at the first symbol in the queue to do the replacement, without need for further 'look ahead' tokens, this is $LL(1)$ parsing.

But this grammar was a bit strange. Normally we would write

$$\text{Expr} \longrightarrow \text{number} \mid \text{number} + \text{Expr} \mid \text{number} * \text{Expr}$$

If our parser can now see the first *two* symbols in the queue, it can form

initial queue:	$2 * 5 + 3$	
start symbol on stack:		Expr
replace		number * Expr
match	$5 + 3$	Tail
replace		number + Expr
match	3	Expr
replace	3	number
match	ϵ	

This is called $LL(2)$ parsing: we need one token look ahead.

2.6.1.1 Problems with LL parsing

If our grammar had been written

$$\text{Expr} \longrightarrow \text{number} \mid \text{Expr} + \text{number} \mid \text{Expr} * \text{number}$$

an $LL(k)$ parser, no matter the value of k, would have gone into an infinite loop.

In another way too, there are many constructs that can not be parsed with an $LL(k)$ parser for any k. For instance if both A<B and A<B> are legal expressions, where B can be of arbitrary length, then no finite amount of look-ahead will allow this to be parsed.

2.6.1.2 LL and recursive descent

The advantages of $LL(k)$ parsers are their simplicity. To see which rule applies at a given point is a recursive-descent search, which is easily implemented. The code for finding which rule to apply can broadly be sketched as follows:

```
define FindIn(Sym,NonTerm)
  for all expansions of NonTerm:
    if leftmost symbol == Sym
      then found
      else if leftmost symbol is nonterminal
        then FindIn(Sym,that leftmost symbol)
```

This implies that a grammar is LL-parsable if distinct rules for some non-terminal can not lead to different terminals. In other words, by looking at a terminal, it should be clear what production was used.

The LR parsers we will study next are more powerful, but much more complicated to program. The above problems with $LL(k)$ are largely non-existent in languages where statements start with unique keywords.

2.6.2 Bottom-up parsing: shift-reduce

In this section we will look at the 'bottom-up' parsing strategy, where terminal symbols are gradually replaced by non-terminals.

One easily implemented bottom-up parsing strategy is called 'shift-reduce parsing'. The basic idea here is to move symbols from the input queue to a stack, and every time the symbols on top of the stack form a right hand size of a production, reduce them to the left hand side.

For example, consider the grammar

$$E \longrightarrow \text{number} \mid E + E \mid E * E$$

and the expression $2 * 5 + 3$. We proceed by moving symbols from the left side of the queue to the top of the stack, which is now to the right.

	stack	queue
initial state:		$2 * 5 + 3$
shift	2	*5+3
reduce	E	*5+3
shift	E*	5+3
shift	E*5	+3
reduce	E*E	+3
reduce	E	+3
shift, shift, reduce	E+E	
reduce	E	

(Can you tell that we have ignored something important here?)

The derivation we have reconstructed here is

$$E \Rightarrow E + E \Rightarrow E + 3 \Rightarrow E * E + 3 \Rightarrow E * 5 + 3 \Rightarrow 2 * 5 + 3$$

which proceeds by each time replacing the right-most nonterminal. This is therefore called a 'rightmost derivation'. Analogously we can define a 'leftmost derivation' as one that proceeds by replacing the leftmost nonterminal.

For a formal definition of shift-reduce parsing, we should also define an 'accept' and 'error' action.

2.6.3 Handles

Finding the derivation of a legal string is not trivial. Sometimes we have a choice between shifting and reducing, and reducing 'as soon as possible' may not be the right solution. Consider the grammar

$$S \longrightarrow aAcBe$$
$$A \longrightarrow bA \mid b$$
$$B \longrightarrow d$$

and the string `abbcde`. This string can be derived (writing the derivation backwards for a change) as

`abbcde` $\Leftarrow$ `abAcde` $\Leftarrow$ `aAcde` $\Leftarrow$ `aAcBe` $\Leftarrow$ S.

However, if we had started

`abbcde` $\Leftarrow$ `aAbcde` $\Leftarrow aAAcde \Leftarrow ?$

we would be stuck because no further reductions would be applicable.

The problem then is to know where to start replacing terminal symbols and, later in the derivation, non-terminals. The shift-reduce strategy of the previous section is here seen to lead to problems, so some extra power is needed. We introduce the concept of 'handle' as a formal definition of 'the right production and place to start reducing'. The following definition is totally unhelpful:

If $S \Rightarrow^* \alpha A w \Rightarrow \alpha \beta w$ is a right-most derivation, then $A \to \beta$ at the position after α is a handle of $\alpha A w$.

Clearly, if we can identify handles, we can derive a parse tree for a given string. However, the story so far has not been constructive. Next we will look at ways of actually finding handles.

2.6.4 Operator-precedence grammars

It is easy to find handles if a grammar is of an 'operator grammar' form. Loosely, by this we mean that expressions in the language look like expression-operator-expression. More strictly, we look at grammars where there are never two adjacent nonterminals, and where no right hand side is ϵ. We also assume that precedence relations between operators and terminals are known.

Let us look again at arithmetic expressions; we will introduce relations $op_1 \lessdot op_2$ if the first operator has lower precedence, and $op_1 \gtrdot op_2$ if it has higher precedence. If the two operators are the same, we use predence to force associativity rules. For instance, right associativity corresponds to definitions such as $+ \gtrdot +$.

For the $+$ and $*$ operators we then have the following table:

	number	$+$	$\times$
number		$\gtrdot$	$\gtrdot$
$+$	$\lessdot$	$\gtrdot$	$\lessdot$
$\times$	$\lessdot$	$\gtrdot$	$\gtrdot$

2.6. PARSING CONTEXT-FREE LANGUAGES

Now we can find a handle by scanning left-to-right for the first $>$ character, then scanning back for the matching $<$. After reducing handles thus found, we have a string of operators and nonterminals. Ignoring the nonterminals, we insert again the comparisons; this allows us to find handles again.

For example, $5 + 2 * 3$ becomes $<5> + <2> * <3>$; replacing handles this becomes $E + E * E$. Without the nonterminals, the precedence structure is $< + < * >$, in which we find $<E * E>$ as the handle. Reducing this leaves us with $E + E$, and we find that we have parsed the string correctly.

This description sounds as if the whole expression is repeatedly scanned to insert precedence relations and find/reduce handle. This is not true, since we only need to scan as far as the right edge of the first handle. Thus, a shift/reduce strategy will still work for operator grammars.

2.6.5 LR parsers

We will now consider LR parsers in more detail. These are the parsers that scan the input from the left, and construct a rightmost derivation, as in the examples we have seen in section 2.6.2. Most constructs in programming languages can be parsed in an LR fashion.

An LR parser has the following components

- A stack and an input queue as in the shift-reduce examples you have already seen in section 2.6.2. The difference is that we now also push state symbols on the stack.
- Actions 'shift', 'reduce', 'accept', 'error', again as before.
- An `Action` and `Goto` function that work as follows:
    - Suppose the current input symbol is a and the state on top of the stack is s.
    - If $\text{Action}(a, s)$ is 'shift', then a and a new state $s' = \text{Goto}(a, s)$ are pushed on the stack.
    - If $\text{Action}(a, s)$ is 'reduce $A \to \beta$' where $|\beta| = r$, then $2r$ symbols are popped from the stack, a new state $s' = \text{Goto}(a, s'')$ is computed based on the newly exposed state on the top of the stack, and A and s' are pushed. The input symbol a stays in the queue.

An LR parser that looks at the first k tokens in the queue is called an LR(k) parser. We will not discuss this issue of look-ahead any further.

It is clear that LR parser are more powerful than a simple shift-reduce parser. The latter has to reduce when the top of the stack is the right hand side of a production; an LR parser additionally has states that indicate whether and when the top of the stack is a handle.

2.6.5.1 A simple example of LR parsing

It is instructive to see how LR parsers can deal with cases for which simple shift/reduce parsing is insufficient. Consider again the grammar

$$E \longrightarrow E+E \mid E*E$$

and the input string $1+2*3+4$. Give the + operator precedence 1, and the $*$ operator precedence 2. In addition to moving tokens onto the stack, we also push the highest precedence seen so far. In the beginning we declare precedence 0, and pushing a non-operator does not change the precedence.

Shift/reduce conflicts are now resolved with this rule: if we encounter at the front of the queue a lower precedence than the value on top of the stack, we reduce the elements on top of the stack.

	$1+2*3+4$	push symbol; highest precedence is 0
1 S_0	$+2*3+4$	highest precedence now becomes 1
1 $S_0 + S_1$	$2*3+4$	
1 $S_0 + S_1$ 2 S_1	$*3+4$	highest precedence becoming 2
1 $S_0 + S_1$ 2 $S_1 * S_2$	$3+4$	
1 $S_0 + S_1$ 2 $S_1 * S_2$ 3 S_2	$+4$	reduce because P(+) < 2
1 $S_0 + S_1$ 6 S_1	$+4$	the highest exposed precedence is 1
1 $S_0 + S_1$ 6 $S_1 + S_1$	4	
1 $S_0 + S_1$ 6 $S_1 + S_1$ 4 S_1		at the end of the queue we reduce
1 $S_0 + S_1$ 10 S_1		
11		

Even though this example is phrased very informally, we see the key points:
- only the top of the stack and the front of the queue are inspected;
- we have a finite set of rules governing shift/reduce behaviour.

As we shall see, this mechanism can also identify handles.

2.6.5.2 States of an LR parser

An LR parser is constructed automatically from the grammar. Its states are somewhat complicated, and to explain them we need a couple of auxiliary constructs.

item An 'item' is a grammar rule with a location indicated. From the rule A $\to$ B C we get the items A $\to$ .B C, A $\to$ B .C, A $\to$ B C.. The interpretation of an item will be that the symbols left of the dot are on the stack, while the

2.6. PARSING CONTEXT-FREE LANGUAGES

right ones are still in the queue. This way, an item describes a stage of the parsing process.

closure The closure of an item is defined as the smallest set that
- Contains that item;
- If the closure contains an item A $\to \alpha$ .B β with B a nonterminal symbol, then it contains all items B $\to$.γ. This is a recursive notion: if γ starts with a non-terminal, the closure would also contain the items from the rules of γ.

The states of our LR parser will now be closures of items of the grammar. We motivate this by an example.

Consider now an item A $\to \beta_1.\beta_2$ in the case that we have recognized $\alpha\beta_1$ so far. The item is called *valid* for that string, if a rightmost derivation $S \Rightarrow^* \alpha A w \Rightarrow \alpha\beta_1\beta_2 w$ exists. If $\beta_2 = \epsilon$, then $A \to \beta_1$ is a handle and we can reduce. On the other hand, if $\beta_2 \neq \epsilon$, we have not encountered the full handle yet, so we shift β_2.

As an example, take the grammar

$$E \longrightarrow \text{E+T} \mid \text{T}$$
$$T \longrightarrow \text{T*F} \mid \text{F}$$
$$F \longrightarrow \text{(E)} \mid \text{id}$$

and consider the partially parsed string E+T*. The (rightmost) derivation

$$E \Rightarrow E + T \Rightarrow E + T * F$$

shows that T $\to$ T*.F is a valid item,

$$E \Rightarrow E + T \Rightarrow E + T * F \Rightarrow E + T * (E)$$

gives F $\to$.(E) as a valid item, and

$$E \Rightarrow E + T \Rightarrow E + T * F \Rightarrow E + T * \text{id}$$

gives F $\to$ .id as a valid item.

2.6.5.3 States and transitions

We now construct the actual states of our parser.
- We add a new start symbol S', and a production S' $\to$ S.
- The starting state is the closure of S' $\to$ .S.
- The transition function $d(s, \text{X})$ of a state s and a symbol X is defined as the closure of
$$\{\text{A} \to \alpha \text{ X}. \ \beta \mid \text{A} \to \alpha \ .\text{X} \ \beta \text{ is in } s\}$$
- The 'follow' of a symbol A is the set of all terminal symbols that can follow its possible expansions. This set is easy to derive from a grammar.

Here is an example

> We construct the states and transition for the grammar
> $$S \longrightarrow (S)S \mid \epsilon$$

which consists of all strings of properly matched left and right parentheses.

Solution: we add the production $S' \to {}_\bullet S$. We now find the states

1. $\{S' \to {}_\bullet S, S \to {}_\bullet (S)S, S \to {}_\bullet\}$
2. $\{S' \to S_\bullet\}$
3. $\{S \to ({}_\bullet S)S, S \to {}_\bullet (S)S, S \to {}_\bullet\}$
4. $\{S \to (S_\bullet)S\}$
5. $\{S \to (S){}_\bullet S, S \to {}_\bullet (S)S, S \to {}_\bullet\}$
6. $\{S \to (S)S_\bullet\}$

with transitions
$$\begin{aligned} d(0, S) &= 1 \\ d(0, '(') &= 2 \\ d(2, S) &= 3 \\ d(2, '(') &= 2 \\ d(3, ')') &= 4 \\ d(4, S) &= 5 \\ d(4, '(') &= 2 \end{aligned}$$

The only thing missing in our parser is the function that describes the stack handling. The parsing stack consists of states and grammar symbols (alternating). Initially, push the start state onto the stack. The current state is always the state on the top of the stack. Also, add a special endmarker symbol to the end of the input string.

Loop:
(1) **if** the current state contains $S' \to S_\bullet$
    accept the string
(2) **else if** the current state contains any other final item $A \to \alpha_\bullet$
    pop all the tokens in α from the stack, along with the corresponding states;
    let s be the state left on top of the stack: push A, push d(s, A)
(3) **else if** the current state contains any item $A \to \alpha \; {}_\bullet x \; \beta$,
    where x is the next input token
    let s be the state on top of the stack: push x, push d(s, x)
    else report failure

Explanation:

1. If we have recognized the initial production, the bottom-up parse process was successful.

2.6. PARSING CONTEXT-FREE LANGUAGES

2. If we have a string of terminals on the stack, that is the right hand side of a production, replace by the left hand side non-terminal.
3. If we have a string of terminals on the stack that is the *start* of a right hand side, we push the current input symbol.

Exercise 19. Give the states and transitions for the grammar
$$S \longrightarrow x$$
$$S \longrightarrow (L)$$
$$L \longrightarrow S$$
$$L \longrightarrow L\ S$$

Apply the above parsing algorithm to the string (x, x, (x)).

The parsers derived by the above algorithm can only handle cases where there is no ambiguity in condition (3). The class of grammars recognized by this type of parser is called $LR(0)$ and it is not very interesting. We get the more interesting class of $SLR(1)$ by adding to condition (2) the clause that the following symbol is in the follow of A. Another similar class, which is the one recognized by *yacc*, is $LALR(1)$.

2.6.6 Ambiguity and conflicts

The problem of finding out *how* a string was derived is often important. For instance, with a grammar
$$\langle\texttt{expr}\rangle \longrightarrow \langle\texttt{number}\rangle \mid \langle\texttt{expr}\rangle + \langle\texttt{expr}\rangle \mid \langle\texttt{expr}\rangle \times \langle\texttt{expr}\rangle$$

the expression $2 + 5 * 3$ is ambiguous: it can mean either $(2 + 5) * 3$ or $2 + (5 * 3)$.

An LR parser would report a 'shift/reduce conflict' here: after $2 + 5$ has been reduced to <expr> + <expr>, do we reduce that further to <expr>, or do we shift the minus, since <expr> - is the start of a legitimate reducible sequence?

Another example of ambiguity is the 'dangling else' problem. Consider the grammar
$$\langle\texttt{statement}\rangle \longrightarrow \text{if } \langle\texttt{clause}\rangle \text{ then } \langle\texttt{statement}\rangle$$
$$\mid \text{if } \langle\texttt{clause}\rangle \text{ then } \langle\texttt{statement}\rangle \text{ else } \langle\texttt{statement}\rangle$$

and the string

    if c_1 then if c_2 then s_1 else s_2

This can be parsed two ways:

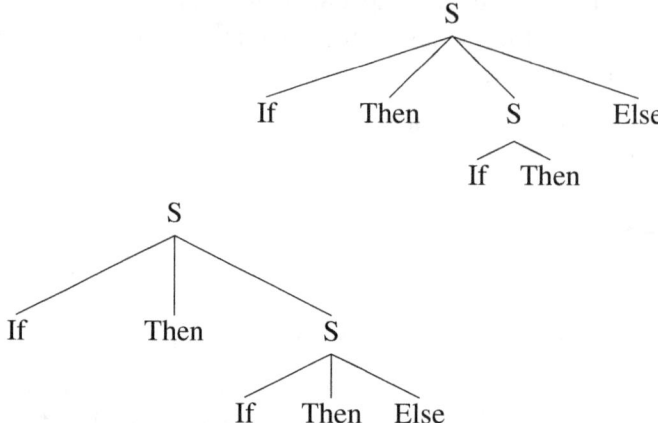

Does the `else` clause belong to the first `if` or the second?

Let us investigate the first example. We can solve the ambiguity problem in two ways:

- Reformulate the grammar as
  $\langle \text{expr} \rangle \longrightarrow \langle \text{mulex} \rangle \mid \langle \text{mulex} \rangle + \langle \text{mulex} \rangle$
  $\langle \text{mulex} \rangle \longrightarrow \langle \text{term} \rangle \mid \langle \text{term} \rangle \times \langle \text{term} \rangle$
  $\langle \text{term} \rangle \longrightarrow \text{number}$

  so that the parser can unambiguously reconstruct the derivation,

  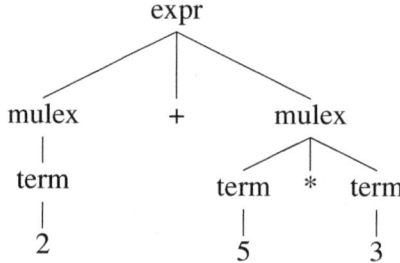

  or

- Teach the parser about precedence of operators. This second option may be easier to implement if the number of operators is large: the first option would require a large number of rules, with probably a slower parser.

  Exercise 20. Rewrite the grammar of the second example to eliminate the dangling else problem.

Since we are not used to thinking of keywords such as `then` in terms of precedence, it is a better solution to eliminate the dangling else problem by introducing a `fi` keyword to close the conditional. Often, however, ambiguity is not so easy to eliminate.

2.6. PARSING CONTEXT-FREE LANGUAGES

Exercise 21. In case of a shift-reduce conflict, yacc shifts. Write an example that proves this. Show what this strategy implies for the dangling else problem.

Another type of conflict is the 'reduce/reduce conflict'. Consider this grammar:

$A \longrightarrow B\,c\,d \mid E\,c\,f$
$B \longrightarrow x\,y$
$E \longrightarrow x\,y$

and the input string that starts x y c.

- An $LR(1)$ parser will shift x y, but can not decide whether to reduce that to B or E on the basis of the look-ahead token c.
- An $LR(2)$ parser can see the subsequent d or f and make the right decision.
- An LL parser would also be confused, but already at the x. Up to three tokens (x y c) is unsufficient, but an $LL(4)$ parser can again see the subsequent d or f.

The following grammar would confuse any $LR(n)$ or $LL(n)$ parser with a fixed amount of look-ahead:

$A \longrightarrow B\,C\,d \mid E\,C\,f$
$B \longrightarrow x\,y$
$E \longrightarrow x\,y$
$C \longrightarrow c \mid C\,c$

which generates $x\,y\,c^n\,\{d|f\}$.

As usual, the simplest solution is to rewrite the grammar to remove the confusion e.g.:

$A \longrightarrow \text{BorE}\,c\,d \mid \text{BorE}\,c\,f$
$\text{BorE} \longrightarrow x\,y$

or assuming we left-factorise the grammar for an $LL(n)$ parser:

$A \longrightarrow \text{BorE}\,c\,\text{tail}$
$\text{tail} \longrightarrow d \mid f$
$\text{BorE} \longrightarrow x\,y$

Another example of a construct that is not LR parsable, consider languages such as Fortran, where function calls and array indexing both look like A(B,C):

⟨expression⟩ ⟶ ⟨function call⟩
| ⟨array element⟩

Victor Eijkhout

⟨function call⟩ ⟶ name(⟨parameter list⟩)
⟨array element⟩ ⟶ name(⟨expression list⟩)
⟨parameter list⟩ ⟶ name
| name, ⟨parameter list⟩
⟨expression list⟩ ⟶ name
| name, ⟨expression list⟩

After we push B on the stack, it is not clear whether to reduce it to the head of a parameter list or of an expression list, and no amount of lookahead will help. This problem can be solved by letting the lexical analyzer have access to the symbol table, so that it can distinguish between function names and array names.

Lex.

2.7 Introduction

The unix utility *lex* parses a file of characters. It uses regular expression matching; typically it is used to 'tokenize' the contents of the file. In that context, it is often used together with the *yacc* utility. However, there are many other applications possible. By itself, *lex* is powerful enough to build interesting programs with, as you will see in a few examples.

2.8 Structure of a *lex* file

A *lex* file looks like

```
    ...definitions...
%%
    ...rules...
%%
    ...code...
```

Here is a simple example:

```
%{
  int charcount=0,linecount=0;
%}

%%

. charcount++;
\n {linecount++; charcount++;}

%%
int main()
{
  yylex();
  printf("There were %d characters in %d lines\n",
          charcount,linecount);
  return 0;
}
```

Victor Eijkhout

In this example, all three sections are present:

definitions All code between %{ and %} is copied to the beginning of the resulting C file.

rules A number of combinations of pattern and action: if the action is more than a single command it needs to be in braces.

code This can be very elaborate, but the main ingredient is the call to `yylex`, the lexical analyser. If the code segment is left out, a default main is used which only calls `yylex`.

2.8.1 Running *lex*

If you store your *lex* code in a file `count.l`, you can build an executable from it by

```
lex -t count.l > count.c
cc -c -o count.o count.c
cc -o counter count.o -ll
```

You see that the *lex* file is first turned into a normal C file, which is then compiled and linked.

If you use the *make* utility (highly recommended!) you can save a few steps because *make* knows about *lex*:

```
counter: count.o
        cc -o counter count.o -ll
```

2.9 Definitions section

There are three things that can go in the definitions section:

C code Any indented code between %{ and %} is copied to the C file. This is typically used for defining file variables, and for prototypes of routines that are defined in the code segment.

definitions A definition is very much like a `#define` cpp directive. For example
```
letter [a-zA-Z]
digit [0-9]
punct [,.:;!?]
nonblank [^ \t]
```
These definitions can be used in the rules section: one could start a rule
```
{letter}+ {...
```

state definitions If a rule depends on context, it's possible to introduce states and incorporate those in the rules. A state definition looks like `%s STATE`, and by default a state `INITIAL` is already given. See section 2.10.2 for more info.

2.10 Rules section

The rules section has a number of pattern-action pairs. The patterns are regular expressions (see section 2.11, and the actions are either a single C command, or a sequence enclosed in braces.

If more than one rule matches the input, the longer match is taken. If two matches are the same length, the earlier one in the list is taken.

It is possible to associate one action with more than one pattern:

```
[0-9]+              process_integer();
[0-9]+\.[0-9]*      |
\.[0.9]+            process_real();
```

2.10.1 Matched text

When a rule matches part of the input, the matched text is available to the programmer as a variable `char* yytext` of length `int yyleng`.

To extend the example from the introduction to be able to count words, we would write

```
%{
 int charcount=0,linecount=0,wordcount=0;
%}
letter [^ \t\n]

%%

{letter}+ {wordcount++; charcount+=yyleng;}
. charcount++;
\n {linecount++; charcount++;}
```

> **Exercise 22.** Write an integer postfix calculator in *lex*: expression such as 1 2 + and 1 2 3 4/*- should be evaluated to 3 and -.5 respectively. White space only serves to separate number, but is otherwise optional; the line end denotes the end of an expression. You will probably need the C function `int atoi(char*)` which converts strings to ints.

2.10.2 Context

If the application of a rule depends on context, there are a couple of ways of dealing with this. We distinguish between 'left context' and 'right context', basically letting a rule depend on what comes before or after the matched token.

See section 2.13.1 for an elaborate example of the use of context.

2.10.2.1 Left context

Sometimes, using regular expression as we have seen so far is not powerful enough. For example:

```
%%
"/*".*"*/"   ;
.            |
\n           ECHO;
```

works to filter out comments in

```
This line /* has a */ comment
```

but not in

```
This /* line has */ a /* comment */
```

What we want is, after the /* string to change the behaviour of *lex* to throw away all characters until */ is encountered. In other words, we want *lex* to switch between two states, and there is indeed a state mechanism available.

We can consider states to implement implement a dependence on the left context of a rule, since it changes the behaviour depending on what came earlier. To use a state, a rule is prefixed as

```
<STATE>(some pattern) {...
```

meaning that the rule will only be evaluated if the specified state holds. Switching between states is done in the action part of the rule:

```
<STATE>(some pattern) {some action; BEGIN OTHERSTATE;}
```

where all state names have been defined with `%s SOMESTATE` statements, as described in section 2.9. The initial state of *lex* is INITIAL.

Here is the solution to the comment filtering problem:

```
%x COMM

%%

.            |
\n           ECHO;
"/*"         BEGIN COMM;
<COMM>"*/"   BEGIN INITIAL;
```

2.11. REGULAR EXPRESSIONS

```
<COMM>.      |
<COMM>\n     ;

%%
```

We see that the state is defined with `%x COMM` rather than as indicated above with `%s`. This is called an 'exclusive state'. If an exclusive state is active, rules without state prefix will not be matched if there is a match in a rule *with* the prefix of the current state.

2.10.2.2 Right context

It is also possible to let a rule depend on what follows the matched text. For instance

```
abc/de {some action}
```

means 'match `abc` but only when followed by `de`. This is different from matching on `abcde` because the `de` tokens are still in the input stream, and they will be submitted to matching next.

It is in fact possible to match on the longer string; in that case the command

```
abcde {yyless(3); .....}
```

pushes back everything after the first 3 characters. The difference with the slash approach is that now the right context tokens are actually in `yytext` so they can be inspected.

2.11 Regular expressions

Many Unix utilities have regular expressions of some sort, but unfortunately they don't all have the same power. Here are the basics:

. Match any character except newlines.
\n A newline character.
\t A tab character.
^ The beginning of the line.
$ The end of the line.
`<expr>*` Zero or more occurrences of the expression.
`<expr>+` One or more occurrences of the expression.
`(<expr1>|<expr2>)` One expression of another.
`[<set>]` A set of characters or ranges, such as `[,.:;]` or `[a-zA-Z]`.
`[^<set>]` The complement of the set, for instance `[^ \t]`.

Victor Eijkhout

Exercise 23. It is possible to have] and - in a character range. The] character has to be first, and - has to be either first or last. Why?

Exercise 24. Write regular expressions that match from the beginning of the line to the first letter 'a'; to the last letter 'a'. Also expressions that match from the first and last 'a' to the end of the line. Include representative input and output in your answer.

2.12 Remarks

2.12.1 User code section

If the *lex* program is to be used on its own, this section will contain a `main` program. If you leave this section empty you will get the default main:

```
int main()
{
  yylex();
  return 0;
}
```

where `yylex` is the parser that is built from the rules.

2.12.2 Input and output to *lex*

Normally, the executable produced from the *lex* file will read from standard in and write to standard out. However, its exact behaviour is that it has two variables

```
FILE *yyin, *yyout;
```

that are by default set that way. You can open your own files and assign the file pointer to these variables.

2.12.3 Lex and Yacc

The integration of *lex* and *yacc* will be discussed in the *yacc* tutorial; here are just a few general comments.

2.12.3.1 Definition section

In the section of literal C code, you will most likely have an include statement:

```
#include "mylexyaccprog.h"
```

2.13. EXAMPLES

as well as prototypes of *yacc* routines such as `yyerror` that you may be using. In some *yacc* implementations declarations like

```
extern int yylval;
```

are put in the `.h` file that the *yacc* program generates. If this is not the case, you need to include that here too if you use `yylval`.

2.12.3.2 Rules section

If you *lex*programmer is supplying a tokenizer, the *yacc* program will repeatedly call the `yylex` routine. The rules will probably function by calling `return` everytime they have constructed a token.

2.12.3.3 User code section

If the *lex* program is used coupled to a *yacc* program, you obviously do not want a main program: that one will be in the *yacc* code. In that case, leave this section empty; thanks to some cleverness you will not get the default main if the compiled *lex* and *yacc* programs are linked together.

2.13 Examples

2.13.1 Text spacing cleanup

(This section illustrates the use of contexts; see section 2.10.2.)

Suppose we want to clean up sloppy spacing and punctuation in typed text. For example, in this text:

```
This    text (all of it  )has occasional lapses , in
   punctuation(sometimes pretty bad) ,( sometimes not so).



   (Ha! ) Is this : fun?Or what!
```
We have

- Multiple consecutive blank lines: those should be compacted.
- Multiple consecutive spaces, also to be compacted.
- Space before punctuation and after opening parentheses, and
- Missing spaces before opening and after closing parentheses.

That last item is a good illustration of where context comes in: a closing paren followed by punctuation is allowed, but followed by a letter it is an error to be corrected.

We can solve this problem without using context, but the *lex* code would be longer and more complicated. To see this, consider that we need to deal with spacing before and after a parenthesis. Suppose that there are m cases of material before, and n of material after, to be handled. A *lex* code without context would then likely have $m \times n$ rules. However, using context, we can reduce this to $m + m$.

2.13.1.1 Right context solution

Let us first try a solution that uses 'right context': it basically describes all cases and corrects the spacing.

```
punct    [,.;:!?]
text     [a-zA-Z]

%%

")"" "+/{punct}            {printf(")");}
")"/{text}                 {printf(") ");}
{text}+" "+/")"            {while (yytext[yyleng-1]==' ') yyleng--; ECHO;

({punct}|{text}+)/"("      {ECHO; printf(" ");}
"("" "+/{text}             {while (yytext[yyleng-1]==' ') yyleng--; ECHO;

{text}+" "+/{punct}        {while (yytext[yyleng-1]==' ') yyleng--; ECHO;

^" "+                      ;
" "+                       {printf(" ");}
.                          {ECHO;}
\n/\n\n                    ;
\n                         {ECHO;}
```

In the cases where we match superfluous white space, we manipulate `yyleng` to remove the spaces.

2.13.1.2 Left context solution

Using left context, we implement a finite state automaton in *lex*, and specify how to treat spacing in the various state transitions. Somewhat surprisingly, we discard spaces entirely, and reinsert them when appropriate.

2.13. EXAMPLES

We recognise that there are four categories, corresponding to having just encountered an open or close parenthesis, text, or punctuation. The rules for punctuation and closing parentheses are easy, since we discard spaces: these symbols are inserted regardless the state. For text and opening parentheses we need to write rules for the various states.

```
punct [,.;:!?]
text [a-zA-Z]

%s OPEN
%s CLOSE
%s TEXT
%s PUNCT

%%

" "+ ;

<INITIAL>"(" {ECHO; BEGIN OPEN;}
<TEXT>"(" {printf(" "); ECHO; BEGIN OPEN;}
<PUNCT>"(" {printf(" "); ECHO; BEGIN OPEN;}

")" {ECHO ; BEGIN CLOSE;}

<INITIAL>{text}+ {ECHO; BEGIN TEXT;}
<OPEN>{text}+ {ECHO; BEGIN TEXT;}
<CLOSE>{text}+ {printf(" "); ECHO; BEGIN TEXT;}
<TEXT>{text}+  {printf(" "); ECHO; BEGIN TEXT;}
<PUNCT>{text}+ {printf(" "); ECHO; BEGIN TEXT;}

{punct}+ {ECHO; BEGIN PUNCT;}

\n {ECHO; BEGIN INITIAL;}

%%
```

Exercise 25. Write a *lex* parser that analyzes text the way the TEX input processor does with the normal category code values. It should print its output with
- `<space>` denoting any space that is not ignored or skipped, and
- `<cs: command>` for recognizing a control sequence `\command`;

- open and close braces should also be marked as <{>, <}>.

Here is some sample input:
```
this is {a line} of text.
handle \control sequences \andsuch
with \arg{uments}.
    Aha!
this line has %a comment


x
y%
z

\comm%
and
```

Yacc.

2.14 Introduction

The unix utility *yacc* (Yet Another Compiler Compiler) parses a stream of token, typically generated by *lex*, according to a user-specified grammar.

2.15 Structure of a *yacc* file

A *yacc* file looks much like a *lex* file:

```
   ...definitions...
%%
   ...rules...
%%
   ...code...
```

definitions As with *lex*, all code between `%{` and `%}` is copied to the beginning of the resulting C file. There can also be various definitions; see section 2.17.

rules As with *lex*, a number of combinations of pattern and action. The patterns are now those of a context-free grammar, rather than of a regular grammar as was the case with *lex*.

code This can be very elaborate, but the main ingredient is the call to `yyparse`, the grammatical parse.

2.16 Motivating example

It is harder to give a small example of *yacc* programming than it was for *lex*. Here is a program that counts the number of *different* words in a text. (We could have written this particular example in *lex* too.)

First consider the *lex* program that matches words:

```
%{

#include "words.h"
int find_word(char*);
extern int yylval;
%}
```

```
%%
[a-zA-Z]+ {yylval = find_word(yytext);
    return WORD;}
.          ;
\n         ;

%%
```

The lexer now no longer has a main program, but instead returns a WORD return code. It also calls a routine `find_word`, which inserts the matched word in a list if it is not already there.

The routine `find_word` is defined in the *yacc* code:

```
%{

#include <stdlib.h>
#include <string.h>
  int yylex(void);
#include "words.h"
  int nwords=0;
#define MAXWORDS 100
  char *words[MAXWORDS];
%}

%token WORD

%%

text : ;
     | text WORD   ; {
           if ($2<0) printf("new word\n");
           else printf("matched word %d\n",$2);
                    }

%%

int find_word(char *w)
{
  int i;
```

2.17. DEFINITIONS SECTION

```
  for (i=0; i<nwords; i++)
    if (strcmp(w,words[i])==0) {
      return i;
    }
  words[nwords++] = strdup(w);
  return -1;
}

int main(void)
{
  yyparse();
  printf("there were %d unique words\n",nwords);
}
```

Other things to note:

- The WORD token that was used in the *lex* code is defined here in the definitions section; *lex* knows about it through including the `words.h` file.
- The *lex* rule also sets a variable `yylval`; this puts a value on the stack top, where *yacc* can find it with `$1`, `$2`, et cetera.

All of this will be explained in detail below.

2.17 Definitions section

There are three things that can go in the definitions section:

C code Any code between `%{` and `%}` is copied to the C file. This is typically used for defining file variables, and for prototypes of routines that are defined in the code segment.

definitions The definitions section of a *lex* file was concerned with characters; in *yacc* this is tokens. These token definitions are written to a `.h` file when *yacc* compiles this file.

associativity rules These handle associativity and priority of operators; see section 2.20.

2.18 Lex Yacc interaction

Conceptually, *lex* parses a file of characters and outputs a stream of tokens; *yacc* accepts a stream of tokens and parses it, performing actions as appropriate. In practice, they are more tightly coupled.

Victor Eijkhout

If your *lex* program is supplying a tokenizer, the *yacc* program will repeatedly call the `yylex` routine. The *lex* rules will probably function by calling `return` every time they have parsed a token. We will now see the way *lex* returns information in such a way that *yacc* can use it for parsing.

2.18.1 The shared header file of return codes

If *lex* is to return tokens that *yacc* will process, they have to agree on what tokens there are. This is done as follows.

- The *yacc* file will have token definitions
  `%token NUMBER`
  in the definitions section.
- When the *yacc* file is translated with `yacc -d -o`, a header file `<file>.h`[3] is created that has definitions like
  `#define NUMBER 258`
  This file can then be included in both the *lex* and *yacc* program.
- The *lex* file can then call `return NUMBER`, and the *yacc* program can match on this token.

The return codes that are defined from `%TOKEN` definitions typically start at around 258, so that single characters can simply be returned as their integer value:

```
/* in the lex program */
[0-9]+ {return NUMBER}
[-+*/] {return *yytext}

/* in the yacc program */
sum : NUMBER '+' NUMBER
```

The *yacc* code now recognizes a `sum` if *lex* returns in sequence a `NUMBER` token, a plus character, and another `NUMBER` token.

See example 2.22.1 for a worked out code.

2.18.2 Return values

In the above, very sketchy example, *lex* only returned the information that there was a number, not the actual number. For this we need a further mechanism. In addition to specifying the return code, the *lex* parser can return a value that is put on top of the stack, so that *yacc* can access it. This symbol is returned in the variable `yylval`. By default, this is defined as an `int`, so the *lex* program would have

---

3. If you leave out the `-o` option to *yacc*, the file is called `y.tab.h`.

2.19. RULES SECTION

```
extern int yylval;
%%
[0-9]+ {yylval=atoi(yytext); return NUMBER;}
```

See section 2.19.1 for how the stack values are used by *yacc*.

If more than just integers need to be returned, the specifications in the *yacc* code become more complicated. Suppose we are writing a calculator with variables, so we want to return double values, and integer indices in a table. The following three actions are needed.

1. The possible return values need to be stated:
   ```
   %union {int ival; double dval;}
   ```
2. These types need to be connected to the possible return tokens:
   ```
   %token <ival> INDEX
   %token <dval> NUMBER
   ```
3. The types of non-terminals need to be given:
   ```
   %type <dval> expr
   %type <dval> mulex
   %type <dval> term
   ```

The generated .h file will now have

```
#define INDEX 258
#define NUMBER 259
typedef union {int ival; double dval;} YYSTYPE;
extern YYSTYPE yylval;
```

This is illustrated in example 2.22.2.

2.19 Rules section

The rules section contains the grammar of the language you want to parse. This looks like

```
name1 :    THING something OTHERTHING {action}
      |    othersomething THING       {other action}
name2 :    .....
```

This is the general form of context-free grammars, with a set of actions associated with each matching right-hand side. It is a good convention to keep non-terminals (names that can be expanded further) in lower case and terminals (the symbols that are finally matched) in upper case.

Victor Eijkhout

The terminal symbols get matched with return codes from the *lex* tokenizer. They are typically defines coming from `%token` definitions in the *yacc* program or character values; see section 2.18.1.

A simple example illustrating the ideas in this section can be found in section 2.22.1.

2.19.1 Rule actions

The example in section 2.22.1 had such rules as:

```
expr:
        expr '+' mulex          { $$ = $1 + $3; }
        | expr '-' mulex        { $$ = $1 - $3; }
        | mulex                 { $$ = $1; }
```

The action belonging to the different right hand sides refer to $$n$$ quantities and to $$. The latter refers to the stack top, so by assigning to it a new item is put on the stack top. The former variables are assigned the values on the top of the stack: if the right hand side has three terms, terminal or nonterminal, then $1 through $3 are assigned and the three values are removed from the stack top.

2.20 Operators; precedence and associativity

The example in section 2.22.1 had separate rules for addition/subtraction and multiplication/division. We could simplify the grammar by writing

```
expr:
        expr '+' expr ;
        expr '-' expr ;
        expr '*' expr ;
        expr '/' expr ;
        expr '^' expr ;
        number ;
```

but this would have $1+2*3$ evaluate to 9. In order to indicate operator precedence, we can have lines

```
%left '+' '-'
%left '*' '/'
%right '^'
```

The sequence of lines indicates increasing operator precedence and the keyword sets the associativity type: we want $5-1-2$ to be 2, so minus is left associative; we want $2\verb|^|2\verb|^|3$ to be 256, not 64, so exponentiation is right associative.

Operators that can be both unary and binary are handled by declaring a non-associative token, and explicitly indicating its precedence.

```
%left '-' '+'
%nonassoc UMINUS
%
expression : expression '+' expression
    | expression '-' expression
    | '-' expression %prec UMINUS
```

2.21 Further remarks

2.21.1 User code section

The minimal main program is

```
int main()
{
  yyparse();
  return 0;
}
```

Extensions to more ambitious programs should be self-evident.

In addition to the main program, the code section will usually also contain subroutines, to be used either in the *yacc* or the *lex* program. See for instance example 2.22.3.

> **Exercise 26.** Try to write *lex* or *yacc* programs for the following languages:
> $$a^n b^m, \quad a^n b^n, \quad a^n b^n c^n$$
> Discuss the theoretical power of *lex* and *yacc*.

2.21.2 Errors and tracing

So far we have assumed that the input to *yacc* is syntactically correct, and *yacc* need only discover its structure. However, occasionally input will be incorrect.

2.21.2.1 Tracing

If you assign `yydebug=1;`, *yacc* will produce trace output. While its states may not make sense to you, at least you will see which tokens it matches, and which rules it can reduce.

2.21.2.2 Syntax errors

Sometimes, *yacc* reports 'syntax error' and stops processing. This means that an unexpected symbol is found. A common source for this is the case that you have made a typo in your grammar, and the symbol it is trying to match is not defined. Example: suppose we have just matched an open token:

```
group : open body close
bodytext : ;
         | character bodytext
```

If you are tracing *yacc*'s workings, you will probably see it matching the character, then giving the syntax error message.

The 'syntax error' message is actually *yacc*'s default implementation of the yyerror routine, but it can be redefined at will. For example, suppose we have a declaration

```
int lineno=1;       /* in yacc */
extern int lineno;  /* in lex */
```

and every line with \n in *lex* increases this variable. We could then define

```
void yyerror(char *s)
{
  printf("Parsing failed in line %d because of %s\n",
        lineno,s);
}
```

2.21.2.3 Error recovery

Error recovery in *yacc* is possible through the error token. In the rule

```
foo : bar baz ;
    | error baz printf("Hope for the best\n");
```

recognizing any token but bar will make *yacc* start skipping tokens, hoping to find baz and recover from that point. This is not guaranteed to work.

2.21.2.4 Semantical errors

Both *lex* and *yacc* are stronger than simple finite-state or pushdown automata, for instance if they are endowed with a symbol table. This can be used to detect semantic errors. For instance, while you would like to write

```
array_slice : array_name '[' int_expr ']'
```

you may be limited to

2.21. FURTHER REMARKS

```
array_slice : ident '[' int_expr ']'
              {if (!is_array($1)) { ....
```

There are a couple of tools here:

`yyerror(char*)` is a default write to `stderr`; you can redefine it.
`YYABORT` is a macro that halts parsing.

2.21.3 Makefile rules for *yacc*

The `make` utility knows about *lex* and *yacc*, but if you want to do things yourself, here are some good rules:

```
# disable normal rules
.SUFFIXES:
.SUFFIXES: .l .y .o

# lex rules
.l.o :
        lex -t $*.l > $*.c
        cc -c $*.c -o $*.o

# yacc rules
.y.o :
        if [ ! -f $*.h ] ; then touch $*.h ; fi
        yacc -d -t -o $*.c $*.y
        cc -c -o $*.o $*.c ;
        rm $*.c

# link lines
lexprogram : $(LEXFILE).o
        cc $(LEXFILE).o -o $(LEXFILE) -ll
yaccprogram : $(YACCFILE).o $(LEXFILE).o
        cc $(YACCFILE).o $(LEXFILE).o -o $(YACCFILE) -ly -ll
```

2.21.4 The power of *yacc*

Theoretically, *yacc* implements an LALR(1) parser, which is essentially an LR parser with one token look-ahead. This describes a large class of useful grammars. As an example of a grammar with *two* tokens look-ahead, consider

    phrase $\longrightarrow$ CART_ANIMAL and cart
    | WORK_ANIMAL and plow

CART_ANIMAL ⟶ horse | goat
WORK_ANIMAL ⟶ horse | ex

Now to distinguish between `horse and cart` and `horse and plow` from the word `horse` takes two tokens look-ahead.

Exercise 27. Use the TEX parser you wrote in *lex* to parse LaTeX documents. The parser should
- Report the documentclass used;
- Check that `\begin{document}` and `\end{document}` are used, with no text before the begin command;
- Know about some commands with one argument, such as `\textbf`, and properly recognize that argument
- Recognize proper matching of begin/end of an environment.

Bonus: let your parser interpret `\newcommand` correctly. You can limit yourself to the the case of commands with one argument, that is

`\newcommand{\foo}[1]{ ...}`

2.22 Examples

2.22.1 Simple calculator

This calculator evaluates simple arithmetic expressions. The *lex* program matches numbers and operators and returns them; it ignores white space, returns newlines, and gives an error message on anything else.

```
%{
#include <stdlib.h>
#include <stdio.h>
#include "calc1.h"
void yyerror(char*);
extern int yylval;

%}

%%

[ \t]+ ;
[0-9]+     {yylval = atoi(yytext);
            return INTEGER; }
```

2.22. EXAMPLES

```
[-+*/]       {return *yytext;}
"("          {return *yytext;}
")"          {return *yytext;}
\n           {return *yytext;}
.            {char msg[25];
              sprintf(msg,"%s <%s>","invalid character",yytext);
              yyerror(msg);}
```

Accepting the *lex* output, the following *yacc* program has rules that parse the stream of numbers and operators, and perform the corresponding calculations.

```
%{
#include <stdlib.h>
#include <stdio.h>
int yylex(void);
#include "calc1.h"
%}

%token INTEGER

%%

program:
        line program
        | line
line:
        expr '\n'           { printf("%d\n",$1); }
        | '\n'
expr:
        expr '+' mulex      { $$ = $1 + $3; }
        | expr '-' mulex    { $$ = $1 - $3; }
        | mulex             { $$ = $1; }
mulex:
        mulex '*' term      { $$ = $1 * $3; }
        | mulex '/' term    { $$ = $1 / $3; }
        | term              { $$ = $1; }
term:
        '(' expr ')'        { $$ = $2; }
        | INTEGER           { $$ = $1; }

%%
```

```
void yyerror(char *s)
{
    fprintf(stderr,"%s\n",s);
    return;
}

int main(void)
{
    /*yydebug=1;*/
    yyparse();
    return 0;
}
```

Here we have realized operator precedence by having separate rules for the different priorities. The rule for plus/minus comes first, which means that its terms, the `mulex` expressions involving multiplication, are evaluated first.

2.22.2 Calculator with simple variables

In this example the return variables have been declared of type double. Furthermore, there can now be single-character variables that can be assigned and used. There now are two different return tokens: double values and integer variable indices. This necessitates the `%union` statement, as well as `%token` statements for the various return tokens and `%type` statements for the non-terminals.

This is all in the *yacc* file:

```
%{
#include <stdlib.h>
#include <stdio.h>
int yylex(void);
double var[26];
%}

%union { double dval; int ivar; }
%token <dval> DOUBLE
%token <ivar> NAME
%type <dval> expr
%type <dval> mulex
%type <dval> term
```

2.22. EXAMPLES

```
%%

program:
        line program
      | line
line:
        expr '\n'            { printf("%g\n",$1); }
      | NAME '=' expr '\n'   { var[$1] = $3; }
expr:
        expr '+' mulex       { $$ = $1 + $3; }
      | expr '-' mulex       { $$ = $1 - $3; }
      | mulex                { $$ = $1; }
mulex:
        mulex '*' term       { $$ = $1 * $3; }
      | mulex '/' term       { $$ = $1 / $3; }
      | term                 { $$ = $1; }
term:
        '(' expr ')'         { $$ = $2; }
      | NAME                 { $$ = var[$1]; }
      | DOUBLE               { $$ = $1; }

%%

void yyerror(char *s)
{
    fprintf(stderr,"%s\n",s);
    return;
}

int main(void)
{
    /*yydebug=1;*/
    yyparse();
    return 0;
}
```

The *lex* file is not all that different; note how return values are now assigned to a component of `yylval` rather than `yylval` itself.

```
%{
#include <stdlib.h>
#include <stdio.h>
#include "calc2.h"
void yyerror(char*);
%}

%%

[ \t]+    ;
((([0-9]+(\.[0-9]*)?)|([0-9]*\.[0-9]+))    {
              yylval.dval = atof(yytext);
              return DOUBLE; }
[-+*/=]        {return *yytext;}
"("            {return *yytext;}
")"            {return *yytext;}
[a-z]          {yylval.ivar = *yytext;
               return NAME;}
\n             {return *yytext;}
.              {char msg[25];
                sprintf(msg,"%s <%s>","invalid character",yytext);
                yyerror(msg);}
```

2.22.3 Calculator with dynamic variables

Basically the same as the previous example, but now variable names can have regular names, and they are inserted into a names table dynamically. The *yacc* file defines a routine for getting a variable index:

```
%{
#include <stdlib.h>
#include <stdio.h>
#include <string.h>
int yylex(void);
#define NVARS 100
char *vars[NVARS]; double vals[NVARS]; int nvars=0;
%}

%union { double dval; int ivar; }
%token <dval> DOUBLE
%token <ivar> NAME
```

2.22. EXAMPLES

```
%type <dval> expr
%type <dval> mulex
%type <dval> term

%%

program:
        line program
        | line
line:
        expr '\n'              { printf("%g\n",$1); }
        | NAME '=' expr '\n'   { vals[$1] = $3; }
expr:
        expr '+' mulex         { $$ = $1 + $3; }
        | expr '-' mulex       { $$ = $1 - $3; }
        | mulex                { $$ = $1; }
mulex:
        mulex '*' term         { $$ = $1 * $3; }
        | mulex '/' term       { $$ = $1 / $3; }
        | term                 { $$ = $1; }
term:
        '(' expr ')'           { $$ = $2; }
        | NAME                 { $$ = vals[$1]; }
        | DOUBLE               { $$ = $1; }

%%

int varindex(char *var)
{
  int i;
  for (i=0; i<nvars; i++)
    if (strcmp(var,vars[i])==0) return i;
  vars[nvars] = strdup(var);
  return nvars++;
}

int main(void)
{
    /*yydebug=1;*/
    yyparse();
```

```
        return 0;
}
```

The *lex* file is largely unchanged, except for the rule that recognises variable names:

```
%{
#include <stdlib.h>
#include <stdio.h>
#include "calc3.h"
void yyerror(char*);
int varindex(char *var);
%}

%%

[ \t]+ ;
(([0-9]+(\.[0-9]*)?)|([0-9]*\.[0-9]+)) {
            yylval.dval = atof(yytext);
            return DOUBLE;}
[-+*/=]    {return *yytext;}
"("        {return *yytext;}
")"        {return *yytext;}
[a-z][a-z0-9]* {
            yylval.ivar = varindex(yytext);
            return NAME;}
\n         {return *yytext;}
.          {char msg[25];
            sprintf(msg,"%s <%s>","invalid character",yytext);
            yyerror(msg);}
```

Hashing. Hashing, hash functions, hash tables, come into play when a compiler, and in particular its parser, needs to store names (of identifiers) and further information about the object of that name.

2.23 Introduction

A compiler, and in particular its parser, needs to store variables and information about them. The data structure for this is in effect addressed by the name of the variable, rather than by any numerical index. This sort of storage is sometimes called 'associative'. The design of a data structure for this is a good example of trade-offs between efficiency and expediency.

- If variables are stored in the order in which they are encountered, storage is very fast, but searching will take time linear in the number of items stored.
- If the list if kept sorted, searching for an item will take logarithmic time. However, insertion is now more expensive, taking linear time because all elements following have to be copied up.
- A naively implemented linked list would give both insertion and retrieval time linearly in the number of stored items. In the insertion phase we avoid the copying, but finding the place to insert is harder, and in fact we can not use bisection here.
- Items can be stored in a treewise fashion:

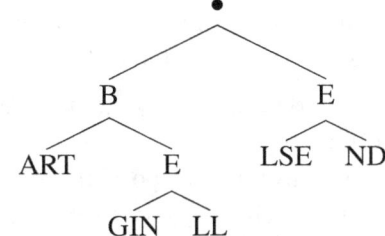

The cost of inserting and retrieving is then linear in the length of the string, at least for as far as is necessary to disambiguate from other strings.

These are then the issues we need to address:

- What is the cost of inserting a new item?
- What is the cost of finding and retrieving an item?
- What is the cost of deleting an item?

Victor Eijkhout

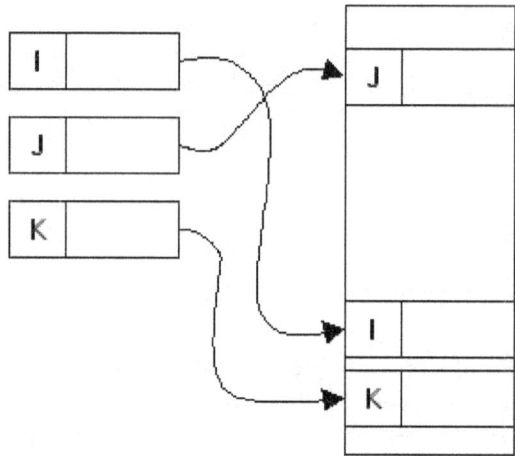

Figure 2.1: A hash function without conflicts

2.24 Hash functions

A hash function is function that maps non-numeric keys into a range of integers, interpreted as the locations in a table. It would be nice if this function was injective, to avoid mapping two keys to the same location but surprisingly hard, as is clear from the 'birthday paradox': it takes only 23 random picks from a 365-entry table to have even chances of a collision. If we know all keys in advance, it is possible to design a function that maps them uniquely into a table of precisely the right size, but this is unrealistic, since the number of possible keys in a programming language is very large, indeed unbounded.

A 'hash function' is then a function that maps keys in some space to a range of integers $0 \ldots M - 1$. A good hash function has the following properties:

- The hash value is fully determined by the data being hashed. For instance, it should not have a 'memory'.
- The hash function uses as much as possible of the input data. Program variables often have names such as `ikey`, so emphasis on the first letter is a bad idea.
- The hash function "uniformly" distributes the data across the entire set of possible hash values.
- The hash function generates very different hash values for similar strings. Variables like `key1`, `key2`, et cetera should not be mapped into a cluster.

Figure 2.1 illustrates a hash function without conflicts.

Let us assume that we have found a way of mapping the names onto a large integer

2.24. HASH FUNCTIONS

space, for instance by interpreting the bit pattern of the name as an integer. A simple hash function would be

$$h(K) = K \bmod M, \qquad (2.2)$$

where M is the size of the hash table.

Certain values of M are less desirable. For instance, if M is even, say $M = 2M'$, then the statement $r = K \bmod M$ (say $K = nM + r$ for some n) implies

$$K = 2K' \Rightarrow r = 2(nM' - K')$$
$$K = 2K' + 1 \Rightarrow r = 2(nM' - K') + 1$$

so the key is even, iff the original number is. This places an undue influence on the last digit. If M is a multiple of 3, we find for numbers stored decimally or in bytes that keys that are a permutation of each other get mapped to numbers that differ by a multiple of 3, since both $10^n \bmod 3 = 1$ and $2^8 \bmod 1 = 1$.

2.24.1 Multiplication and division strategies

A good strategy is to take M prime, and such that $r^k \neq \pm a \bmod M$, where r the radix of the number system, and a, k small. (There is a list of suitable primes on http://planetmath.org/encyclopedia/GoodHashTablePrimes.html.)

Equation (2.2) requires you to perform a division. The same equation based on multiplication would use an integer $A \approx w/M$, where w is the maxint value. Then $1/M = A/w$, which is simply A with an imaginary decimal point to its left. Observing that

$$K \bmod M = M(K/M \bmod 1)$$

we define

$$h(K) = \lfloor M\left(\left(\frac{A}{w}K\right) \bmod 1\right)\rfloor.$$

As an example of the value of using a prime table size, consider hashing the Bible, which consists of 42,829 unique words, into an open hash table with 30,241 elements (a prime number). In the end, 76.6 percent of the slots were used and that the average chain was 1.85 words in length (with a maximum of 6). The same file run into a hash table of 30,240 elements (evenly divisible by integers 2 through 9) fills only 60.7 percent of the slots and the average chain is 2.33 words long (maximum: 10).

2.24.2 String addition strategies

One could Derive a hash key by adding or XORing together all bytes in a string.

```
h = <some value>
for (i=0; i<len(var); i++)
    h = h + <byte i of string>;
```

This runs into the problem that anagrams map into the same key, and nearby strings into nearby keys. This could be remedied by introducing a table of random numbers:

```
h = <some value>
for (i=0; i<len(var); i++)
    h = Rand( h XOR <byte i of string> );
```

> **Exercise 28.** This algorithm only gives a one-byte key. How would you derive longer keys? Give pseudo-code for the algorithm.

2.24.3 Examples

Here are a couple of published hash functions:

```
/* UNIX ELF hash
 * Published hash algorithm used in the UNIX ELF format for object f
 */
unsigned long hash(char *name)
{
    unsigned long h = 0, g;

    while ( *name ) {
        h = ( h << 4 ) + *name++;
        if ( g = h & 0xF0000000 )
            h ^= g >> 24;
        h &= ~g;
    }

}
```

This hash key is then reduced to an index in the hash table by

```
#define HASHSIZE 997
    static int M = HASHSIZE;
    return h % M;
```

Another hash function:

```
/* djb2
 * This algorithm was first reported by Dan Bernstein
 * many years ago in comp.lang.c
 */
```

```
unsigned long hash(unsigned char *str)
{
        unsigned long hash = 5381;
        int c;
        while (c = *str++) hash = ((hash << 5) + hash) + c;
        return hash;
}
```

Note the use of bit shifts to implement multiplication.

2.25 Collisions

The above techniques for generating randomly spread out addresses are generally sufficient. The problem to worry about is how to handle collisions, that is, if $h(k_1) = h(k_2)$ for different keys k_1, k_2. We will investigate several techniques for dealing with this.

For all of the strategies below, any performance analysis is statistical in nature. The average expected behaviour is often excellent, but the worst case behaviour is always very bad. In the worst case, all hash addresses map to the same location, and search time is propertional to the number of elements in the table.

The question is now how to find the storage locations for the elements with conflicting hash keys. We will look at one strategy that allocates space outside the hash table ('open hash table'), and two that resolve the conflict by finding different locations in the table ('closed hash table').

2.25.1 Separate chaining

A simple solution to hash conflicts is the create a linked list from each table entry, as shown in figure 2.5. This way of implementing a hash table is called 'separate chaining' or 'open hashing'. One problem with this approach is that we need to maintain two different kinds of storage: static in the table and dynamic for the linked lists.

The linked lists can be created by `malloc` (and released by `free`) calls. However, these are very expensive compared to using a freespace pointer in a list. To amortize the cost, one could allocate a block of cells, and dole them out gradually. The problem with this strategy is dealing with deletions. If a cell is deleted, rerouting the pointers is easy, but additionally we have to keep track of which cells in the allocated chunk are free. This makes the open hash table somewhat complicated to implement.

Another problem is that, while this strategy is fairly efficient if the number of collisions is low, in order to get the number of collisions low, one typically chooses the table size

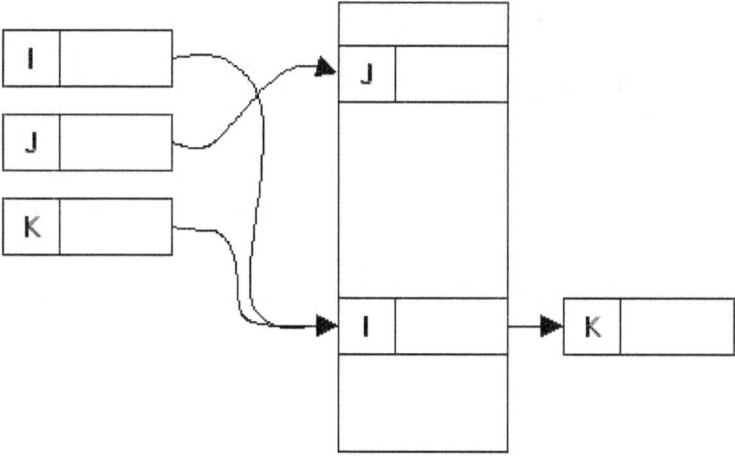

Figure 2.2: Separate chaining as a solution for hash conflicts

fairly large, and then this solution is wasteful of storage. It is then better to store all elements in the hash table and maintain links in the table.

Exercise 29. Discuss the value of keeping the lists ordered by key: how does this influence the run time of insertion and retrieval? Programming languages like C have local variables. Does this change your argument?

2.25.2 Linear probing

The easiest solution is to store a conflicting element in the location immediately after the computed hash address.

```
struct { ... } node;
node Table[M]; int Free;
/* insert K */
addr = Hash(K);
if (IsEmpty(addr)) Insert(K,addr);
else {
   /* see if already stored */
  test:
    if (Table[addr].key == K) return;
    else {
      addr = Table[addr].link; goto test;}
   /* find free cell */
   Free = addr;
```

2.25. COLLISIONS

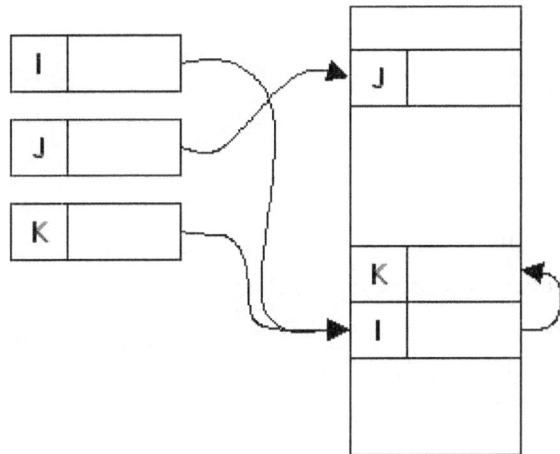

Figure 2.3: Linear probing as a solution for hash conflicts

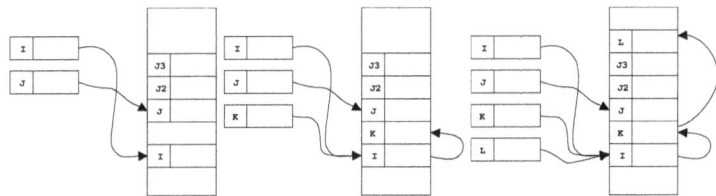

Figure 2.4: Coalescing of blocks in linear probing

```
    do { Free--; if (Free<0) Free=M-1; }
    while (!IsEmpty(Free) && Free!=addr)
    if (!IsEmpty(Free)) abort;
    else {
       Insert(K,Free); Table[addr].link = Free;}
}
```

However, this is not the best solution. Suppose that the blocks of size N is occupied, then the free pointer will search $N/2$ locations on average for an address that maps into this block. While this is acceptable, if two blocks coalesce, this makes the search time double. Note that the chance of the cell between two blocks filling up is much larger than the chance of that exact address being generated as hash: each hash in the top block will cause the address to be filled.

This is illustrated in figure 2.4. There is a gap of size one between $h(I)$ and a block starting at $h(J)$. When a conflict $h(K) = h(I)$ occurs, the free space pointer fills the gap. A subsequent conflict $h(L) = h(I)$ (or $h(L) = h(K)$) needs the free space pointer to traverse the whole J block to find the next location.

With $\alpha = N/M$ the ratio between occupied cells and total table size, the expected search time with this algorithm is

$$T \approx \begin{cases} \frac{1}{2}\left(1 + \left(\frac{1}{1-\alpha}\right)^2\right) & \text{unsuccessful} \\ \frac{1}{2}\left(1 + \frac{1}{1-\alpha}\right) & \text{successful} \end{cases}$$

It is clear that when α approaches 1, this time will go up unbounded.

The clumping behaviour of this algorithm makes it sensitive to the hash algorithm used. Care has to be taken that successive keys, such as `Ptr1`, `Ptr2`..., do not get mapped to successive hash values $K, K+1, \ldots$.

2.25.3 Chaining

The problems with linear probing can be prevented by storing conflicting elements at the start or end of the table.

```
struct { ... } node;
node Table[M]; int Free = M;
/* insert K */
addr = Hash(K);
if (IsEmpty(addr)) Insert(K,addr);
else {
    /* see if already stored */
  test:
    if (Table[addr].key == K) return;
    else {
      addr = Table[addr].link; goto test;}
    /* find free cell */
    do { Free--; }
    while (!IsEmpty(Free)
    if (Free<0) abort;
    else {
      Insert(K,Free); Table[addr].link = Free;}
}
```

This algorithm does the same list traversal as linear probing in the case a search is ultimately successful. However, for an unsuccessful search the `Free` pointer will usually be decreased by one, and only occasionally by two or more, when it runs into already occupied positions. Since these are likely to be spread out, having to search more than two steps will be rare.

2.25. COLLISIONS

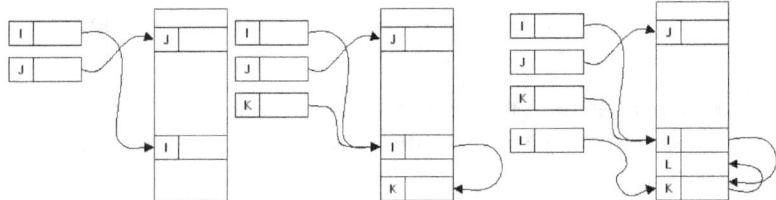

Figure 2.5: Chaining as a solution for hash conflicts

In this algorithm, occasionally a hash address will be an address that has further links. We say that we have lists coalescing. This increases search time slightly, but not by much, and preventing this increases insertion time, because we would have to move cells.

With $\alpha = N/M$ the fraction of used to total table entries, find that the number of entries searched is

$$T \approx \begin{cases} 1 + (e^{2\alpha} - 1 - 2\alpha)/4 & \text{unsuccessful} \\ 1 + (e^{2\alpha} - 1 - 2\alpha)/8\alpha + \alpha/4 & \text{successful} \end{cases}$$

The hash algorithm of TeX is a variant of this chaining algorithm.

2.25.4 Other solutions

The solutions to the conflict problem given so far can be called 'linear rehashing'. The following strategies are called 'nonlinear rehashing'.

Random probing Try $(h(m) + p_i) \bmod s$, where p_i is a sequence of random numbers. This requires either reproducible random numbers, or storing these numbers. In order to prevent colliding keys to collide on the next try too, the random number needs to depend on the key.

Add the hash Try $(i \times h(m)) \bmod s$. This requires s to be a prime number; with this approach clumping is prevented.

They have the advantage that occupied locations in the table remain fairly scattered. On the other hand, they require further hash calculations. Also, because of the irregular memory access pattern, the cost of memory operations may become significant here.

2.25.5 Deletion

A surprising aspect of closed hash table algorithms is that generally it is hard to delete elements. Since most algorithms give coalescing lists, we can not mark a cell empty if its key is to be removed. Instead, we mark a cell 'deleted', which removes the key, but leaves the link intact. There are algorithms that can deal with deletions, but they have a fairly high complexity.

On the other hand, deleting in an open hash table algorithm is simple. The complication there is the freeing of the memory. If the cells are allocated in chunks, the decision to free a chunk becomes complicated.

2.26 Other applications of hashing

The foremost application of hashing is in compilers. However, there are other uses.

2.26.1 Truncating searches

In applications such as chess programs, you want to avoid evaluating a configuration twice if it's arrived at two different ways. This can be done by storing evaluations in a table. This table can be addressed by the configuration as a key itself, but these keys are long and span a large space, so searching will probably be expensive. Instead, one can use a hash table.

If two configurations generate the same hash key, they can be, but need not be the same, so further decision might be needed. To avoid this second stage work, a good quality hash function is essential.

(This example comes from `http://www.seanet.com/~brucemo/topics/hashing.htm`.)

2.26.2 String searching

The question 'does a string of length M appear anywhere in a document of length N' can be answered in $O(NM)$ time by a sequence of string comparisons. However, we can do considerably better, reducing the complexity to $O(N + M)$.

A hash function that adds characters together will give the same hash key for strings that are anagrams of each other. This means that instead of doing a string comparison we can compare hash keys, and only if they are equal resort to a full string comparison. To get the complexity down, we note that if the hash function is of the form

$$h(k) = \left\{\sum_i k[i]\right\} \bmod K,$$

where k is a character string, then (for a text t long enough)

$$h(t[2\ldots n+1]) = h(t[1\ldots n]) + t[n+1] - t[1]$$

(with addition/subtraction modulo K) so we can cheaply update the hash key in $O(1)$ time.

2.27 Discussion

In a comparison between hash tables and, for instance, tree-based storage, there is no clear preference. Hash tables can be faster, because, until the table fills up, access is $O(1)$. A similar complexity can be obtained for trees, but

- memory access in trees is more chaotic, leading to worse cache or paging behaviour;
- memory is allocated and freed dynamically; circumventing that takes considerable programming effort;
- trees can become unbalanced, and balancing them is tricky to program, and takes time;
- the optimal search time can be made approximately equal, but that is again hard to code.

Closed hash tables have the advantage of simpler storage management, and, until they fill up, no worse performance than open tables.

Projects for this chapter.

Project 2.1. Use the *lex* and *yacc* programs you have written for LaTeX to write a full LaTeX-to-HTML translator.

Project 2.2. A number of projects involve parsers or code generators for (parts of) TeX or LaTeX.

> **formulas** Reinhold Heckmann and Reinhard Wilhelm. 1997. A functional description of TeX's formula layout. Journal of Functional Programming 7(5):451-485. Available online at `http://rw4.cs.uni-sb.de/users/heckmann/doc.html`. For software, see `ftp://ftp.cs.uni-sb.de/formulae/`.
>
> **also formulas** Preview-LaTeX (`http://preview-latex.sourceforge.net/`) displays formulas right in the emacs edit buffer.
>
> **math on web pages** see `http://www.forkosh.com/mimetex.html`.
>
> **LaTeX to HTML** HeVeA, TtH, TeX4ht and LaTeX2HTML.
>
> **front end for LaTeX** `http://www.lyx.org/` Ages ago there was 'griff'. Scientific Word still exists but is commercial.
>
> **reimplementation of TeX** TeX in Python: `http://www.pytex.org/`
>
> Investigate these parsers: what is their basic approach and theoretical power, what are they good at, what are they bad at.

Project 2.3. Develop the full theory of the compound NFA that does lexical analysis.

- This automaton basically parses the whole file, rather than small chunks; every once in a while it will report that it has recognized an identifier, number, special symbol &c. This means that the definition of the output alphabet has to be expanded. Analyze the structure of this output language.
- As explained, the returning ϵ-transition only has to be taken if a maximal string is recognized. Formalyze this notion.
- The automaton may need look-ahead of one or more tokens. Formalize this notion and give equivalence proofs.

Project 2.4. Do an experimental study of hashing. Implement open and closed hash table algorithms, and do a search on the web for hash functions. Compare to storing the names in a tree. Find some documents to hash: the source of some programs, books. Construct some input data sets to trip up the various algorithms. Measure statistics and do timings.

Chapter 3

Breaking things into pieces

The line breaking algorithm of TeX is interesting, in that it produces an aesthetically optimal solution in very little time.

Handouts and further reading for this chapter

If you still have the book 'Introduction to Algorithms' by Cormen *et al.*, you can find a discussion of Dynamic Programming and NP-completeness there. The books by Bellman are the standard works in this field. Bellman's 'Applied Dynamic Programming' [1] has been put on reserve, *QA264.B353*. The TeX line breaking algorithm is described in an article by Knuth and Plass [13], reprinted in [9].

The standard work on Complexity Theory, including NP-completeness, is Garey and Johnson 'Computers and intractibility' [7]. There is excellent online material about this subject on Wikipedia, for instance http://en.wikipedia.org/wiki/Complexity_classes_P_and_NP. Issues in page breaking are discussed in Plass' thesis [18].

Dynamic Programming. Dynamic programming is an optimization technique, that is, a way of solving problems where a yield function is to be maximized, or a cost function minimized, under certain constraints. Certain optimization problems can be solved using calculus – unconstrained optimization being a prime example – and others by such linear algebra techniques as the simplex method. However, such continuous methods have a hard time dealing with integer constraints. For instance, in computing the yield of a car factory, the number of cars has to be integer.

The type of problems that dynamic programming is suited for is the type where the problem can be formulated as a series of decisions. For instance, in work allocation problems, there is a separate decision for the amount of work to be allocated in each month.

We will start with some examples that show the essential features of the dynamic programming approach.

3.1 Some examples

3.1.1 Decision timing

Our first example concerns the problem of when to make a one-time decision, giving a number of opportunities to do so. This example illustrates the concept of a series of decisions, and of starting at the final stage and working backward from that.

The surprise menu in a new restaurant works as follows. You will be shown 5 dishes in sequence, and you can pick one that you like, but if you turn one down, you can not reconsider. Let us say that each dish scores between 0 and 1 on your attractiveness scale. How do you maximize your choice of dish?

Call the scores you give the dishes x_i, and N the number of dishes.
- If you wait till the last dish, you have no choice.
- The last dish can be anything, so the best you can say is that it will have an expected attractiveness of 0.5. Therefore, if $x_{N-1} > 0.5$, you take that one, since it is better than what you can expect in the next step.
- Now, you will take dish $N-1$ in half the cases, giving you on average a .75 score, and the other half of the cases you take dish N, with a score of .5. Therefore, you are expecting to score .625, and you will take dish $N-2$ if it scores more than that.
- In .375 of the cases, dish $N-3$ will score higher than that.
- Et cetera.

From this example we see some characteristics:

3.1. SOME EXAMPLES

Stages The optimization problem involves a sequence of stages, each involving a choice.

Principle of optimality Once you arrive at a certain stage, the optimal solution for the rest of the path is independent of how you got to that stage.

Stepwise solution The solution (here: solution strategy) is arrived at by starting at the final and working backward. We will also examples that are solved forward; in general it is a characteristic that dynamic programming problems are solved stage-by-stage.

Often, the fact that the problem is solved starting at the last stage is considered an essential feature. We will not do so: many dynamic programming problems can also be solved forward.

> **Exercise 30.** For this example, draw up the recurrence relation between the expected scores. Prove that the relation is monotonically increasing (for decreasing index), and bounded above by 1, in fact with limit 1. Bonus: solve this relation explicitly.

3.1.2 A manufacturing problem

Suppose a factory has N months time to produce a quantity S of their product, which we will for now assume to be bulk. Because of seasonal variations, in month k the cost of producing an amount p_k is $w_k p_k^2$. The problem is to produce the requested amount in the given time, at minimal cost, that is

$$\min_{\sum p_k = S} \sum w_k p_k^2.$$

We break down the problem by looking at the cost for producing the remaining amount in the remaining time. Define the minimum cost as

$$v(s|n) = \min_{\sum_{k>N-n} p_k = s} \sum w_k p_k^2$$

and $p(s|n)$ as the work that has to be done n months from the end, given that s work is left, then, by splitting this into the cost this month plus the cost for the then remaining time, we get

$$\begin{aligned} v(s|n) &= \min_{p_n \leq s} \left\{ w_n p_n^2 + \sum_{\substack{k > N-n+1 \\ \sum p_k = s - p_n}} w_k p_k^2 \right\} \\ &= \min_{p_n \leq s} \left\{ w_n p_n^2 + v(s - p_n | n - 1) \right\} \end{aligned}$$

That is, we get a recurrence where the remaining work for n months is expressed in that for $n - 1$ months.

Starting off is easy: $p(s|1) = s$, and $v(s|1) = w_1 s^2$. By the above rule then

$$v(s|2) = \min_{p_2}\{w_2 p_2^2 + v(s - p_2|1)\} = \min_{p_2} c(s, p_2)$$

where $c(s, p_2) = w_2 p_2^2 + w_1(s-p_2)^2$. We find the minimum by taking $\delta c(s, p_2)/\delta p_2 = 0$, which gives us $p(s|2) = w_1 s/(w_1 + w_2)$ and $v(s|2) = w_1 w_2 s^2/(w_1 + w_2)$.

Solving one or two more steps like this, we notice the general form:

$$p(s|n) = \frac{1/w_n}{\sum_{i=1}^{n} 1/w_i} s, \qquad v(s|n) = s^2 \sum_{i=1}^{n} 1/w_i.$$

This solution can in fact be derived by a variational approach to the constraint minimization problem

$$\sum_k w_k p_k^2 + \lambda(\sum_k p_k - S)$$

for which we set the derivatives to both p_n and λ to zero.

This problem shows another characteristic of dynamic programming:

State The cost (yield) function that we define as a function of the stage, also has a state parameter. It typically describes the amount of some constrained quantity that is still left. In this case, that is the amount still to be produced.

We see that for this problem there is both an analytical solution, and one found by dynamic programming, using analytical techniques for local optimization. However, these techniques would become increasingly cumbersome, if we imposed restrictions such as that the factory does not have unlimited production capacity, or even impossible, if the product can only be made in discrete units, meaning that the p_n have to be integers.

The next problem is a good example of the sort of discrete choices that dynamic programming is well suited for.

3.1.3 The stagecoach problem

A business man in the Old West needs to travel from city 0 to city 8. For this, he has to go through 3 other cities, but in each stage of the trip there are choices. This being the Wild West, he decides to get travel insurance. However, not all routes are equally safe, so the cost of insurance varies. The problem is to find the trip that minimizes the total cost of the insurance.

3.1. SOME EXAMPLES

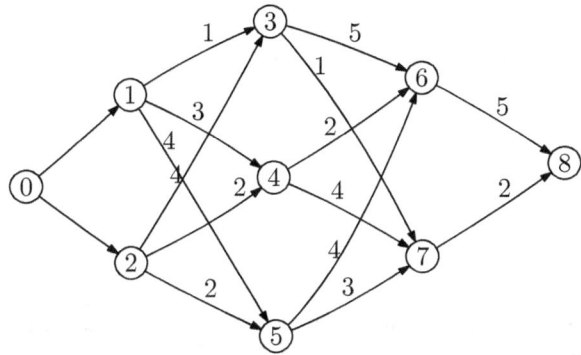

We will look at various ways of solving this problem. First let us define the data.

```
table = [ [0, 5, 4, 0, 0, 0, 0, 0, 0], # first stage: 0
          [0, 0, 0, 1, 3, 4, 0, 0, 0], # second: 1 & #2
          [0, 0, 0, 4, 2, 2, 0, 0, 0],
          [0, 0, 0, 0, 0, 0, 5, 1, 0], # third: 3, #4, #5
          [0, 0, 0, 0, 0, 0, 2, 4, 0],
          [0, 0, 0, 0, 0, 0, 4, 3, 0],
          [0, 0, 0, 0, 0, 0, 0, 0, 5], # fourth: 6 & #7
          [0, 0, 0, 0, 0, 0, 0, 0, 2]
        ]
final = len(table);
```

3.1.3.1 The wrong way to solve this

The solution to the stage coach problem is easy to formulate recursively, given that you are in some city:

- If you are in the final city, the cost is zero;
- Otherwise it is the minimum – over all cities reachable from here – of the cost of the next leg plus the minimum cost from that city.

```
# the wrong way
def cost_from(n):
    # if you're at the end, it's free
    if n==final: return 0
    # otherwise range over cities you can reach
    # and keep minimum value
    val = 0
    for m in range(n+1,final+1):
        # for all later cities
        local_cost = table[n][m]
```

```
            if local_cost==0: continue
            # if there is a connection from here,
            # compute the minimum cost
            local_cost += cost_from(m)
            if val==0 or local_cost<val:
                val = local_cost
    return val
print "recursive minimum cost is",cost_from(0)
```

If there are N cities, divided into S stages of L cities in each stage, and assuming that in each stage all cities of the next stage are reachable, the cost of this algorithm is $O(L^S)$.

3.1.3.2 Dynamic programming solution

The implementation strategy of the previous section is wasteful. Consider some city 1, and cities 2 and 3 in the stage before that. The cost computations from 2 and 3 both compute the cost from 1, which is clearly redundant. We call this characteristic

Overlapping subproblems: A straightforward (recursive) solution to the problem would revisit a subproblem, meaning that different solution attempts have a common subproblem.

Recognizing this leads us to a better solution strategy: once the minimum cost from one city has been computed, we store it for future reference.

An equivalent interpretation of this strategy is that we compute in each stage a cost function $f_n(x_n)$, describing the cost of reaching the end starting at the nth step, giving that we start there in city x_n. This is in fact a dynamic programming solution, with x_n the state variable in the nth stage.

Formally, $f_k(s)$ is the minimum cost for traveling the from stage k given that your are in city s in that stage. Then
$$f_{k-1}(s) = \min_t \{c_{st} + f_k(t)$$
where c_{st} is the cost of traveling from city s to t.

Initially, the cost from every city till the final one (in particular from the final one itself) is zero:

```
# initialization
cost = (final+1)*[0]
```

Now we loop backwards over the stages, computing in each stage the cost of all city we can go through. These two loops – the stages, and the cities in each stage – can actually be collapsed into one loop:

3.1. SOME EXAMPLES 111

```
# compute cost backwards
for t in range(final-1,-1,-1):
    # computing cost from t
```

For each city `t` we consider the ones `i` that are reachable from it. By induction, for these later ones we already know the cost of going from them to the final one, so the cost from `t` to the final one is the cost from `t` to `i` plus the cost from `i`:

```
for i in range(final+1):
    local_cost = table[t][i]
    if local_cost==0: continue
    local_cost += cost[i]
```

If there was no cost yet associated with `t`, we set it now, otherwise we compare the cost from `t` over `i` with the cost of an earlier evaluated route:

```
if cost[t]==0 or local_cost<cost[t]:
    cost[t] = local_cost
```

In the end, the minimum cost is given in `cost[0]`.

We see that the main difference between this solution and the recursive one given above, is that the recursive function call has been replaced by a lookup in a table.

The running time of this algorithm is $O(N \cdot L)$ or $O(L^2 S)$, which is a considerable improvement over L^S for the straightforward implementation. This solution carries an extra cost of N memory locations; on the other hand, it does not build up a recursion stack.

3.1.3.3 Forward dynamic programming solution

This problem was solved by starting at the end point. We can also work our way to the solution forwards, with a code that is essentially the same. Instead of computing the cost of reaching the final city from an intermediate, we now compute the cost of reaching the intermediate city from the initial one.

We loop over all cities and all their connections:

```
cost = (final+1)*[0]
for t in range(final):
    for i in range(final+1):
        local_cost = table[t][i]
        if local_cost == 0: continue
```

Now we can compute the cost to the connecting city as the transition cost, plus the known minumum cost to get where we are:

Victor Eijkhout

```
            cost_to_here = cost[t]
            newcost = cost_to_here+local_cost
            if cost[i]==0 or newcost<cost[i]:
                cost[i] = newcost
```

The result is now in `cost[final]`.

The minimization problem corresponding to this algorithm concerns $f_k s$, the cost to get to city s in stage k. Then

$$f_{k+1}(t) = \min_s \{c_{st} + f_k(s)\}$$

which is equivalent to the earlier problem.

Exercise 31. A 'sparse matrix' is a matrix where a number of matrix elements are zero, sufficiently many that you do not want to store them. To compute the matrix vector product $y = Ax$ you then do not compute the full sum $y_i = \sum_j a_{ij} x_j$, but only those terms for which $a_{ij} \neq 0$. This sort of operation is easy enough to code, but is pretty inefficient in execution.

Suppose that for small k the product with k consecutive matrix elements (that is $a_{ij} x_j + a_{ij+} x_{j+1} + \cdots + a_{ij+k-1} x_{j+k-1}$ can be executed more efficiently than doing it as k separate operations. For instance, suppose that with $k = 3$ the time per $a_i.x.$ reduced to .4 of the normal multiply time, that is, doing three consecutive multiplications as a block takes time 1.2, while doing them separately takes time 3.

Now, if $a_{11} \neq 0, a_{12} = 0, a_{13} \neq 0$, the multiplication $a_{11} x_1 + a_{13} x_3$ takes time 2, but if we store the intermediate zero at a_{12}, the size 3 block multiplication takes time 1.2. This means that doing some superfluous operations (multiplying by zero) we can actually speed up the matrix-vector product.

Let a pattern of nonzeros and reduction factors be given. The pattern stands for the locations of the nonzeros in a matrix row, for instance
`row = [1,0,0,1,0,1,1,0,0,1,0,0,0,1,1,0,1,1]`
`redux = [1, .75, .4, .28]`
Formulate a principle of optimality for this problem, and write a dynamic programming solution for finding the covering of the sparse row that will lead to the shortest multiplication time. Tinker with the `redux` times (but make sure the n-th is more than $1/n$ in base-1 indexing) and see how the solution changes.

3.1.4 Traveling salesman

The above problems all had dynamic programming solutions with a cost slightly more than linear in the input problem size. Dynamic programming does not always give that low a complexity.

The traveling salesman problem looks a bit like the stagecoach problem above. However, now the traveler does not only need to go from a starting to a final city, he also has to visit every city on his travel.

This problem can be solved by dynamic programming, but the concept of stage is now more complicated. We can no longer map the cities into a linear ordered set of stages since they can be visited in any sequence.

The solution is to let stage n correspond to picking the nth city, and to define the current state as the last visited city, plus the set of the remaining ones. Initially we loop over all possible last cities, so the cost is the sum of the single leg trip to the end point, plus the minimum cost through remaining cities. unvisited cities.

To be precise: a state is a pair (S, f) of a set of cities left to be visited, and the current city $f \in S$.

We can now construct a cost function that depends on the stage and the current state.

$$\begin{aligned} C(\{1\}, 1) &= 0 \\ C(\{f\}, f) &= a_{1f} \quad \text{for } f = 2, 3, \ldots \\ C(S, f) &= \min_{m \in S - f} [C(S - f, m)] + a_{mf}] \end{aligned}$$

This is easily enough implemented:

```
def shortest_path(start,through,lev):
    if len(through)==0:
        return table[start][0]
    l = 0
    for dest in through:
        left = through[:]; left.remove(dest)
        ll = table[start][dest]+shortest_path(dest,left,lev+1)
        if l==0 or ll<l:
            l = ll
    return l
to_visit = range(1,ntowns);
s = shortest_path(0,to_visit,0)
```

This solution has factorial complexity.

3.2 Discussion

In the example above we saw various properties that a problem can have that make it amenable to dynamic programming.

Stages The optimization problem involves a sequence of stages, each involving a choice, or a discrete or continuous parameter to be determined.

Stepwise solution The solution is arrived at by solving the subproblems in the stages one by one. Often this is done starting at the final stage and working backward.

State The cost (yield) function that we define as a function of the stage, also has a state parameter. It typically describes the amount of some constrained quantity that is still left to be consumed or produced.

Overlapping subproblems This is the property that a straightforward (recursive) solution to the problem would revisit a subproblem, meaning that different solution attempts have a common subproblem.

Principle of optimality This is the property that the restriction of a global solution to a subset of the stages is also an optimal solution for that subproblem.

The principle of optimality is often phrased thus:

> An optimal policy has the property that whatever the initial state and initial decision are, the remaining decisions must be an optimal policy with regard to the state resulting from the first decision.

It is easy to show that the principle of optimality holds for certain functions and constraints. For example, consider the problem of maximizing $\sum_i^N g_i(x_i)$ under the constraint $\sum_i x_i = X$ where $x_i \geq 0$. Call this maximal sum $f_N(X)$, then

$$
\begin{aligned}
f_N(X) &= \max_{\sum_i^N x_i = X} \sum_i^N g_i(x_i) \\
&= \max_{x_N < X} \left\{ g_N(x_N) + \max_{\sum_i^{N-1} x_i = X - x_N} \sum_i^{N-1} g_i(x_i) \right\} \\
&= \max_{x_N < X} \left\{ g_N(x_N) + f_{N-1}(X - x_N) \right\}
\end{aligned}
$$

We see here that the form of the g_i functions does not enter the argument, but the fact that the total utility is a sum of g_is does. Utility functions that are not symmetric in the component g_i functions clearly can not straightforwardly be solved with dynamic programming.

"Diglio A. Simoni" <diglio@simoni.org> wrote in message
news:ouFTc.27970$Kt5.1192@twister.nyroc.rr.com...
> Suppose C(m,dist[d]) is the optimal solution to travel distance d
> gas stations

3.2. DISCUSSION 115

That won't do, because:

```
> Two cases arise
>     a) Buy gas at station m, in which case:
>
>            cost = C(m-1,dist[m]) + price[m] * ( (dist[m] - dist[j] ) / 10 )
> + D( dist[m] - dist[j] )
```

You can't do that. The problem says you have to fill your tank, and since the parameters of the cost function don't capture how much gas you have left, you don't know how much filling your tank will cost.

In fact, the number of gas stations you've used at any point is irrelevant. If you could put in however much gas you liked, you wouldn't need to use dynamic programming to find a solution.

Since your prof asked for complexity analysis in terms of distance, I can tell that he expects you to use something like C(n,i) = the minimum price paid to get to dist[i] with n gallons of gas left in the tank, which works just fine.

You'll probably get extra marks if you expain how you can use a different cost function, or just a little finesse in the implementation, to get a better complexity result in terms of the number of gas stations.

Victor Eijkhout

TEX paragraph breaking. Breaking a paragraph into lines is the problem of, given a string of words and other material with intervening spaces, breaking that string into chunks (lines) of approximately equal length, and doing so in a visually attractive way. Simple strategies (see the 'first fit' algorithm below) give a result that is easy to compute, but that can be visually very unappealing. While the problem of finding globally optimal line breaks sounds very hard – with n words there are 2^n ways of breaking the paragraph; also, this problem resembles the bin-packing problem which is NP-complete – it can actually be solved fairly efficiently.

TEX's basic strategy is to calculate the badness of breaking the lines at certain points, and to minimize the badness over the whole paragraph.

3.3 The elements of a paragraph

TEX's paragraph breaking algorithm is based around the concepts of

- Boxes: this comprises letters, formulas, TEX boxes, and other material of a fixed with.
- Glue: this is white space; a glue item has a natural width, stretchability, and shrinkability.
- Penalties: these are items that express the desirability or undesirability of breaking a line at a particular point.

The same elements are also present in a vertical list; in both cases there are some other, more rare items, that we will ignore here.

3.3.1 Some details

3.3.1.1 Boxes

The boxes in a paragraph are such things as words, rules, math formulas, and actual TEX \boxes. A box can not be broken: it is completely described by its height, depth, width. Actually, looking at words as boxes is too simplistic, since words can often be hyphenated. This means that a word is a sequence of boxes alternating with penalties.

3.3.1.2 Penalties

A penalty item describes the desirability or undesirability of breaking a list at some point. Penalties can be inserted by hand (most often as the \nobreak macro, which is equivalent to \penalty10000), or in a macro, or are inserted by TEX itself. An

3.3. THE ELEMENTS OF A PARAGRAPH

example of the latter case is the `\hyphenpenalty` which discourages breaking at a hyphen in a word.

Hyphenating a word can be simulated by having a penalty of zero at the hyphenation location. Since this usually introduces a hyphen character, TeX internally pretends that penalties can have a width if the list is broken at that place.

The most common types of penalty are the infinite penalty that starts a non-breaking space, and the penalty associated with breaking by hyphenating a word. The latter kind is called a 'flagged penalty', and TeX has an extra amount of demerits associated with them, for instance to prevent two consecutive lines ending in a hyphen.

Penalties can have positive and negative values, to discourage or encourage breaking at a specific place respectively. The values $+\infty$ and $-\infty$ are also allowed, corresponding to a forbidden and forced break respectively.

3.3.1.3 Glue

A 'glue' is a dimension with possible stretch and/or shrink. There are glue denotations, such as `2cm plus .5cm minus .1cm`, or glue parameters, such as `\leftskip` or `\abovedisplayskip`. The parameters are inserted automatically by the various TeX mechanisms.

Glue can be measured in points `pt`, centimeters `cm`, millimeters `mm`, inches `in`. There is also infinite glue: `fil`, `fill`, and `filll`. Presence of TeX's infite glue (`fill`) causes all other glue to be set at natural width, that is, with zero stretch and shrink.

If there is more than one glue item in a list, the natural widths and the stretch and shrink amounts are added together. This means that a list with both `2cm plus 1cm` and `2cm plus -1cm` has no stretch since the stretch amounts add up to zero. On the other hand, with `2cm plus 1cm` and `2cm minus 1cm` it has both stretch and shrink.

The stretch and shrink components of glue are not treated symmetrically. While in a pinch we can allow a line to be stretched further than the indicated maximum, we can not allow spaces to be shrunk to zero, or even close to that.

3.3.1.4 Stretch and shrink

Each space can have stretch and shrink. When we consider a line, we add up all the stretch and shrink and compute an 'adjustment ratio' as the ratio of the shortfall or excess space to the available stretch or shrink repectively. This ratio r is negative for lines that need to be shrunk.

A simple algorithm would be to impose a limit of $|r| \leq 1$ (and then to minimize the number of hyphenations under that restriction), but that might be too restrictive. Instead, TeX uses a concept of 'badness'. The badness of a line break is infinite if $r < -1$; otherwise it is cubic in the absolute size of r.

3.3.1.5 Line break locations

Here are the main (but not the only) locations where TeX can decide to break a line.

- At a penalty
- At a glue, if it is preceeded by a non-discardable item, meaning, not a penalty or other glue
- At a hyphen in a word
- At a place where TeX knows how to hyphenate the word. (There is actually a mechanism, called 'discretionaries' that handles these last two cases.)

3.3.2 Examples

Here are a few examples of the things that the boxes/penalties/glue mechanism is capable of.

3.3.3 Centered text

By using \leftskip and \rightskip we can get centered text.

```
\begin{minipage}{4cm}
\leftskip=0pt plus 1fil \rightskip=0pt plus 1fil
\parfillskip=0pt
This paragraph puts infinitely stretchable glue at
the left and right of each line.
The effect is that the lines will be centered.
\end{minipage}
```

Output:

> This paragraph puts
> infinitely stretchable glue
> at the left and right of
> each line. The effect is
> that the lines will be
> centered.

The following centers only the last line. This is done by letting the \leftskip and \rightskip cancel each other out, except on the last line.

3.3. THE ELEMENTS OF A PARAGRAPH 119

```
\begin{minipage}{5cm}
\leftskip=0pt plus 1fil \rightskip=0pt plus -1fil
\parfillskip=0pt plus 2fil
This paragraph puts infinitely stretchable glue at
the left and right of each line, but the amounts cancel out.
The parfillskip on the last line changes that.
\end{minipage}
```

Output:

> This paragraph puts infinitely stretchable glue at the left and right of each line, but the amounts cancel out. The parfillskip on the last line changes that.

3.3.3.1 Hanging punctuation

Hanging punctuation is a style of typesetting where punctuation that would wind up against the right margin is actually set *in* the right margin. Optically, this makes the margin look straighter.

```
\newbox\pbox  \newbox\cbox
\setbox\pbox\hbox{.}  \wd\pbox=0pt
\setbox\cbox\hbox{,}  \wd\cbox=0pt
\newdimen\csize  \csize=\wd\cbox
\newdimen\psize  \psize=\wd\pbox

\catcode`,=13 \catcode`.=13
\def,{\copy\cbox \penalty0 \hskip\csize\relax}
\def.{\copy\pbox \penalty0 \hskip\psize\relax}
```

> Here is a bit of text in a minipage, with too much punctuation. Every sentence, long or short, is overly, yes, overly, punctuated. This should show off 'hanging punctuation'.

Victor Eijkhout

3.3.3.2 Mathematical Reviews

In 'Mathematical Reviews' the name of the reviewer should be separated sufficiently from the review, but fit on the same line if space allows.

> This review is rather negative, almost devastating.   A. Reviewer
>
> This review is als very negative but it's longer than the other.
>   A. Nother-Reviewer

We do this by having two separate infinite glues with a break in between, and with a total natural width equal to the minimum separation. The trick is to make sure that the second glue is not discarded after a break, which we do by putting an invisible box at the beginning.

```
\def\signed#1{\unskip
  \penalty10000 \hskip 40pt plus 1fill
  \penalty0
  \hbox{}\penalty10000
            \hskip 0pt plus 1fill
  \hbox{#1}%
            \par
}
```

3.4 TeX's line breaking algorithm

3.4.1 Elements

3.4.1.1 Glue setting and badness

In order to make a list fit a prescribed dimension, there is a process called 'glue setting'. The natural size of the list and the desired size are compared. Let ρ be the ratio of the amount stretched (shrunk) to the possible amount of stretch (shrink). The exact definition is such that the ratio is positive for stretch and negative for shrink: let ℓ be the desired length of the line, L the natural width, X the available stretch and Y the available shrink, then

$$\rho = \begin{cases} 0 & \ell = L \\ (\ell - L)/X & \text{(stretch:)}\ \ell > L\ \text{and}\ X > 0 \\ (\ell - L)/Y & \text{(shrink:)}\ \ell < L\ \text{and}\ Y > 0 \\ \text{undefined} & \text{otherwise} \end{cases}$$

3.4. TEX'S LINE BREAKING ALGORITHM

Then the 'badness' of the needed glue setting is

$$b = \begin{cases} 10\,000 & \rho < 1 \text{ or undefined} \\ \min\{10\,000, 100|\rho|^3\} & \text{otherwise} \end{cases}$$

Since 10 000 is considered infinite in glue arithmetic, this algorithm allows glue to be stretched further than the indicated amount, but not shrunk beyond what is available.

A list that is stretched or shrunk is put in one of the following four categories:

tight (3) if it has shrunk with $b \geq 13$
decent (2) if $b \leq 12$
loose (1) if it has stretched with $100 > b \geq 13$
very loose (0) if it has stretched with $b \geq 100$

Note that $100 \times (1/2)^3 = 12.5$, so the crossover values denote that half the stretch or shrink is used.

Lines that differ by more than one in their classifications are called 'visually incompatible'.

3.4.1.2 Demerits

Breaking a line at a certain points gives the penalty p associated with that point, and the badness b of the resulting stretch/shrink. These are combined into a 'demerits' figure:

$$d = \begin{cases} b^2 + p^2 & 0 \leq p < 10\,000 \\ b^2 - p^2 & -10\,000 < p < 0 \end{cases}$$

The demerits for breaking a paragraph along a certain sequence of break points is then the sum of the demerits of the lines, plus \adjdemerits for every two lines that are not visually compatible (section 3.4.1.1), \doublehyphendemerits for pairs of lines that end in a hyphen, and \finalhyphendemerits if the last full line ends in a hyphen.

TEX acts as if before the first line there is a line that is 'decent'; the last line will typically contain infinite glue, so all spaces are set at natural width.

For full generality, the last line of a paragraph is handled like any other. Filling out the line to the margin is realized by added infinite glue plus a trailing penalty that forces a line break at the end of the paragraph.

3.4.2 Breaking strategies

We will now look at a couple of line breaking strategies. The first two will be strictly local; the third – TEX's algorithm – is able to optimize in a more global sense.

The problem with local algorithms is that they can not take a slightly worse solution in one line to prevent much worse from happening later. This will for instance allow tight and very loose lines to occur next to each other.

3.4.2.1 First fit

The traditional algorithm for line breaking only looks at the current line. Once a word is starting to exceed the right margin, the following cases are investigated.

1. If the spaces in the line can be compressed without exceeding some maximum shrinkage, break after this word.
2. Otherwise, if the spaces can be stretched short of some maximum, break before this word.
3. Otherwise, try hyphenating this word.
4. If no hyphenation point can be found, accept a line with spaces stretched to whatever degree is needed to break before this word.

If you have set text with TeX, you will have noticed that TeX's solution to the last point is slightly different. It will let a word protrude into the right margin as a visual indicator that no good breakpoint could be found. (TeX's tolerance to bad breaks can be increased by setting the `\emergencystretch` parameter.)

This method can be called 'first fit', because it will the first option (compress), without comparing if later options (stretching) look better. This is remedied in TeX by, instead of having an all-or-nothing it fits / it doesn't fit distinction, there is a continuous scale of evaluation.

3.4.2.2 Best fit

A slight improvement on the first fit algorithm results from deciding between the possibilities 1–3 based on badness calculations. This can be termed 'best fit', and while it may work slightly better than fit, it is still a local decision process.

3.4.2.3 Total fit

TeX's actual algorithm calculates the 'demerits' of a line break as a compound of badness, the breakpoint penalty, plus any flagged penalties. It then adds together the demerits of the whole paragraph, and minimizes this number. This makes it possible to use a slightly worse line break early in the paragraph, to prevent a much worse one later.

3.4. TEX'S LINE BREAKING ALGORITHM 123

Exercise 32. In dynamic programming, many solutions start from a final stage and work backwards. Why is this approach inappropriate for TEX's line breaking algorithm? Why would it be even less appropriate for a page breaking algorithm?

3.4.3 Model implementation

We will here only discuss implementations of solutions based on dynamic programming.

The line breaking algorithm goes linearly through the items in the horizontal list, and for each considers whether there is a valid breakpoint after it, and with what cost. For the latter point, it needs to know what the beginning of the line is, so there is an inner loop over all preceeding words. This would make the running time of the algorithm quadratic in the number of words, which is much better than the initial estimate of 2^n.

However, the situation is better than that. The number of words that can fit on a line is limited by what can fit when all spaces are sqeezed to zero. The easiest way to implement this is by maintaining an 'active list' of possible words to begin the line with. A word can be removed from the active list if the material from it to the current word does not fit: if it does not fit now, it will certainly not fit when the next word is considered.

This is then the main program; we will mainly vary the function that computes the breakpoint cost.

```
active = [0]
nwords = len(paragraph)
for w in range(1,nwords):
    # compute the cost of breaking after word w
    for a in active:
        line = paragraph[a:w+1]
        ratio = compute_ratio(line)
        if w==nwords-1 and ratio>0:
            ratio = 0 # last line will be set perfect
        print "..line=",line,"; ratio=",ratio
        if ratio<-1:
            active.remove(a)
            print "active point",a,"removed"
        else:
            update_cost(a,w,ratio)
    report_cost(w)
```

```
active.append(w)
print
```

The only thing different between various strategies is how the cost of a line break is computed by `update_cost(a,w,ratio)`.

> **Exercise 33.** Not every word should be added to the active list. For instance, for any realistic line length, the second word in the paragraph will not have a valid breakpoint after it, so we need not consider it. Take the model implementation and add this modification. Measure the improvement in running time, for instance by counting the number of calls to some inner routine. Give a theoretical argument for how this reduces the complexity of the algorithm.

3.4.3.1 First fit implementation

Since at first we are looking only locally, for each breakpoint we only keep track of the cost and the previous breakpoint that the cost was computed from. Here we set up the data structure `cost`. Element `cost[w]` describes the cost of breaking after word w; the `'from'` component is the number of the first word of the line.

```
def init_costs():
    global cost
    cost = len(paragraph)*[0]
    for i in range(len(paragraph)):
        cost[i] = {'cost':0, 'from':0}
    cost[0] = {'cost':10000, 'from':-1}
```

The essential function is the cost computation. In first fit we accept any stretch or shrink that is $|\rho| < 1$.

```
def update_cost(a,w,ratio):
    global cost
    if a>0 and cost[a-1]['cost']<10000:
        if ratio<=1 and ratio>=-1:
            to_here = abs(ratio)
        else: to_here = 10000
        if cost[w]['cost']==0 or to_here<cost[w]['cost']:
            cost[w]['cost'] = to_here; cost[w]['from'] = a-1
```

(The first test serves to make sure that the previous point being considered is in fact a valid breakpoint.)

Here is the remaining function that constructs the chain of breakpoints:

3.4. TEX'S LINE BREAKING ALGORITHM 125

```
def final_report():
    global cost,nwords,paragraph
    print "Can break this paragraph at cost",\
        cost[nwords-1]['cost']
    cur = len(paragraph)-1; broken = []
    while cur!=-1:
        prev = cost[cur]['from']
        line = paragraph[prev+1:cur+1]
        broken.insert(0,line)
        cur = prev;
    set_paragraph(broken)
```

A small example text, faked in monospace:

```
You  may  never  have  thought  of  it,  but  fonts  (better:     -0.111111111111
typefaces)  usually  have  a  mathematical  definition  somehow.   -0.666666666667
If   a   font   is   given   as   bitmap,   this   is   often      0.888888888889
a   result   originating   from   a   more   compact   description. 0.0
Imagine  the  situation  that  you  have  bitmaps  at  300dpi,  and -0.777777777778
you   buy   a   600dpi   printer.   It   wouldn't   look   pretty.  0.25
There   is   then   a   need   for   a   mathematical   way   of    0.555555555556
describing   arbitrary   shapes.   These   shapes   can   also   be 0.0
three-dimensional;  in  fact,  a~lot  of  the  mathematics  in      -0.285714285714
this  chapter  was  developed  by  a  car  manufacturer  for        0.0
modeling   car   body   shapes.   But   let   us   for   now   only 0.222222222222
look   in   two   dimensions,   which   means   that   the   curves 0.125
are   lines,   rather   than   planes.
```

We see ugly stretched break in line 3, especially after the compressed line 2. However, both of them fit the test.

It is in fact simple to turn this into a dynamic programming solution that considers a global minimum:

```
def update_cost(a,w,ratio):
    global cost
    if ratio<=1 and ratio>=-1:
        to_here = abs(ratio)
    else: to_here = 10000
    if a>0:
        from_there = cost[a-1]['cost']
        to_here = to_here+from_there
    else: from_there = 0
    if cost[w]['cost']==0 or to_here<cost[w]['cost']:
        cost[w]['cost'] = to_here; cost[w]['from'] = a-1
```

3.4.3.2 Best fit

In the best fit strategy, we compute badness from the stretch/shrink ratio. This involves only a slight change in the cost computation function:

```
def update_cost(a,w,ratio):
    global cost
    to_here = 100*abs(ratio)**2
    if a>0:
        from_there = cost[a-1]['cost']
        to_here = to_here+from_there
    else: from_there = 0
    if cost[w]['cost']==0 or to_here<cost[w]['cost']:
        cost[w]['cost'] = to_here; cost[w]['from'] = a-1
```

The same text:

You may never have thought of it, but fonts (better: typefaces) usually have a mathematical definition somehow. If a font is given as bitmap, this is often a result originating from a more compact description. Imagine the situation that you have bitmaps at 300dpi, and you buy a 600dpi printer. It wouldn't look pretty. There is then a need for a mathematical way of describing arbitrary shapes. These shapes can also be three-dimensional; in fact, a~lot of the mathematics in this chapter was developed by a car manufacturer for modeling car body shapes. But let us for now only look in two dimensions, which means that the curves are lines, rather than planes.	-0.111111111111 -0.666666666667 0.5 0.5 -0.777777777778 0.25 0.555555555556 0.0 -0.285714285714 0.0 0.222222222222 0.125

While there are no lines stretched with $\rho >$, the quadratic function has improved the break in line 3.

3.4.3.3 Total fit

For the algorithm that TEX uses, we have to distinguish between lines that are tight, decent, loose. This makes our datastructure more complicated:

```
def init_costs():
    global cost
    nul = [0,0,0]
    cost = len(paragraph)*[ 0 ]
    for i in range(len(paragraph)):
        cost[i] = nul[:]
        for j in range(3):
            cost[i][j] = {'cost':10000, 'from':-2}
```

3.4. TEX'S LINE BREAKING ALGORITHM 127

```
for j in range(3):
    cost[0][j] = {'cost':10000, 'from':-1}
```

An element `cost[i]` is now an array of three possible breakpoints, one in each of the classifications. An actual breakpoint is now in `cost[word][type]['from']` and `cost[word][type]['cost']`.

The cost computation becomes more complicated:

```
def minimum_cost_and_type(w):
    global cost
    c = 10000; t = 0
    for type in range(3):
        nc = cost[w][type]['cost']
        if nc<c:
            c = nc; t = type
    return [c,t]
def update_cost(a,w,ratio):
    global cost
    type = stretch_type(ratio)
    to_here = 100*abs(ratio)**2
    if a>0:
        [from_there,from_type] = minimum_cost_and_type(a-1)
        to_here += from_there
    else: from_there = 0
    if cost[w][type]['cost']==0 or\
        to_here<cost[w][type]['cost']:
        cost[w][type]['cost'] = to_here;
        cost[w][type]['from'] = a-1
```

Exercise 34. The total fit code does not yet contain the equivalent of TEX's `\adjdemerits`. Add that.

Let us look at the same test text again:

```
You may never have thought of it, but fonts (better:      -0.111111111111
typefaces) usually have a mathematical definition          1.2
somehow. If a font is given as bitmap, this is often a     -0.454545454545
result originating from a more compact description.        0.5
Imagine the situation that you have bitmaps at             1.0
300dpi, and you buy a 600dpi printer. It wouldn't look     -0.333333333333
pretty. There is then a need for a mathematical way of     -0.4
describing arbitrary shapes. These shapes can also be      0.0
three-dimensional; in fact, a lot of the mathematics in    -0.285714285714
this chapter was developed by a car manufacturer for       0.0
modeling car body shapes. But let us for now only          0.222222222222
look in two dimensions, which means that the curves        0.125
```

Victor Eijkhout

```
are   lines,   rather   than   planes.
```

In this output, line 2 is stretched further than before, to prevent lower badnesses later.

Exercise 35. Add the functionality for hanging indentation to this code.

Exercise 36. (bonus point exercise) TeX has the possibility of forcing a paragraph to be a line longer or shorter than optimal. Implement that.

3.4.3.4 Utility parts

File header: we read a text and store it.

```
#! /usr/bin/env python

import sys

max_line_length = 60

paragraph = []
while 1:
    try:
        a = raw_input()
        paragraph.extend(a.split())
    except (EOFError):
        break
```

In order to fake stretch and shrink with a monospace font, we let a 'space' be two spaces by default.

```
def line_length(words):
    l = 2*(len(words)-1)
    for w in words:
        l += len(w)
    return l
#
# ratio = -1 : shrink each double space to one
# ratio = 1 : stretch each double space to three
#
def compute_ratio(line):
    spaces = len(line)-1
    need = 1.*(max_line_length-line_length(line))
```

3.4. TEX'S LINE BREAKING ALGORITHM

```
    #print "ratio:",need,spaces
    if spaces==0: return 10000
    else: return need/spaces
```
Output formatting with this idea:
```
def set_paragraph(para):
    for l in range(len(para)-1):
        line = para[l]
        set_line(line)
    set_last_line(para[len(para)-1])
def set_line(line):
    shortfall = max_line_length-line_length(line)
    for w in range(len(line)-1):
        sys.stdout.write(line[w])
        if shortfall>0:
            sys.stdout.write('  '); shortfall = shortfall-1
        elif shortfall<0:
            sys.stdout.write(' '); shortfall = shortfall+1
        else:
            sys.stdout.write(' ')
    sys.stdout.write(line[len(line)-1])
    print " ",compute_ratio(line)
def set_last_line(line):
    for w in range(len(line)-1):
        sys.stdout.write(line[w])
        sys.stdout.write(' ')
    sys.stdout.write(line[len(line)-1])
    print
```

NP completeness.

3.5 Introduction

The 'NP' stands for 'nondeterministic polynomial time', which stands for the fact that a solution can be checked (not: found) in polynomial time. This class of algorithms is informally characterized by the fact there is polymomial time for checking their solution. However, it is also true that there is no polynomial algorithm known for solving them.

"I can't find an efficient algorithm, I guess I'm just too dumb."

The fact that there is no efficient algorithms *known* would not be bad if it could be proved that no efficient algorithm *exists*.

3.5. INTRODUCTION 131

"I can't find an efficient algorithm, because no such algorithm is possible!"

However, also there exists no non-polynomial lower bound on the solution time. Thus, the question whether they can be solved in polynomial time is still open. Since methods in this class can all be translated into each other, having a solution method for one implies that methods exist for all of them. This also means that none of the problems in this class have been solved so far.

"I can't find an efficient algorithm, but neither can all these famous people."

Victor Eijkhout

3.6 Basics

3.6.1 Optimization versus decision problems

Many problems that are said to be NP-complete are optimization problems. For instance, in the traveling salesman problem the shortest route through a set of cities is asked. However, it is more convenient to look at decision problems, that is, problems that have a yes or no answer for each input.

It is not hard to transform an optimization problem into a decision problem. Rather than asking for an optimal solution, we determine a bound B, and ask whether there is a solution that is within that bound.

> **Exercise 37.** Finish this argument. Show that, if we can solve the optimization problem, we can solve the decision problem. Now, supposing we can solve the decision problem, how does that give a solution of the optimization problem? Assume that the outcome of the optimization problem is an integer quantity. Do you have to make other assumptions; discuss? What is the complexity of the one solution method given a certain complexity for the other?

3.6.2 Language of a problem

For each optimization or decision problem we can defined 'instances', which are ways of setting all the free variables of the problem. Since these variables are in sets of types that depend on the problem, we can not be more precise here. A problem can then be phrased as a question over this set of instances: which instances optimize the cost function, or which give a yes answer. That last set we will denote Y_Π.

Again depending on the problem, we can encode instances of a problem. For instance, in the traveling salesman problem, an instance would be encoded as the ordered list of cities to pass through.

With this, we can define the language of a problem:

$$L[\Pi, e] = \{\text{the instances in } Y_\Pi \text{ encoded under } e\}$$

3.6.3 Turing machines

A Turing machine, given some input, can halt with the yes state q_Y, the no state q_N, or can never halt. We say that a string is accepted if it leads the Turing machine to halt with q_Y. The language L_M of a Turing machine M is the set of strings that are accepted.

3.7. COMPLEXITY CLASSES

A deterministic Turing machine (DTM) M is said to solve a problem Π (under some encoding e), or equivalently to recognize $L[\Pi, e]$, if

- it halts for all strings over its input alphabet, and
- its language L_M is $L[\Pi, e]$.

Note that 'solving a problem' here actually means 'recognizing a solution of the problem'. This DTM is a solution checker, not a solution generator.

As an example, consider the recast the traveling salesman problem 'does a route, shorter than B, exist?'. The set of purported solutions are then lists of cities, and the DTM gives for each list a verdict 'yes, this route is shorter than B' or 'no, this route is not shorter than B'.

3.7 Complexity classes

3.7.1 Class P

This allows us to define class P:

$$P = \{L : \text{there is DTM that recognizes } L \text{ in polynomial time}\}$$

and with this

$$\begin{aligned}\Pi \in P &\equiv L[\Pi, e] \in P \quad \text{for some encoding } e \\ &\equiv \text{there is a polynomial time DTM that recognizes } L[\Pi, e]\end{aligned}$$

What this means is that for problems in P there is a polynomial time Turing machine that recognizes strings in Y_Π as valid, and that on strings not in Y_Π it both halts, and gives a negative verdict.

3.7.2 Class NP

Solving the traveling salesman problem may be hard, but if we have a network and some bound, and someone gives us an itinerary with the claim that it satisfies that bound, we can check this with a DTM in polynomial time. We can now build a non-deterministic Turing machine (NDTM) which 'solves' such problems: given a decision problem it 'guesses' some purported solution, and then checks (with a DTM) whether that solves the decision problem. The guessed solution is called a 'certificate'.

Clearly, only if the decision problem has an answer of 'true' can the NDTM guess a solution, so the Y_Π of this problem is precisely the set of decision problem instances with a yes answer.

For instance, for the traveling salesman problem, the instances in Y_Π are a combination of a cities network plus a feasible bound on the travel time. The non-deterministic

Turing machine would then guess an itinerary, and it can be checked in polynomial time that that is indeed a valid route, and that is satisfies the bound.

We can write this whole story compactly: a problem Π is in NP if there is a polynomial time function $A(\cdot, \cdot)$ such that
$$w \in Y_\Pi \Leftrightarrow \exists_C : A(w, C) = \text{true}$$
and C itself can be polynomially generated.

The final condition on the generation of the certificate is needed for a total polynomial runtime, but in practice it is not much of a limitation. For instance, in the traveling salesman problem, a list of cities can be guessed in linear time.

Exercise 38. Prove that NP is closed under union and intersection. What difficulty is there in showing that it is closed under complement taking?

3.7.3 Examples

As was indicated above, while finding a solution to a problem is often hard, checking that something is a solution is often fairly simply and doable in polynomial time. A nontrivial example of a polynomial time problem is checking whether a number is prime. This question was only settled in 2002. Before that there were polynomial time probabilistic testers, which would test a number and return a verdict with high reliability, or with a high probability of polynomial running time.

Exercise 39. Why is the following algorithm not a linear time solution to the PRIME problem?
for $i = 0 \ldots \sqrt{n}$:
   if $\mod(n, i) \equiv 0$
     return true

Other algorithms have provably an exponential running time. Examples here are finding the best move in chess, or checking statements in Pressburger arithmetic.

It is possible to find levels in between polynomial and exponential. The problem of factoring an integer (note that this is more powerful than primality testing) has a runtime of $O(\exp((n \cdot 64/9)^{1/3})(\log n)^{2/3})$. Interestingly, on a quantum computer, a polymial algorithm is known; see http://en.wikipedia.org/wiki/Shors_algorithm.

In the next section we will go further into the middle ground, of algorithms for which no polymomial time algorithm is known, but for which no exponential bound is known either.

3.8 NP-completeness

3.8.1 Transformations

Often it is possible to transform one problem into another. This has the advantage that, if you prove that one problem is in a certain class, the other one is also in that class. Of course this depends on the nature of the transformation.

We will here consider 'polynomial transformations'. Let L_1 and L_2 be the languages of two problems over alphabets Σ_1^* and Σ_2^* respectively, then f is a polymomial transformation of problem 1 into problem 2 if

- There is a DTM that computes $f(x)$ in time $T_f(x) \leq p_f(|x|)$ for some polynomial p_f, and
- For all $x \in \Sigma_1^*$, $x \in L_1$ iff $f(x_1) \in L_2$.

The transformation does not have to be a one-to-one mapping, so it is sometimes explicitly terms a 'many-to-one polynomial transformation'.

Lemma 1 *Suppose f is a polynomial transformation from L_1 to L_2, then*

$$L_2 \in P \Rightarrow L_1 \in P$$

Proof: assume that $M_2 : L_2 \to \{0, 1\}$ is a DTM that recognizes L_2, then $M_2 \circ f$ is a DTM that recognizes L_1, and this composition still runs in polynomial time $T_{M_2 \circ f}(x) \leq p_{T_2}(|p_f(|x|)|)$.

If L_1 transforms to L_2 (in polynomial time), we notate that as $L_1 \leq L_2$. This notation also suggests the idea that L_1 is easier than L_2.

It is easy to see that

$$L_1 \leq L_2 \wedge L_2 \leq L_3 \Rightarrow L_1 \leq L_3,$$

that is, the 'transforms into' relation is transitive.

3.8.2 NP-complete

A language L is said to be NP-complete if

- $L \in NP$, and
- for all $L' \in NP$: $L' \leq L$

(Languages that satisfy the second clause but not the first are called 'NP-hard'. One example is the halting problem, which is known not to be decidable. In other words, the DTM that should recogize the language does not always halt with yes or no.)

Victor Eijkhout

Informally, the class NP-complete is that of the problems where a solution can be verified quickly (meaning, in polynomial time). On the other hand, P is the class of problems where the solution can be *computed* quickly. The question whether these classes are disjoint is open. In fact, you can win a million dollars by settling it one way or another.

Lemma 2 *If $L_1, L_2 \in NP$, L_1 is NP-complete, and $L_1 \leq L_2$, then L_2 is NP-complete.*

Proof: the only thing we need to check is that every $L' \leq L_2$ for all $L_2 \in NP$. Since L_1 is NP-complete, $L' \leq L_1$. Now use the transitivity of the transform relation.

3.8.3 Proving NP-completeness

Above we saw that, given one NP-complete problem, others can easily be proved NP-complete by constructing a mapping between the one problem and the other. This raises a bootstrapping question.

Stephen Cook was the first to prove the NP-completeness of any problem (1971), in his case the satisfiability problem. This is the problem of, given boolean variables $x_1 \ldots x_n$ and a logical formula $F(x_1, \ldots, x_n)$, deciding whether there is a way of specifying the variables such that the result is true.

Examples: the formula $x_1 \vee \neq x_1$ is always true; $x_1 \wedge \neq x_1$ is always false, and $x_1 \wedge \neq x_2$ is only true for the pair $(x_1 = T, x_2 = F)$. For the first and third examples, there are values of x_1, x_2 for which the formula is true, so these are satisfiable. The second example is not satisfiable.

The Boolean satisfiability problem is in NP because a non-deterministic Turing machine can guess an assignment of truth values to the variables, determine the value of the expression under that assignment, and accept if the assignment makes the entire expression true.

Now, to prove that the satisfiability problem is NP-complete, it remains to show that any language $L \in NP$ can polynomially be transformed into it. This is done by assuming a NDPT Turing machine for L, and transforming it into a logical formula, so that there is a correspondence between successful computation in the NDTM, and a satisfied logical formula.

Let the Turing machine be
$$M = \langle Q, s, \Sigma, F, \delta \rangle$$
where

3.8. NP-COMPLETENESS

Q is the set of states, and $s \in Q$ the initial state,
Σ the alphabet of tape symbols,
$F \subset Q$ the set of accepting states, and
$\delta \subset Q \times \Sigma \times Q \times \Sigma \times \{-1, +1\}$ the set of transitions,

and that M accepts or rejects an instance of the problem in time $p(n)$ where n is the size of the instance and $p(\cdot)$ is a polynomial function.

We describe for each instance I a Boolean expression which is satisfiable if and only if the machine M accepts I.

The Boolean expression uses the variables set out in the following table, where $q \in Q$, $-p(n) \leq i \leq p(n)$, $j \in \Sigma$, and $0 \leq k \leq p(n)$:

Variables	Intended interpretation	How many
T_{ijk}	True iff tape cell i contains symbol j at step k of the computation	$O(p(n)^2)$
H_{ik}	True iff the M's read/write head is at tape cell i at step k of the computation.	$O(p(n)^2)$
Q_{qk}	True iff M is in state q at step k of the computation.	$O(p(n))$

Define the Boolean expression B to be the conjunction of the clauses in table **??**, for all $-p(n) \leq i \leq p(n)$, $j \in \Sigma$, and $0 \leq k \leq p(n)$.

This table describes how to construct a logical formula in the variables T_{ijk}, H_{ik}, Q_{qk} (describing tape contents, head positions, and states, respectively) that corresponds to the Turing machine. If there is an accepting computation for M on input I, then B is satisfiable, by assigning T_{ijk}, H_{ik} and Q_{ik} their intended interpretations. On the other hand, if B is satisfiable, then there is an accepting computation for M on input I that follows the steps indicated by the assignments to the variables.

How large is B? There are $O(p(n)^2)$ Boolean variables, each of which may be encoded in space $O(\log p(n))$. The number of clauses is $O(p(n)^2)$. So the size of B is $O((\log p(n))p(n)^2)$. This is polynomial in n, the size of the input, so the transformation is certainly a polynomial-time reduction, as required.

Victor Eijkhout

For all:	Add the clauses	Interpretation	How many clauses?
initial conditions			
Tape cell i of the input I contains symbol j.	T_{ij0}	Initial contents of the tape.	$O(p(n))$
	Q_{s0}	Initial state of M	$O(1)$
	H_{00}	Initial position of read/write head.	$O(1)$
physical constraints			
symbols $j \neq j'$	$T_{ijk} \to \neg T_{ij'k}$	One symbol per tape cell.	$O(p(n)^2)$
states $q \neq q'$	$Q_{qk} \to \neg Q_{q'k}$	Only one state at a time.	$O(p(n))$
cells $i \neq i'$	$H_{ik} \to \neg H_{i'k}$	Only one head position at a time.	$O(p(n))$
Turing machine basics			
i, j, k	$T_{ijk} = T_{ij(k+1)} \lor H_{ik}$	Tape remains unchanged unless written.	$O(p(n)^2)$
$f \in F$	The disjunction of the clauses $Q_{f,p(n)}$	Must finish in an accepting state.	$O(1)$
transition table			
$(q, \sigma, q', \sigma', d) \in \delta$	The disjunction of the clauses $(H_{ik} \land Q_{qk} \land T_{i\sigma k}) \to (H_{(i+d)(k+1)} \land Q_{q'(k+1)} \land T_{i\sigma'(k+1)})$	Possible transitions at computation step k when head is at position i.	$O(p(n)^2)$

Table 3.1: Translation table from a NDPT Turing machine to a logic formula

Page breaking.

3.9 Introduction

T_EX's page breaking algorithm is simpler than the line breaking one. The reason for this is probably that global optimization of breakpoints, the way it is done in the paragraph algorithm, would take prohibitively much memory, at least, for the amount of memory that computers around 1980 had. The algorithm used is related to the 'best fit' algorithm we discussed in the line breaking chapter.

Theoretically, page breaking is a more complicated problem than line breaking. We will explore the issues in section 3.11, but first we will briefly go into the algorithms that TeX actually uses.

3.10 TeX's page breaking algorithm

The problem of page breaking has two components. One is that of stretching or shrinking available glue (mostly around display math or section headings) to find typographically desirable breakpoints. The other is that of placing 'floating' material, such as tables and figures. These are typically placed at the top or the bottom of a page, on or after the first page where they are referenced. These 'inserts', as they are called in TeX, considerably complicate the page breaking algorithms, as well as the theory.

3.10.1 Typographical constraints

There are various typographical guidelines for what a page should look like, and TeX has mechanisms that can encourage, if not always enforce, this behaviour.

1. The first line of every page should be at the same distance from the top. This changes if the page starts with a section heading which is a larger type size.
2. The last line should also be at the same distance, this time from the bottom. This is easy to satisfy if all pages only contain text, but it becomes harder if there are figures, headings, and display math on the page. In that case, a 'ragged bottom' can be specified.
3. A page may absolutely not be broken between a section heading and the subsequent paragraph or subsection heading.
4. It is desirable that
   (a) the top of the page does not have the last line of a paragraph started on the preceding page
   (b) the bottom of the page does not have the first line of a paragraph that continues on the next page.

3.10.2 Mechanisms

The basic goal of page breaking in TeX is to fill up a box of height `\vsize`. The is the goal size of the material without header and footer lines. The box is constructed by adding material to the vertical list until an optimal breakpoint is found. The material before that breakpoint is then put in `\box255`, and the code in `\output`, the 'output routine' is executed. The command to send a box to the output file is `\shipout`.

The typographical rules in the previous section can be realized fairly simply in TeX.

Victor Eijkhout

1. The vertical location of the first line on a page is controlled by \topskip. If the baseline of the first line is closer to the top than this parameter, glue is inserted to make up for the difference.
2. The vertical location of the last line of a page is controlled by \maxdepth. If the last line of the page is deeper than this amount, the reference point of the box is shifted down accordingly.
3. Preventing page breaks between vertical material of different kinds can be done by the proper use of penalties and glue.
4a. A break after the first line of a paragraph is prevented by setting the \clubpenalty.
4b. A break before the last line of a paragraph is prevented by setting the \widowpenalty.

3.10.3 Breakpoints

TEX builds up a current page that is a vertical list of material. It regularly tests whether there is enough material to fill a box of height \vsize while incurring a badness less than $10,000$. The breakpoints are similar to those in the line breaking algorithm, mostly occurring at a penalty, or at a glue that follows non-discardable material.

3.10.4 Some output routines

The very simplest output routine simply takes the vertical list and ships it to the output file:

```
\output={\shipout\box255}
```

Slighly more sophisticated, a header and footer are added:

```
\output={
  \setbox255=\vbox{ <header>
                    \box255
                    <footer>
                  }
  \shipout\box255
  }
```

The following example makes the page one line longer if a widow (break before the last line of a paragraph) occurs. First we save the original \vsize and we declare a recognizable value for the \widowpenalty:

```
\newif\ifEnlargedPage  \widowpenalty=147
\newdimen\oldvsize  \oldvsize=\vsize
```

The output routine now works by testing for the widow penalty, and if it is found, increasing the \vsize and returning the page material to the list by \unvbox255:

3.11. THEORY OF PAGE BREAKING

```
\output={
   \ifEnlargedPage <output the page>
   \else \ifnum \outputpenalty=\widowpenalty
            \global\EnlargedPagetrue
            \global\advance\vsize\baselineskip
            \unvbox255 \penalty\outputpenalty
         \else   \shipout\box255
   \fi    \fi}
```

Here is the missing bit of code that outputs the enlarged page:

```
\ifEnlargedPage \shipout\box255
        \global\LargePagefalse
        \global\vsize=\oldvsize
```

3.10.5 Insertions

Floating material, such as tables and figures, are handled by a mechanism called 'insertions'. Insertions fall in different classes, and insertion material is specified by

```
\insert<class number>{ <material> }
```

If the class number is n, then

- When the output routine is active, \box$n$ contains the material of insertion class n.
- \dimen$n$ specifies the maximum amount of insertion material that is allowed to be placed on one page. If there is more material, it is split with the remainder carried over to the next page.
- There are further fine points to this algorithm.

Insertions are thus added, for as far as possible, to the page being formed when the \insert command is given. TeX has no way of moving insertions to an earlier page, although moving material to a later page – presumable where more space is available – is possible.

3.11 Theory of page breaking

At first glance, the page breaking problem is much like the line breaking problem, except with larger basic blocks, and vertically instead of horizontally. In the line breaking problem, a long list of words is broken into lines, adjusting the margins by stretching or shrinking the interword space. In the page breaking problem, a vertical list of lines, display formulas, and other vertical material, is broken into equal sized pages, using the various amounts of vertical space for taking up the slack.

Victor Eijkhout

However, the page breaking problem becomes much harder if we include the possibility of figures and other floating material. In that case, the computed badness (the measure we try to minimize in the breaking process) will include reflect that we want a figure to be close to pages that reference it, or satisfy other ordering rules involving references to it. Maybe surprisingly, even rather simple cost functions make page breaking into an NP-complete problem.

To get an appreciation of the issues, consider this sequence of pages with figures:

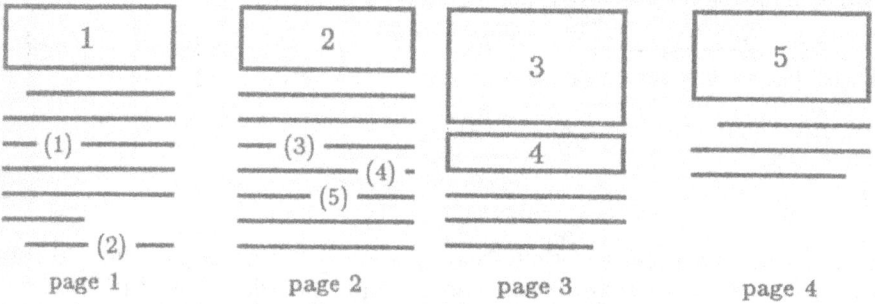

References to the figures are here indicated with parenthesized numbers. We see that out of 5 references, 3 are not to a figure on the same page. However, if we move one line from page 1 to 2, and move figure 3 forward a page, we get:

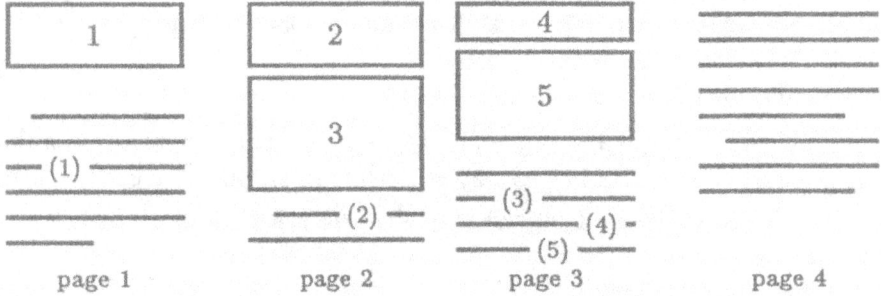

where we see that only one reference is not to the same page. Unfortunately this is a backward reference.

In the remainder of this chapter we will investigate theoretical aspects of functions that try to optimize placement of floating material in a global fashion. It should be noted that this is considerably more sophisticated than what is implemented in TeX. The available algorithm is closer to a 'first fit' strategy.

We will investigate two closely related page breaking algorithms. We show how a

3.11. THEORY OF PAGE BREAKING

particular form of the page breaking problem (the 'MQ' problem) is equivalent to the 2-satisfyability problem, which is known NP-complete. As is usual in the context of proving NP-completeness, we transform our minimization problem 'give the solution with minimum cost' into a decision problem by asking 'is there a solution with a cost $\leq B$' where B is some predetermined bound.

The very similar 'ML' problem, which only differs in the form of the badness function, does have a polynomial time solution.

3.11.1 The MQ problem is NP-complete

We consider the MQ page breaking problem: Multiply referenced figures, and Quadratic badness measure. Under the simplifying assumptions that each figure takes a whole page, we then have a set $T = \{t_1, \ldots, t_N\}$ of text blocks and a set $F = \{f_1, \ldots, f_N\}$ of figures and a function $W : T \times F$ such that $W(t_i, f_j)$ describes how many times text block i references figure j. We assume a bound $W(t_i, f_j) \leq q(N)$ (where q is a polynomial) dependent on the size of the problem.

The MQ problem is now the question whether there is an page ordering of text blocks and figures, that is, a mapping $P : (T \cup F) \to \{1, 2, \ldots, 2N\}$ such that

$$\begin{aligned} P(t_i) < P(t_j) \\ P(f_i) < P(f_j) \end{aligned} \qquad \forall_{1 \leq i < j \leq N}$$

and so that

$$S = \sum_{i,j} W(t_i, f_j)(P(t_i) - P(f_j))^2 \leq B$$

In order to show that this problem is NP-complete, we show that it can be transformed into an instance of the maximum 2-satisfiability problem. This means that solving the one problem is equivalent to solving the other, and since the transformation is done in polynomial time, the two problems have the same complexity.

The maximum 2-satisfiability (MAX 2-SAT problem can be formulated as follows. Let there be given n binary variables $x_1, \ldots, x_n$ and m clauses $\{u_1 \vee v_1, \ldots, u_m \vee v_m\}$, where $u_i = x_j$ or $u_i = \neg x_j$ for some j. Given a bound K, is there a way of setting the x_i variables such that at least K of the clauses are satisfied? This problem is known to be NP-complete.

We will now make a pagination problem that 'translates' an instance of the 2-satisfyability problem. That is, given a configuration of binary variables and clauses and a bound K to satisfy, we will make a pagination problem with bound B such that the one bound is satisfied if and only if the other is. Then, since MAX 2-SAT is NP-complete, it follows that this particular pagination problem is also NP-complete.

Victor Eijkhout

3.11.1.1 Construction of the translation

We make the translation between the two types of problems by constructing the page assignment function P, and the weight function W. There are three aspects we need to take care of, so we let $B = B_1 + B_2 + B_3$, and we will determine the B_i bounds separately.

First of all we set $W(t_i, f_i) = b_1$ sufficiently large that only configuration with $|P(t_i) - P(f_i)| = 1$ will satisfy the bound. (Recall that the badness is a sum of $W(t_i, f_j)(P(t_i) - P(f_j))^2$ terms.) To allow for the pages to be ordered this way, we let $B_1 = Nb_1$. The b_1 quantity will be defined in terms of B_2 and B_3 as

$$b_1 = \lceil (B_2 + B_3)/3 \rceil + 1$$

Supposing that at least one t_i, f_i pair is not adjacent, then it follows from this bound that the badness will be

$$S \geq (N-1)b_1 + 2^2 b_1 = (N+3)b_1 > B$$

where the $N-1$ corresponds to the pairs that are adjacent, and the 2^2 to at least one pair at distance 2.

Since text blocks and are next to each other, the only remaining question is which comes first. This limits the number of cases we need to consider in the remainder of this proof.

Now let parameters n for the number of variables and m for the number of clauses be as described above, then our pagination problem will have N text blocks and figures, where $N = 2n + 2m$. The first $4n$ pages encode the values of the variables x_i, with each consecutive 4 pages corresponding to one variable:

$4i-3$	$4i-2$	$4i-1$	$4i$	
t_{2i-1}	f_{2i-1}	f_{2i}	t_{2i}	if x_i is true
f_{2i-1}	t_{2i-1}	t_{2i}	f_{2i}	if x_i is false

To ensure that these are the only configuration that will satisfy the bound, set $W(t_{2i-1}, f_{2i}) = W(f_{2i-1}, t_{2i}) = b_2$ large enough. Either of the above patterns then contributes $2 \cdot 2^2 b_2 = 8b_2$, while the other possibilities ($t\,f\,t\,f$ and $f\,t\,f\,t$) would contribute $(1^2 + 3^2)b_2 = 10b_2$.

Correspondingly, we allow a bound of $B_2 = 4b_2 \sum (i-j)^2$ where i,j range over the pairs that satisfy $W(t_i, f_j) = b_2$. Defining

$$b_2 = 8(m-k) + 5$$

is sufficient to make violation of this condition outweigh the gain from more clauses being satisfied.

TEX – LATEX – CS 594

3.11. THEORY OF PAGE BREAKING

Next, the $4m$ remaining pages will encode the clauses in a similar manner:

$4n+4j-3$	$4n+4j-2$	$4n+4j-1$	$4n+4j$	
$t_{2n+2j-1}$	$f_{2n+2j-1}$			if u_j is true
$f_{2n+2j-1}$	$t_{2n+2j-1}$			if u_j is false
		t_{2n+2j}	f_{2n+2j}	if v_j is true
		f_{2n+2j}	t_{2n+2j}	if v_j is false

Further conditions on W ensure that the u_j variables indeed correspond to the proper x_i. For instance

$$W(t_{2n+2j-1}, f_{2i}) = W(t_{2i} = f_{2n+2j-1}) = b_2 \quad \text{if } u_j = x_i$$

This term contributes $2d^2 b_2$ to the badness, where d is twice the difference between the subscripts, in this case $d = (2n+2j-2i)$. With a mismatch, a t and f page assignment are reversed, so the contribution becomes $((d-1)^2 + (d+1)^2) = 2(d^2+1)b_2$.

Proper truth values of the clauses are enforced as follows. Observe that the combination where u_j and v_j are both false is the only one that gives a false result. This corresponds to the pagination

$$f_{2n+2j-1} \quad t_{2n+2j-1} \quad f_{2n+2j} \quad t_{2n+2j}$$

In this configuration f_{2n+2j_1} and t_{2n+2j} are spread the furthest apart, so we penalize that with

$$W(t_{2n+2j}, f_{2n+2j_1}) = 5, \qquad W(t_{2n+2j-1}, f_{2n+2j}) = 3.$$

This gives a contribution of 32 for the three true cases, and 48 for the false result. Correspondingly, to allow for K clauses to be satisfied we allow $B_3 = 48(m-K) + 32K$.

Finally, by defining the polynomial $q(i) = 64(i+1)^4$, we have $q(N) > b_1 \geq b_2 > 5 > 3$, so W is bounded as required.

3.11.1.2 NP-completeness

In order to establish NP-completeness of the problem MQ, we need to establish that something is a true instance of MAX 2-SAT iff the translated instance is true for MQ.

Given a truth assignment of the x_is that makes K clauses true, we can now construct a pagination P with a satisfied bound of B.

Conversely, let a pagination with bound B be given, then the corresponding truth assignment makes K clauses true. To see this, inspect each of the details of the translation between the problems, and observe that any violation will cause the bound B to be exceeded.

Victor Eijkhout

3.11.2 The ML problem has a polynomial time solution

The 'ML' problem (Multiply referenced figures, Linear badness function) is identical to MQ, except for the form of the badness function. Having a linear badness function makes it possible to solve this problem by dynamic programming in linear time.

As in MQ, we have text blocks t_i and figures f_j that take up whole pages. We generalize the problem slightly to having different numbers of text and figure blocks:

$$T = \{t_1, \ldots, t_N\}, \qquad F = \{f_1, \ldots, f_M\}$$

The function $W : T \times F$ is such that $W(t_i, f_j) \geq 0$ describes how many times text block i references figure j.

The ML problem is now the question whether, given the above, and given a bound B, there is an page ordering of text blocks and figures, that is, a mapping $P : (T \cup F) \to \{1, 2, \ldots, M + N\}$ such that

$$\begin{aligned} P(t_i) &< P(t_j) \\ P(f_i) &< P(f_j) \end{aligned} \qquad \forall_{1 \leq i \leq N, 1 \leq j \leq M}$$

and so that

$$S = \sum_{i,j} W(t_i, f_j) |P(t_i) - P(f_j)| \leq B$$

3.11.2.1 Dynamic programming solution

The key to a dynamic programming solution of ML is to identify subproblems. The subproblem we consider is

> Given i text blocks and j figures, what is the least badness of placing these on the first $i + j$ pages. Call this partial badness B_{ij}.

The problem here is the 'dangling' references (t_r, f_s) with $r > i, s \leq j$ or $r \leq i, s > j$. The measure $R_{i,j}$ is defined as the number of dangling references after these blocks and figures have been placed.

A dangling reference is either

A forward reference: A text block refering to a figure not yet placed. The number of forward references from the $i + j$ block is

$$F_{ij} = \sum_{\substack{1 \leq r \leq i \\ j < s \leq M}} W(t_r, f_s)$$

A backward reference: A figure that will be reference on a text block not yet placed.) The number of backward references from the $i + j$ block is

$$B_{ij} = \sum_{\substack{i < r \leq N \\ 1 \leq s \leq j}} W(t_r, f_s)$$

3.11. THEORY OF PAGE BREAKING

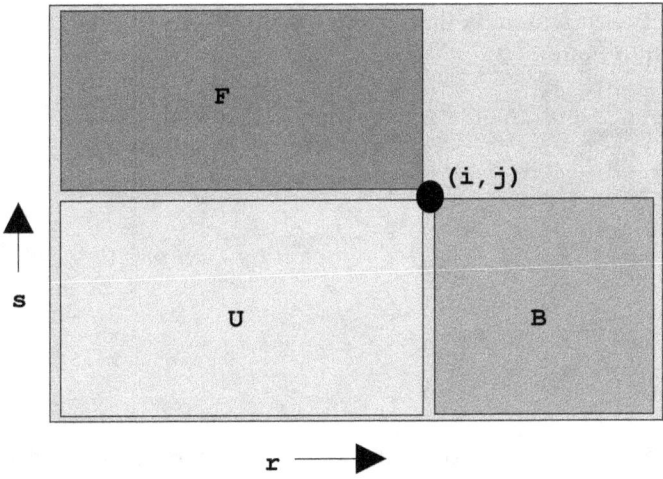

Figure 3.1: The F_{ij}, B_{ij}, and U_{ij} areas in (r,s) space

which makes $R_{ij} = F_{ij} + B_{ij}$.

For badness calculations involving dangling references, we count only the part to the boundary of the i, j region. Formally:

$$B_{ij} = B_{ij}^{(1)} + B_{ij}^{(2)}$$

where

$$B_{ij}^{(1)} = \sum_{\substack{r \le i \\ s \le j}} W(t_r, f_s) \, |P(t_r) - P(f_s)|$$

is the part of the badness due to references that are fully resolved within the pages already placed; the part of the badness due to dangling references is

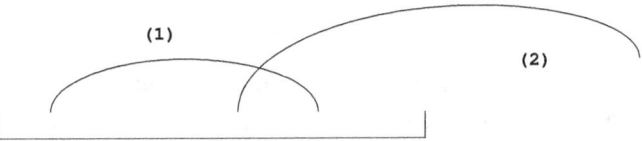

Figure 3.2: Resolved and dangling references of a block of pages

$$B_{ij}^{(2)} = \sum_{\substack{r > i \\ s \le j}} W(t_r, f_s) \, \ell(i,j;r,s) + \sum_{\substack{r \le i \\ s > j}} W(t_r, f_s) \, \ell(i,j;r,s)$$

where

$$\ell(i,j;r,s) = \begin{cases} i + j - P(f_s) & \text{if } r > i \\ i + j - P(t_r) & \text{if } s > j \end{cases}$$

describes the part of the arc between t_r and f_2 that lies in the first $i+j$ pages. These two types of arcs are illustrated in figure 3.2.

Figure 3.3 illustrates how reference arcs change status when we go from $i+j-1$ to $i+j$ pages, say by placing text block t_i:

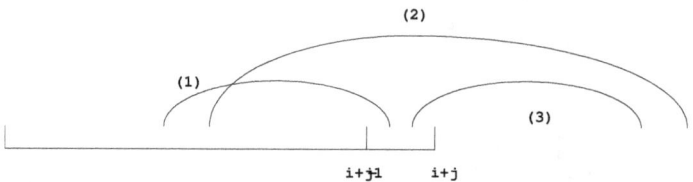

Figure 3.3: Change in status of resolved and dangling references upon extending a block of pages

(1) References that were unresolved with references originating in t_i move their contribution from the $B^{(2)}$ term to the $B^{(1)}$ term. (Note that a reference to a page one location outside the current block is already fully counted in the badness.)

(2) Dangling references that stay unresolved increase their contribution to the $B^{(2)}$ term by $(\sum_{r \leq i-1, s>j} + \sum_{r>i-1, s \leq j}) W(t_r, f_s)$

(3) Arcs that used to fall completely outside the page block, but that are now dangling in the new page block, add a contribution of $\sum_{r=i, s>j} W(t_r, f_s)$ to the $B^{(2)}$ term.

$\sum_{r>i, s \leq j} W(t_r, f_s)$ In sum, $B_{ij} = B_{i-1,j} + R_{ij}$. The same story holds for extending $i+j-1$ pages by placing figure f_j, so we have the recurrence

$$B_{ij} = \min(B_{i-1,j}, B_{i,j-1}) + R_{ij}.$$

We still need to compute the R_{ij} quantities, describing the number of dangling references from placing i text blocks and j figures. Above we saw $R_{ij} = F_{ij} + B_{ij}$. For efficient calculation of these sums, it is convenient to make a table of

$$U_{ij} = \sum_{\substack{1 \leq r \leq i \\ 1 \leq s \leq j}} W(t_r, f_s)$$

which takes time $O(NM)$, that is, quadratic in the total number of pages. Then

$$R_{ij} = U_{iM} + U_{Nj} - 2U_{ij},$$

as is easily seen from figure 3.1.

3.11.3 Discussion

It is interesting to note that certain details of the NP-completeness proof of MQ rely on the quadratic badness function, rather than on more 'structural' properties of the problem.

> **Exercise 40.** Find a place in the NP-completeness proof of MQ that uses the quadratic badness function, and show that the underlying fact does not hold for linear functions. Does it hold for other functions than quadratic?

Similarly, ML only has a dynamic programming solution thanks to the linear badness function.

> **Exercise 41.** Explain how the linearity of the badness function is essential for the dynamic programming solution of ML.

> **Exercise 42.** The discussion of the ML problem only gave the cost computation. How can the actual page assignment be derived from the given construction? What is the time and space complexity of this part of the algorithm?

Projects for this chapter.

Project 3.1. What is the paragraph breaking algorithm of OpenOffice? Replace by TeX's algorithm.

Project 3.2. Write a paragraph breaking algorithm that prevents 'rivers' in the text.

Project 3.3. TeX's line breaking algorithm is not just for good looks. Many aesthetic decisions in typography actually influence readability of the document. Read 'Digital Typography' by Rubinstein [19] and find an issue to investigate.

Project 3.4. Many page layout parameters (Rubinstein [19] and the references therein) have an influence on legibility. Has typographic design deteriorated in that sense now that authors publish their own works? Do a study, using various books in the library.

Project 3.5. The following sentence

> Only the fool would take trouble to verify that this sentence was composed of ten a's, three b's, four c's, four d's, forty-six e's, sixteen f's, four g's, thirteen h's, fifteen i's, two k's, nine l's, four m's, twenty-five n's, twenty-four o's. five p's, sixteen r's, forty-one s's, thirty-seven t's, ten u's, eight v's, eight w's, four x's, eleven y's, twenty-seven commas, twenty-three apostrophes, seven hyphens and, last but not least, a single !

is called a pangram. (There are other pangrams. Google for the combination of 'pangram' and 'Lee Sallows' for this particular type.) Given a beginning of the sentence ('Only the fool...'), solve the rest of the sentence by dynamic programming.

Chapter 4

Fonts

Knuth wrote a font program, Metafont, to go with TeX. The font descriptions involve some interesting mathematics.

Handouts and further reading for this chapter

Bezier curves and raster graphics are standard topics in computer graphics. The book by Foley and Van Dam (section 11.2 about Splines) has been placed on reserve, *T385.C587*. More theoretical information can be found de Boor's Practical Guide to Splines [2], which unfortunately limits itself to spline functions.

Digital typography is a very wide area, spanning from perception psychology and physiology to the electronics and mathematics of display equipment. The book by Rubinstein [19] is a good introduction. This book has been placed on reserve, *Z253.3.R8*.

The relation between Bezier curves and aesthetics is explicitly discussed in `http://www.webreference.com/dlab/9902/examples-ii.html`.

Bezier curves.

4.1 Introduction to curve approximation

You may never have thought of it, but fonts (actually, typefaces) usually have a mathematical definition somehow. If a font is given as a bitmap, this is typically the result from a more compact description. Imagine the situation that you have bitmaps at 300dpi, and you buy a 600dpi printer. It wouldn't look pretty.

There is then a need for a mathematical way of describing arbitrary shapes. These shapes can also be three-dimensional; in fact, a lot of the mathematics in this chapter was developed by a car manufacturer for modeling car body shapes. But let us for now only look in two dimensions, which means that the curves are lines, rather than planes.

A mathematical formalism for curves should have these properties:

- The description should be clear and unambiguous.
- It should be easy to tinker with the shapes. This is important for the design phase.
- Constructing and evaluating the curves should be computationally cheap.
- The curves should be well behaved: small changes in the definition should not lead to unexpected bulges or spikes.
- Curves should be easily composable: if two curves describe adjacent pieces of the shape, they should connect smoothly.

We actually have two problems that we want to solve:

1. The exact curve is known, and we want to approximate it, for instance by something that is cheaper to compute, or
2. Only certain points are given, and we want to draw a smooth curve through them.

We will tackle the second problem first.

4.1.1 Interpolation

The interpolation problem is that of, given points $(x_1, f_1) \ldots (x_n, f_n)$, drawing a curve through them, for instance for purposes of computing intermediate values. Suppose that we have decided on a polynomial for the interpolating curve. With n points we need an $n - 1$st degree polynomial $p(x) = p_{n-1}x^{n-1} + \cdots + p_1 x + p_0$, which takes

4.1. INTRODUCTION TO CURVE APPROXIMATION

n coefficients. We can draw up the set of equations $p(x_i) = f_i$ and solve that. The system
$$p_{n-1}x_1^{n-1} + \cdots + p_1 x_1 + p_0 = f_1$$
$$\cdots$$
$$p_{n-1}x_n^{n-1} + \cdots + p_1 x_n + p_0 = f_n$$
can be written as $X\bar{p} = \bar{f}$, where
$$X = (x_i^j), \quad \bar{p} = \begin{pmatrix} p_1 \\ \vdots \\ p_{n-1} \end{pmatrix}, \quad \bar{f} = \begin{pmatrix} f_1 - p_0 \\ \vdots \\ f_n - p_0 \end{pmatrix}$$
Solving this system is not overly expensive, but its numerical stability is questionable. A better way of computing the same polynomial p is to define auxiliary polynomials $p^{(k)}$:
$$p^{(k)}(x) = c_k(x - x_1) \cdots (x - x_{k-1})(x - x_{k+1}) \cdots (x - x_n)$$
where c_k is chosen so that $p^{(k)}(x_k) = 1$. From the fact that $p^{(i)}(x_j) = \delta_{ij}$, it follows that
$$p(x) = \sum_i f_i p^{(i)}(x), \qquad p^{(i)}(x) = \prod_{j \neq i} \frac{x - x_j}{x_i - x_j} \qquad (4.1)$$
interpolates the points as intended. It is easy enough to prove that polynomials are uniquely defined by these interpolation points, so we have now computed the same polynomial in a more stable way. A polynomial that is based on exact interpolation of values in a number of points is called a 'Lagrange interpolation' polynomial.

Another type of interpolation is 'Hermite interpolation', where the derivatives are dictated, rather than function values. Analogous to the above construction, we can define polynomials
$$q^{(k)} = c_k(x - x_1)^2 \cdots (x - x_{k-1})^2 \cdot (x - x_k) \cdot (x - x_{k+1})^2 \cdots (x - x_n)^2$$
where c_k is chosen so that $q^{(k)\prime}(x_k) = 1$.

4.1.2 Approximation

The above notion of interpolation is sometimes applied to known curves. For instance, by finding an interpolating polynomial we may aim to find a cheaper way of computing values on the curve. This raises the question how well the interpolation curve approximates the original curve.

In classical approximation theory there is usually a family of functions $\{f_n\}$, typically polynomials of increasing degree, such that $\|f_n - f\| \to 0$, typically on a closed interval I. The Weierstrass approximation theorem tells us that every continuous function on a closed bounded interval can be approximated by polynomials.

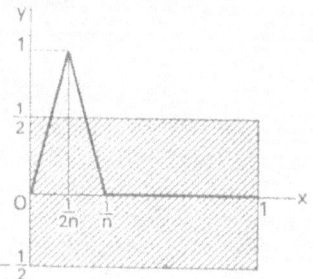

Figure 4.1: A family of functions that converges pointwise but not uniformly.

Note that this is uniform convergence:
$$\forall_\epsilon \exists_N \forall_{x \in I, n \geq N} : |f_n(x) - f(x)| \leq \epsilon.$$
This is a stronger statement than pointwise convergence:
$$\forall_{x \in I, \epsilon} \exists_N \forall_{n \geq N} : |f_n(x) - f(x)| \leq \epsilon.$$
It is easy to find families of functions f_n that convergence in the pointwise sense, but not uniformly; see figure 4.1.

The spline curves that we will study later in this chapter are a special case of Bernstein polymials: the n-th Bernstein polynomials for a function f is
$$B_n(f)(t) = \sum_{p=0}^{n} \binom{n}{p} f(\frac{p}{n})(1-t)^{n-p} t^p.$$
If f is continuous on $[0, 1]$, this sequence converges uniformly to f. It is worth remarking that these polynomials do not require computation of derivatives.

While the ideas behind Lagrange and Hermite interpolation will find applicability later in this story, the idea of interpolating with a single, high degree, polynomial may not be a good one from a point of uniform convergence. The error can be unacceptably large, as can be seen in figure 4.2, where the dashed line is an interpolation on equispaced points. In this case there is in fact not even pointwise convergence. There are a few ways out of that, such as better choice of interpolation points or of basis functions. In figure 4.2 the dotted line uses Tchebyshev interpolation points which is seen to remedy the problem to a large extent.

However, the approach we will use here is that of piecewise approximations with relatively low degree polynomials. This simplifies certain aspects, but we need to take care to piece together such curves smoothly. For instance, with Lagrange interpolation the direction of the curve at the end points can not be specified.

4.1. INTRODUCTION TO CURVE APPROXIMATION

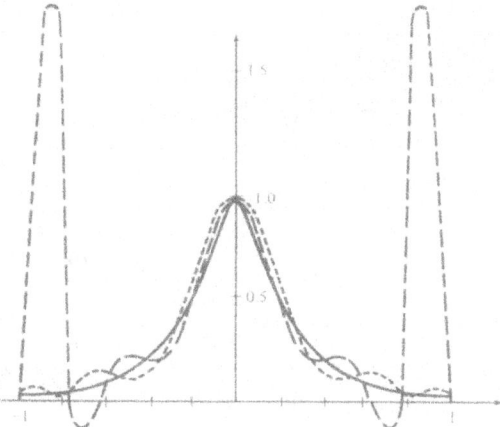

Figure 4.2: The Runge effect of interpolating with a high degree polynomial

4.1.3 Computation with interpolation curves

While we will mostly investigate theoretical properties of interpolation curves, the practical matter of how efficient it is to work with them, also deserves attention. In equation (4.1) there are n terms involving n multiplications and additions each, making for an $O(n^2)$ cost. This can be considerably reduced by rewriting the formula as

$$p(x) = \prod_i (x - t_i) \cdot \sum_i \frac{y_i}{x - t_i}, \qquad y_i = f_i / \prod_{j \neq i}(x_i - x_j),$$

which takes n additions, multiplications, and additions if the y_i quantities are precomputed. We will now see a formulation that dispenses with the divisions, and that will also be simpler if derivatives need to be computed.

The k-th 'divided difference' of a function g in the points $\tau_1 \ldots \tau_{k+1}$, notation $[\tau_1, \ldots, \tau_{k+1}]g$, is the leading coefficient of the k-th order[1] polynomial p_{k+1} that agrees with g in the points $\tau_1 \ldots \tau_{k+1}$.

The simplest examples of divided differences are:

- The zeroeth divided difference of a function is the leading coefficient of a zeroth order polynomial $p(x) = c$ that agrees with that function in one point: $g(\tau_1) = g_1$. Clearly $[\tau_1]g = g_1$.
- The first divided difference is the leading coefficient of a linear function that

---

1. It is convenient to talk about polymomials of a certain order rather than degree: a polynomial of order k has a degree no more than k. We denote this set with $\prod_{<k+1}$. One advantage of this set is that it is closed under summing.

agrees in two points:
$$[\tau_1, \tau_2]g = \frac{g(\tau_2) - g(\tau_1)}{\tau_2 - \tau_1} = \frac{[\tau_2]g - [\tau_1]g}{\tau_2 - \tau_1}$$
This equation may suggest to the reader a relation for higher divided differences. We shall see in lemma 4 that this indeed holds.

We now prove some facts about divided differences.

Lemma 3 *Let* $p_{k+1} \in \prod_{<k+1}$ *agree with* g *in* $\tau_1 \ldots \tau_{k+1}$, *and* $p_k \in \prod_{<k}$ *with* g *in* $\tau_1 \ldots \tau_k$, *then*

$$p_{k+1}(x) - p_k(x) = [\tau_1, \ldots, \tau_{k+1}]g \prod_{i=1}^{k}(x - \tau_i). \tag{4.2}$$

Proof. Since p_k is of a lower order, we immediately have
$$p_{k+1} - p_k = [\tau_1, \ldots, \tau_{k+1}]g x^k + c x^{k-1} + \cdots.$$
Observing that $p_{k+1} - p_k$ is zero in t_i for $i \leq k$, it follows that
$$p_{k+1} - p_k = C \prod_{i=1}^{k}(x - \tau_i).$$
From this we get that $C = [\tau_1, \ldots, \tau_{k+1}]g$. •

If we repeat this lemma we find that
$$p_{k+1}(x) = \sum_{m=1}^{k+1}[\tau_1, \ldots, \tau_m]g \prod_{i=1}^{m-1}(x - \tau_i), \tag{4.3}$$
which we can evaluate as
$$\begin{aligned} p_{k+1}(x) &= [\tau_1, \ldots, \tau_{k+1}]g \prod^{k}(x - \tau_i) + [\tau_1, \ldots, \tau_k]g \prod^{k-1}(x - \tau_i) \\ &= [\tau_1, \ldots, \tau_{k+1}]g(x - \tau_k)(c_k + [\tau_1, \ldots, \tau_k]g(x - \tau_{k-1})(c_{k-1} + \cdots \end{aligned}$$
where $c_k = [\tau_1, \ldots, \tau_k]g / [\tau_1, \ldots, \tau_{k+1}]g$. This is a very efficient evaluation by Horner's rule.

The remaining question is how to construct the divided differences. We approach this recursively.

Lemma 4 *Divided differences can be constructed by, eh, dividing differences*
$$[\tau_1, \ldots, \tau_{n+1}]g = ([\tau_1, \ldots, \tau_n]g - [\tau_2, \ldots, \tau_{n+1}]g) / (\tau_1 - \tau_{n+1}). \tag{4.4}$$

Proof. Let three polynomials be given:
- $p_n^{(1)} \in \prod_{<n}$ agrees with g on $\tau_1 \ldots \tau_n$;
- $p_n^{(2)} \in \prod_{<n}$ agrees with g on $\tau_2 \ldots \tau_{n+1}$;

4.2. PARAMETRIC CURVES

- $p_{n-1} \in \prod_{<n-1}$ agrees with g on $\tau_2 \ldots \tau_n$.

Then by lemma 3
$$p_n^{(1)} - p_{n-1} = [\tau_1, \ldots, \tau_n]g \prod_{j=2}^{n}(x - \tau_j)$$
$$p_n^{(2)} - p_{n-1} = [\tau_2, \ldots, \tau_{n+1}]g \prod_{j=2}^{n}(x - \tau_j)$$

Now let p_{n+1} be the polynomial that agrees with g on $\tau_1 \ldots \tau_{n+1}$, then
$$p_{n+1} - p^{(1)} = [\tau_1, \ldots, \tau_{n+1}]g \prod_{j=1}^{n}(x - \tau_j)$$
$$p_{n+1} - p^{(2)} = [\tau_1, \ldots, \tau_{n+1}]g \prod_{j=2}^{n+1}(x - \tau_j)$$

Subtracting both pairs of equations, we find two expressions for $p_n^{(1)} - p_n^{(2)}$:

$$([\tau_1, \ldots, \tau_n]g - [\tau_2, \ldots, \tau_{n+1}]g)\prod_{j=2}^{n}(x - \tau_j) = [\tau_1, \ldots, \tau_{n+1}]g \left(\prod_{j=2}^{n+1} - \prod_{j=1}^{n}\right)(x - \tau_j)$$

Filling in $\tau_2 \ldots \tau_n$ in this equation, we find zero for both sides. Using $x = \tau_1$ we find

$$([\tau_1, \ldots, \tau_n]g - [\tau_2, \ldots, \tau_{n+1}]g)\prod_{j=2}^{n}(\tau_1 - \tau_j) = [\tau_1, \ldots, \tau_{n+1}]g \prod_{j=2}^{n+1}(\tau_1 - \tau_j)$$

from which the lemma follows. ●

From this lemma, we see easily that $[\tau_1, \ldots, \tau_n]g$ can be computed in approximately $n^2/2$ additions and divisions.

4.2 Parametric curves

So far we have been looking at approximation by a function of a single value. That is, we have y as a function of x. This rules out many curves, such as circles. We could try expressing x as a function of y, or more generally rotating them, but that is a big hassle, and it would still rule out some curves.

Another approach is to let the curve be defined implicitly by $f(x, y, z) = 0$. This suffers from several problems. We could get too many solutions, for instance as in $x^2 + y^2 - 1 = 0$, requiring constraints. Tracking a path is possible in theory, but is not trivial in practice. Finally, many shapes are defined piecewise, and joining shapes in a smooth way is also tricky.

Rather than considering a curve in the plane as a function, it is more productive to describe the shape of the curve, as some imaginary point moves over the curve. That is, we have a description of the points on the curve as
$$P = P(t) = \begin{pmatrix} x(t) \\ y(t) \end{pmatrix}.$$

(Feel free to think of t as time.)

A simple example of how this works is to consider two points P_1 and P_2, and the curve $P = tP_2 + (1-t)P_1$. Then for $t = 0$, $P(0) = P_1$, for $t = 1$, $P(1) = P_2$, and for intermediate values of t we get some point between P_1 and P_2.

That this solves our problems with multiple solutions that were present in both function and implicit approaches is clear if we look at the example $P(t) = (\cos 2\pi t, \sin 2\pi t)$, which traces out a circle as t goes from 0 to 1.

While a description in terms of piecewise linear functions would be very simple, it is not smooth. Using the various ideas sketched above, we will now concentrate on curves that are piecewise parametric cubic splines. Cubics have the following property that they are the lowest degree that allows specification of location and direction in the end points. Higher degree functions would allow for instance the specification of higher derivatives, but unless great care is taken, they would introduce unwanted 'wiggles' in the curves.

Using piecewise cubic parametric curves then is a good mean between ease of use and power of approximation.

4.2.1 Parametrized basis functions

To begin with we will concentrate on a single curve $Q(t)$ where $t = 0 \ldots 1$. We often write this as $Q(t) = C \cdot T$ where the coefficient matrix

$$C = \begin{pmatrix} c_{11} & c_{12} & c_{13} & c_{14} \\ c_{21} & c_{22} & c_{23} & c_{24} \\ c_{31} & c_{32} & c_{33} & c_{34} \end{pmatrix}, \qquad T = \begin{pmatrix} 1 \\ t \\ t^2 \\ t^3 \end{pmatrix}$$

The direction of the curve is then given by

$$\frac{dQ(t)}{dt} = C \cdot \frac{dT}{dt} = C \cdot \begin{pmatrix} 0 \\ 1 \\ 2t \\ 3t^2 \end{pmatrix}$$

We see that the C matrix can be derived if we know a total of four locations or directions of the curve. For instance, if $P_1 = Q(0)$, $R_1 = Q'(0)$, $P_2 = Q(1)$, and $R_2 = Q'(1)$ are given, then

$$C \cdot \begin{pmatrix} 1 & 0 & 1 & 0 \\ 0 & 1 & 1 & 1 \\ 0 & 0 & 1 & 2 \\ 0 & 0 & 1 & 3 \end{pmatrix} = [P_1, R_1, P_2, R_2],$$

4.2. PARAMETRIC CURVES

from which C follows.

Now, often we have a set of basis polynomials given, and we want to take combinations of them to satisfy the constraints. That can be done by splitting $C = GM$, where M describes the basis polynomials, and G is the 'geometry matrix'. We get the equation

$$Q(t) = G \cdot M \cdot T = \begin{pmatrix} g_{11} & g_{12} & g_{13} & g_{14} \\ g_{21} & g_{22} & g_{23} & g_{24} \\ g_{31} & g_{32} & g_{33} & g_{34} \end{pmatrix} \cdot \begin{pmatrix} m_{11} & \cdots & m_{14} \\ \vdots & & \vdots \\ m_{41} & \cdots & m_{44} \end{pmatrix} \cdot T \quad (4.5)$$

If we introduce new basis polynomials $\pi_i(t) = M_{i*} \cdot T$, then we see that $Q_x = G_{11}\pi_1 + G_{12}\pi_2 + G_{13}\pi_3 + G_{14}\pi_4$, $Q_y = G_{21}\pi_1 + \cdots$, et cetera.

4.2.2 Hermite basis functions

In equation (4.5) the matrix M describes the basis functions, so it is fixed for a certain class of curves: we will have one set of basis functions for Lagrange type curves, one for Hermite curves, et cetera. However, we have not yet seen a way to compute the matrix M.

The geometry matrix G is used to derive a specific curve in the class described by M: each choice of G corresponds to one curve. The columns of G will be points or direction vectors that somehow describe the intended curve.

Let us now consider Hermite curves. Here we want G to be the matrix of geometric constraints, $[P_1, R_1, P_2, R_2]$ in the above example. Recall that these constraints, using the locations of the end points and the derivatives of the curve there, give us indeed an example of Hermite interpolation.

We write out the equations. From $Q = G \cdot M \cdot T$ we get

$$Q(t) = G_H \cdot M_H \cdot T(t), \qquad Q'(t) = G_H \cdot M_H \cdot T'(t).$$

Applying both these formulas to $t = 0$ and $t = 1$, we get

$$Q_H \equiv [Q(0), Q'(0), Q(1), Q'(1)] = G_H \cdot M_H \cdot T_H$$

where

$$T_H = [T(0), T'(0), T(1), T'(1)] = \begin{pmatrix} 1 & 0 & 1 & 0 \\ 0 & 1 & 1 & 1 \\ 0 & 0 & 1 & 2 \\ 0 & 0 & 1 & 3 \end{pmatrix}$$

But this Q_H is the matrix that we had stipulated as the matrix of geometry constraints,

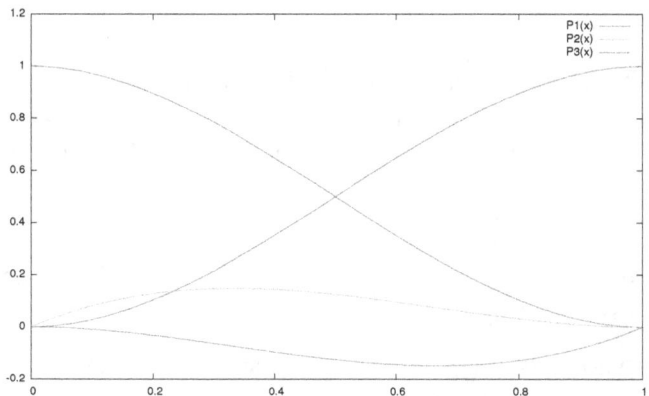

Figure 4.3: Hermite polynomials

in other words: $G_H = Q_H$. It now follows that
$$M_H = T_H^{-1} = \begin{pmatrix} 1 & 0 & -3 & 2 \\ 0 & 1 & -2 & 1 \\ 0 & 0 & 3 & -2 \\ 0 & 0 & -1 & 1 \end{pmatrix}.$$

Writing this out, we find the cubic Hermite polynomials
$$P_1(t) = 2t^3 - 3t^2 + 1, \quad P_2(t) = t^3 - 2t^2 + t, \quad P_3(t) = -2t^3 + 3t^2, \quad P_1(t) = t^3 - t^2$$
illustrated in figure 4.3, and we get $Q(t) = G \cdot B_H$ where $B_H = M \cdot T$ is the matrix of 'Hermite blending functions'.

With this formula, we can take a set of geometric constraints, in this case the two endpoints and the directions there, and derive the formula for the Hermite curve that satisfies these constraints. As an example, figure 4.5 is the curve $.3P_1 - 2P_2 + P_3 - 2P_4$, that is, the curve through $(0, .3)$ and $(1, 1)$, with slope -2 in both $x = 0, 1$.

We make the transition to parametric curves by expressing both components as Hermite curves. For instance, figure 4.7 shows the curve

```
#
# 4 cubic Hermite polynomials
#
set terminal pdf
set xrange [0:1]
set yrange [-.2:1.2]
```
```
P1(x) = 2*x**3-3*x**2+1
P2(x) = x**3-2*x**2+x
P3(x) = -2*x**3+3*x**2
P4(x) = x**3-x**2
plot P1(x), P2(x), P3(x), P4(x) title ""
```

Figure 4.4: The gnuplot source for figure 4.3

4.2. PARAMETRIC CURVES

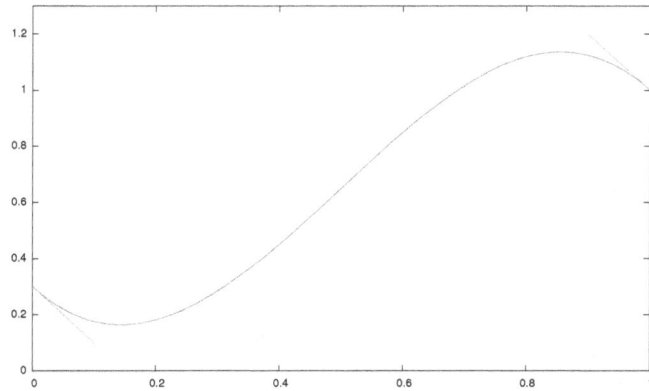

Figure 4.5: An example of Hermite interpolation

$$Q_x(t) = .1 * P_1(t) + P_2(t) + .9 * P_3(t), \quad Q_y(t) = .2 * P_1(t) + .3 * P_3(t) - P_4(t)$$

that is

$$Q = \begin{pmatrix} .1 \\ .2 \end{pmatrix} P_1 + \begin{pmatrix} 1 \\ 0 \end{pmatrix} P_2 + \begin{pmatrix} .9 \\ .3 \end{pmatrix} P_3 + \begin{pmatrix} 0 \\ -1 \end{pmatrix} P_4.$$

There is one aspect of these Hermite curves worth remarking on. In figure 4.9 we have replaced the direction vector $\begin{pmatrix} 1 \\ 0 \end{pmatrix}$ in $(0,0)$ by $\begin{pmatrix} x \\ 0 \end{pmatrix}$, where $x = 1, 1.5, 2, 2.5$, which all have the same direction, but a different magnitude. Clearly there is a visual effect.

```
#
# Hermite interpolation
#
set terminal pdf
set multiplot
set xrange [0:1]
set yrange [0:1.3]
P1(x) = 2*x**3-3*x**2+1
P2(x) = x**3-2*x**2+x
P3(x) = -2*x**3+3*x**2
P4(x) = x**3-x**2
p1y = .3
p1slope = -2
p2y = 1
p2slope = -2
plot p1y*P1(x) + p1slope*P2(x) \
    + P3(x) + p2slope*P4(x) title ""
set parametric
set style function lines
plot [t=0:.1] t,  p1y+t*p1slope \
    title "" with lines 2
plot [t=0:.1] 1-t,p2y-t*p2slope \
    title "" with lines 2
```

Figure 4.6: The source for figure 4.5

Victor Eijkhout

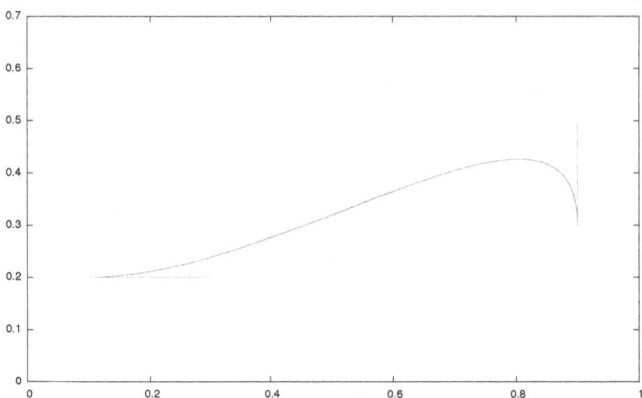

Figure 4.7: A Hermite interpolation curve

4.2.3 Splines

We will now take a close look at Bernshtein polynomials of degree 3:

$$z(t) = (1-t)^3 z_1 + 3(1-t)^2 t z_2 + 3(1-t)t^2 z_3 + t^3 z_4, \qquad (4.6)$$

also known as Bezier curves or Bezier cubics after Pierre Bezier, an engineer at Renault[2].

There are a couple of ways of looking at these polynomials. Consider the function $z(t)$ to be the sum of four basis functions, $(1-t)^3$, $(1-t)^2 t$, $(1-t)t^2$, and t^3, each

---

2. Pierre Bézier was born September 1, 1910 and died November 25, 1999 at the age of 89. In 1985 he was recognized by ACM SIGGRAPH with a 'Steven A. Coons' award for his lifetime contribution to computer graphics and interactive techniques.

```
#                                          p1x  = .1 ; p1y  = .2
# Parametric Hermite curve                 p1dx = 1  ; p1dy = 0
#                                          p2x  = .9 ; p2y  = .3
set terminal pdf                           p2dx = 0  ; p2dy = -1
set parametric                             plot [t=0:1] \
set multiplot                                 p1x*P1(t)+p1dx*P2(t)+p2x*P3(t)+p2dx*P4(t), \
set xrange [0:1]                              p1y*P1(t)+p1dy*P2(t)+p2y*P3(t)+p2dy*P4(t) \
set yrange [0:.7]                             title ""
P1(t) = 2*t**3-3*t**2+1                    plot [t=0:.2] p1x+t*p1dx,p1y+t*p1dy \
P2(t) = t**3-2*t**2+t                         title "" with lines 2
P3(t) = -2*t**3+3*t**2                     plot [t=0:.2] p2x-t*p2dx,p2y-t*p2dy \
P4(t) = t**3-t**2                             title "" with lines 2
```

Figure 4.8: The source of figure 4.7

4.2. PARAMETRIC CURVES

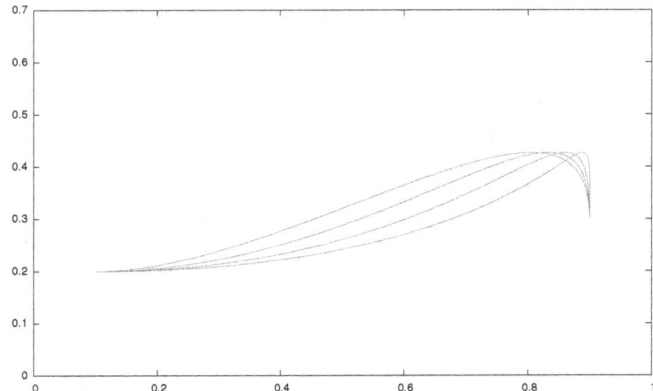

Figure 4.9: The same curve, tinkering with the direction vector

multiplied by a factor deriving from a control point. From the formulas, and from a picture (figure 4.11) we see that the first term $p_1(t) = (1-t)^3$ is the only one with $p(0) \neq 0$. Likewise, p_4 is the only one with $p(1) \neq 0$. That means $z(0) = z_1$ and $z(1) = z_4$. Furthermore, the second term is (after the first term) the only remaining one with $p'(0) \neq 0$, so by choosing z_2 we can change $z'(0)$ without changing $z(0)$ or $z(1)$. Likewise z_3 for $z'(1)$.

Bezier curves can be derived from cubic Hermite splines by replacing the direction vectors R_1, R_2 by control points P'_1, P'_2, so that $R_1 = 3(P'_1 - P1)$ and $R_2 = 3(P_2 - P'_2)$. For the Bezier geometry vector we then have

$$G_B = [P_1, P'_1, P'_2, P_2]$$

and the relation with the Hermite geometry vector

$$G_H = [P_1, R_1, P_2, R_2] = [P_1, P'_1, P'_2, P_2] M_{BH} = G_B \cdot M_{BH}$$

where

$$M_{BH} = \begin{pmatrix} 1 & -3 & 0 & 0 \\ 0 & 3 & 0 & 0 \\ 0 & 0 & 0 & -3 \\ 0 & 0 & 1 & 3 \end{pmatrix} \tag{4.7}$$

Defining

$$M_B = M_{BH} \cdot M_H = \begin{pmatrix} 1 & -3 & 3 & -1 \\ 0 & 3 & -6 & 3 \\ 0 & 0 & 3 & -3 \\ 0 & 0 & 0 & 1 \end{pmatrix} \tag{4.8}$$

we now get for Bezier curves

$$Q(t) = G_H \cdot M_H \cdot T(t) = G_B \cdot M_{BH} \cdot M_H \cdot T(t) = G_B \cdot M_B \cdot T(t)$$

We can also write that as $Q_x(t) = g_{11}B_1(t) + g_{12}B_2(t) + \cdots$ where

$$\begin{aligned} B_1(t) &= 1 - 3t + 3t^2 - t^3 &= (1-t)^3 \\ B_2(t) &= 3t - 6t^2 + 3t^3 &= 3t(1-t)^2 \\ B_3(t) &= 3t^2 - 3t^3 &= 3t^2(1-t) \\ B_4(t) &= &= t^3 \end{aligned}$$

which are the Bernstein polynomials we started this section with.

The sum of these polynomials (this is equivalent to setting the z_i coefficients to one in equation (4.6)) is $z(t) = (t + (1-t)))^3 \equiv 1$. Also, the polynomials are positive on $[0,1]$, so the components Q_x, Q_y, Q_z are weighted averages of the polynomials. This means that the curve, consisting of weighted sums of the control points, is contained in the convex hull of the control points.

Exercise 43. One could also define quadratic Bezier curves. These have only a single control point, and the curve is such that in both the endpoints it is aimed at the control point.

```
set terminal pdf                        # direction 2:
set parametric                          p1dx = 1.5 ; p1dy = 0
set multiplot                           plot [t=0:1] \
set dummy t                                 p1x*P1(t)+p1dx*P2(t)+p2x*P3(t)+p2dx*P4(t), \
set xrange [0:1]                            p1y*P1(t)+p1dy*P2(t)+p2y*P3(t)+p2dy*P4(t) \
set yrange [0:.7]                           title ""
P1(t) = 2*t**3-3*t**2+1                 # direction 3:
P2(t) = t**3-2*t**2+t                   p1dx = 2 ; p1dy = 0
P3(t) = -2*t**3+3*t**2                  plot [t=0:1] \
P4(t) = t**3-t**2                           p1x*P1(t)+p1dx*P2(t)+p2x*P3(t)+p2dx*P4(t), \
p1x = .1 ; p1y = .2                         p1y*P1(t)+p1dy*P2(t)+p2y*P3(t)+p2dy*P4(t) \
p2x = .9 ; p2y = .3                         title ""
p2dx = 0 ; p2dy = -1                    # direction 4:
# direction 1:                          p1dx = 2.5 ; p1dy = 0
p1dx = 1 ; p1dy = 0                     plot [t=0:1] \
plot [t=0:1] \                              p1x*P1(t)+p1dx*P2(t)+p2x*P3(t)+p2dx*P4(t), \
    p1x*P1(t)+p1dx*P2(t)+p2x*P3(t)+p2dx*P4(t), \   p1y*P1(t)+p1dy*P2(t)+p2y*P3(t)+p2dy*P4(t) \
    p1y*P1(t)+p1dy*P2(t)+p2y*P3(t)+p2dy*P4(t) \    title ""
    title ""
```

Figure 4.10: The source for figure 4.9

4.2. PARAMETRIC CURVES

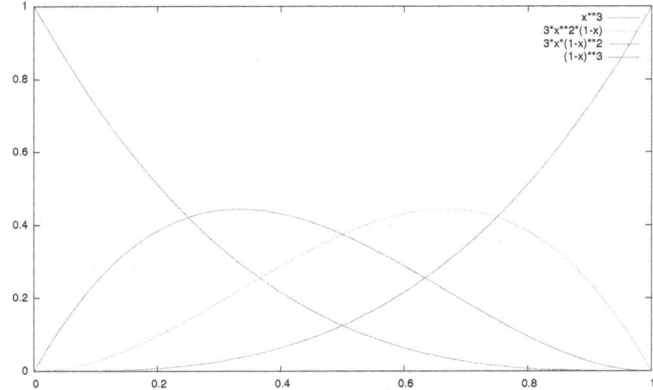

Figure 4.11: Bernshtein polynomials

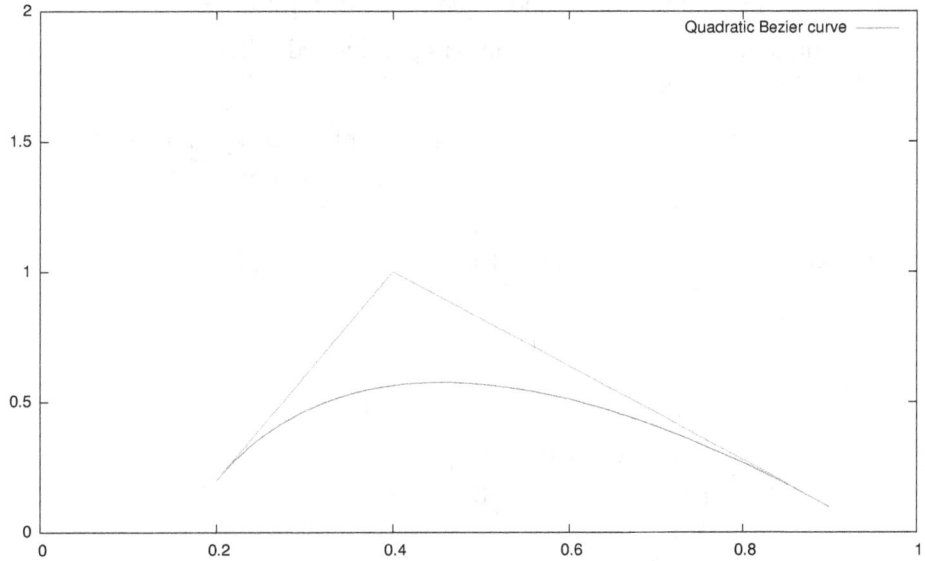

Derive the basis functions and geometry matrix for this case. Make a `gnuplot` figure of a single quadratic Bezier curve, and of two curves joined smoothly.

Hint: you can follow the construction of the cubic splines in the lecture notes. The only problem is defining the control point. First draw up the Hermite geometry matrix based on end points q_0 and q_1, and the derivative q'_0 in the first end point. Derive from them the derivative q'_1 in the other end point. The control point then lies on the intersection of two lines. Solving this looks like a single equation in two unknowns, but it can be solved: write it as a matrix-vector equation that is satisfied no matter the choice of the geometry matrix.

4.2.4 Calculation of Bezier curves

Suppose we have a Bezier curve defined by four control points, and we want to draw points on the curve, meaning that we have to evaluate the function $Q(t)$ for a number of values of t. The relation $Q(t) = G \cdot M \cdot T(t)$ allows us to do this calculation in

- 2 multiplications to form the terms t^2 and t^3 in T;
- 16 multiplications and 12 additions forming $M \cdot T$;
- 12 multiplications and 9 additions forming $G \cdot (M \cdot T)$.

An obvious improvement is to store $\tilde{M} = G \cdot M$, which brings the cost down to two multiplications for T and

- 12 multiplications and 9 additions for forming $\tilde{M} \cdot T$.

A similar count is arrived at by looking at divided differences. Additionally, this way of computing is more stable.

From the formula $Q(t) = G \cdot M \cdot T(t)$ we get for each component

$$q_i(t) = \sum_j G_{ij}(MT)_j = \sum_{j,k} G_{ij} M_{jk} t^{k-1}.$$

Looking at only one component for simplicity, we find, for instance

$$x(t) = \sum_k c_k t^{k-1} \qquad c_k = \sum_j G_{1j} M_{jk}.$$

We recall equation (4.8):

$$M_B = \begin{pmatrix} 1 & -3 & 3 & -1 \\ 0 & 3 & -6 & 3 \\ 0 & 0 & 3 & -3 \\ 0 & 0 & 0 & 1 \end{pmatrix}$$

and writing $g_j \equiv G_{1j}$ we find

$$c_1 = g_1, \quad c_2 = 3(g_2 - g_1), \quad c_3 = 3(g_3 - 2g_2 + g_1), \quad c_4 = g_4 - 3g_3 + 3g_2 - g_1.$$

In this we recognize divided differences of g:

$$\begin{aligned}
[2,1]g &= g_2 - g_1, \\
[3,2,1]g &= [3,2]g - [2,1]g = (g_3 - g_2) - (g_2 - g_1) \\
&= g_3 - 2g_2 + g_1 \\
[4,3,2,1] &= [4,3,2]g - [3,2,1]g = (g_4 - 2g_3 + g_2) - (g_3 - 2g_2 + g_1) \\
&= g_4 - 3g_3 + 3g_2 - g_1
\end{aligned}$$

using lemma 4.

4.3. PRACTICAL USE

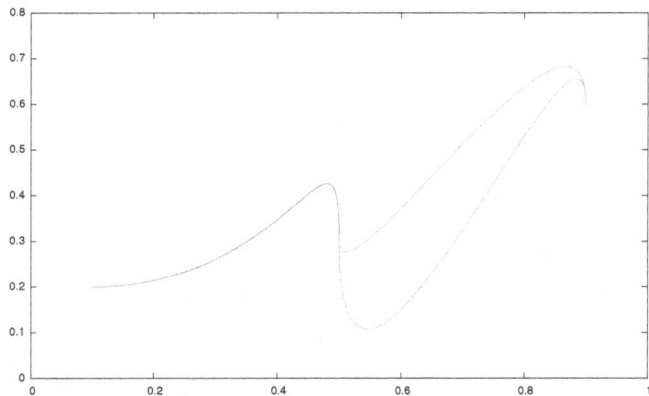

Figure 4.12: Two Hermite curves, joined together smoothly in (.5, .3)

4.3 Practical use

4.3.1 Piecewise curves

As we indicated earlier, complicated shapes can be approximated by piecewise cubics. Figure 4.12 shows two Hermite curves joined together. The curve is continuous and the directions at the join are proportional. This is called 'geometric continuity', and is denoted G^1. So-called B-splines ('basis splines') are constructed by piecing together Bezier curves, not only continuously, but differentiably. For this, if $P_1 \ldots P_4$

```
set terminal pdf                        p1x*P1(t)+p2x*P2(t)+p3x*P3(t)+p4x*P4(t), \
set parametric                          p1y*P1(t)+p2y*P2(t)+p3y*P3(t)+p4y*P4(t) \
set multiplot                             title ""
set dummy t                             p5x = .9 ; p5y =  .6
set xrange [0:1]                        p6x =  0 ; p6y = -1
set yrange [0:.8]                       plot [t=0:1] \
P1(t) = 2*t**3-3*t**2+1                   p3x*P1(t)+.5*p4x*P2(t)+p5x*P3(t)+p6x*P4(t), \
P2(t) = t**3-2*t**2+t                     p3y*P1(t)+.5*p4y*P2(t)+p5y*P3(t)+p6y*P4(t) \
P3(t) = -2*t**3+3*t**2                    title "" with lines 2
P4(t) = t**3-t**2                       plot [t=0:1] \
p1x = .1 ; p1y =  .2                      p3x*P1(t)+2*p4x*P2(t)+p5x*P3(t)+p6x*P4(t), \
p2x =  1 ; p2y =   0                      p3y*P1(t)+2*p4y*P2(t)+p5y*P3(t)+p6y*P4(t) \
p3x = .5 ; p3y =  .3                      title "" with lines 2
p4x =  0 ; p4y = -1
plot [t=0:1] \
```

Figure 4.13: The source for figure 4.12

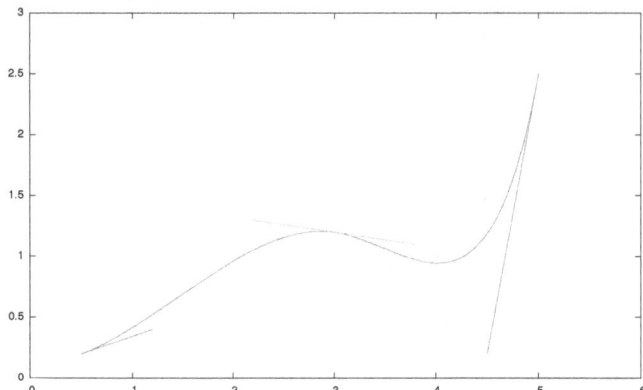

Figure 4.14: Two Bezier curves, joined together smoothly

and $P_4 \ldots P_7$ are the control points of the two curves, then we require

$$P_4 = (P_3 + P_5)/2.$$

This is shown in figure 4.14.

```
set terminal pdf
set xrange [0:6]
set yrange [0:3]
set parametric
B1(x) = x**3
B2(x) = 3*x**2*(1-x)
B3(x) = 3*x*(1-x)**2
B4(x) = (1-x)**3
P1x = .5  ; P1y = .2
P2x = 1.2 ; P2y = .4
P3x = 2.2 ; P3y = 1.3
P4x =   3 ; P4y = 1.2
P5x = 2*P4x-P3x
P5y = 2*P4y-P3y
P6x = 4.5 ; P6y = .2
P7x = 5   ; P7y = 2.5
set multiplot
plot [t=0:1] \
   P1x*B1(t)+P2x*B2(t)+P3x*B3(t)+P4x*B4(t), \
   P1y*B1(t)+P2y*B2(t)+P3y*B3(t)+P4y*B4(t) \
   title ""
plot [t=0:1] \
   P4x*B1(t)+P5x*B2(t)+P6x*B3(t)+P7x*B4(t), \
   P4y*B1(t)+P5y*B2(t)+P6y*B3(t)+P7y*B4(t) \
   title ""
plot [t=-1:1] \
   P4x+t*(P5x-P4x),P4y+t*(P5y-P4y) \
   title "" with lines 2
plot [t=0:1] \
   P1x+t*(P2x-P1x),P1y+t*(P2y-P1y) \
   title "" with lines 3
plot [t=0:1] \
   P7x+t*(P6x-P7x),P7y+t*(P6y-P7y) \
   title "" with lines 3
```

Figure 4.15: The source for figure 4.14

4.3. PRACTICAL USE

4.3.2 Drawing splines

Even if we can evaluate a Bezier curve efficiently (section 4.2.4) in a given point, we can improve on this considerably in the context of line drawing. Consider the problem of drawing a cubic curve on the interval $[0, 1]$ by drawing consecutive points $Q(n\delta)$ for $n = 0, 1, \ldots$.

We will discuss one line-drawing technique in the chapter on raster graphics. A technique that is attractive for splines, and which is used in METAFONT, is recursive subdivision. Here, a curve is subdivided until a segment is a straight line within the pixel resolution, so that a line drawing algorithm can be used. The test for a straight line can be implemented efficiently through using the spline control points.

Curve plotting with `gnuplot`. The `gnuplot` utility can be used for plotting sets of points. However, here we will only discuss drawing curves.

4.4 Introduction

The two modes for running `gnuplot` are *interactive* and *from file*. In interactive mode, you call `gnuplot` from the command line, type commands, and watch output appear (see next paragraph); in the second case you call `gnuplot <your file>`.

The output of `gnuplot` can be a picture on your screen, or drawing instructions in a file. Where the output goes depends on the setting of the *terminal*. By default, `gnuplot` will try to draw a picture. This is equivalent to declaring

```
set terminal x11
```

or `aqua`, `windows`, or any choice of graphics hardware.

For output to file, declare

```
set terminal pdf
```

or `fig`, `latex`, `pbm`, et cetera.

4.5 Plotting

The basic plot command is `plot`. By specifying

```
plot x**2
```

you get a plot of $f(x) = x^2$; `gnuplot` will decide on the range for x. With

```
set xrange [0:1]
plot 1-x title "down", x**2 title "up"
```

you get two graphs in one plot, with the x range limited to $[0, 1]$, and the appropriate legends for the graphs. The variable x is the default for plotting functions.

Plotting one function against another – or equivalently, plotting a parametric curve – goes like this:

```
set parametric
plot [t=0:1.57] cos(t),sin(t)
```

which gives a quarter circle.

To get more than one graph in a plot, use the command `set multiplot`.

4.5.1 Styles

You can change the default drawing style with

```
set style function dots
```

(`lines`, `dots`, `points`, et cetera), or change on a single plot with

```
plot f(x) with points
```

Raster graphics.

4.6 Vector graphics and raster graphics

We may use fancy techniques such as Bezier curves for describing shapes, but at some point the graphic needs to be rendered on an actual device with pixels or ink dots. Thus we need algorithms for deciding which pixels to turn on or off, and, in case the device has a larger bitdepth, with what intensity.

The technical terms here are 'vector graphics' for a description of the lines and curves, and 'raster graphics' for the pixel-by-pixel description. A description of a raster is also called 'bitmap'. Common bitmap-based formats are JPEG, GIF, TIFF, PNG, PICT, and BMP.

Vector graphics make for a much more compact file, but they rely on the presence of a final rendering stage. For instance, Macromedia's Flash format (now an open Internet standard) is a vector graphics format, that relies on a browser plugin. However, presence of a Flash renderer is pretty much standard in browsers these days. Adobe Postscript is also a vector format. The first popular printer to incorporate it, the Apple Laserwriter, had a Motorola 68000 processor, exactly as powerful as the Macintosh computer it connected to.

Two vector standards are being proposed to the W3C: the Precision Graphics Markup Language and the Vector Markup Language. PGML is backed by Adobe Systems, IBM, Netscape, and Sun Microsystems. VML is supported by Microsoft, Hewlett-Packard, Autodesk, Macromedia, and Visio. Both standards are based on Extensible Markup Language (XML).

4.7 Basic raster graphics

4.7.1 Line drawing

We limit the discussion to lines with slope less than 1. For those, on a grid of pixels, one pixel per column will be switched on, and the question to be addressed is which pixel to turn on in each column.

Probably the simplest way to draw a line is by using an 'incremental' drawing algorithm. Let a line $y = mx + B$ be given, and we write the slope as $m = \delta y / \delta x$. In the case of pixel graphics, we set $\delta x \equiv 1$, so $\delta y = m$ and we can recursively state

$$y_{i+1} = y_i + \delta y.$$

The simplest implementation of this is

4.7. BASIC RASTER GRAPHICS

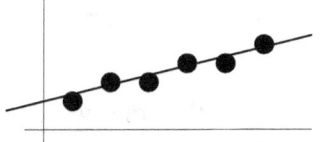

Figure 4.16: Line with slope ≤ 1 and one pixel per column on

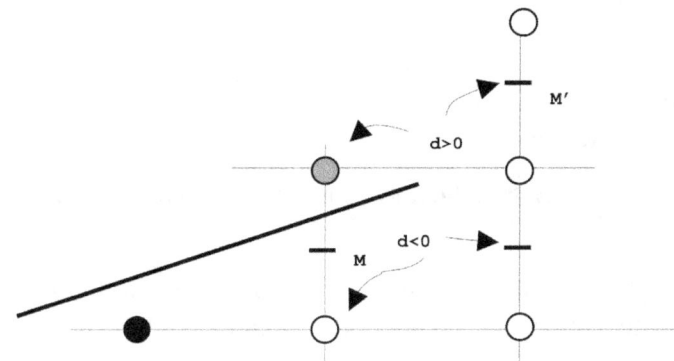

Figure 4.17: The midpoint algorithm for line drawing

let x_0, y_0 and m be given, then
for $i = 0 \ldots n - 1$
    WritePixel(x_i, Round(y_i))
    $x_{i+1} = x_i + 1$
    $y_{i+1} = y_i + m$

Since (x_i, y_i) is never related to the actual formula for the line, there will be an accumulation of round-off error. However, this will be negligible. More seriously, the rounding operation is relatively expensive. In the next algorithm we will eliminate it. If possible, we want to operate completely in integer quantities.

The 'midpoint algorithm' proceeds fully by integer addition. First we write the equation for the line in two different ways as

$$y = \frac{dy}{dx}x + B, \qquad F(x, y) = ax + by + c = 0.$$

Clearly, $a = dy, b = -dx, c = B$, and we can derive dx, dy from the end pixels of the line. The function F is zero on the line, positive in the half plane under it, and negative above it.

Now we consider how to progress given that we have switched on a pixel at (x_p, y_p). With the initial assumption that the line has a slope between 0 and 1, the next pixel will be either $(x_P + 1, y_P + 1)$, or $(x_p + 1, y_p)$, depending on which is closer to the line.

Instead of measuring the distance of the candidate next pixels to the line, we decide whether their midpoint M is above or under the line. For this, we use the function $F(\cdot, \cdot)$ introduced above, and evaluate the 'decision value' of the midpoint:

$$d = F(x_p + 1, y_p + 1/2).$$

The two cases to consider then are

$d < 0$: M lies over the line, so we take $y_{p+1} = y_p$;

$d \geq 0$: M lies under the line, so we take $y_{p+1} = y_p + 1$.

Similarly we update the mid point: if $d \geq 0$, the midpoint moves up. Note that the new midpoint is at $x_{p+1} + 1$.

Now, we do not actually use the midpoint, only the value of d. The algorithm is then complete once we find a way to update d cheaply. For this we look at its next value

$$d' = F(x_{p+1} + 1, y_{p+1} + 1/2).$$

Corresponding to the above two cases:

$$\begin{aligned}
d' = & \ a(x_{p+1} + 1) + b(y_{p+1} + 1/2) + c = \\
d < 0: & \ = a(x_p + 2) + b(y_p + 1/2) & = d + a = d + dy \\
d \geq 0: & \ = a(x_p + 2) + b(y_p + 3/2) + c & = d + a + b = d + dy - dx
\end{aligned}$$

In other words, we update d with dy or $dy - dx$ depending on whether it's negative or non-negative.

To start off the algorithm, dx and dy are computed from the endpoints, and the initial value of d follows from

$$d_0 = F(x_0 + 1, y_0 + 1/2) = F(x_0, y_0) + a + b/2 = 0 + dy - dx/2.$$

To get rid of the division by 2, which would cause real rather than integer values to be used throughout the algorithm, we can redefine $\tilde{F}(x, y) = 2F(x, y)$; correspondingly we update d with $2dy$ and $2(dy - dx)$ in the two cases.

> **Exercise 44.** Can you modify the DDA line drawing algorithm so that it works (as well as possible) when the line is given between points that are not on pixels?

These algorithms are sometimes referred to as 'Digital Differential Analyzers', since they trace out a curve by proceeding with small differences. The line algorithm was first derived by Bressenham.

4.7. BASIC RASTER GRAPHICS

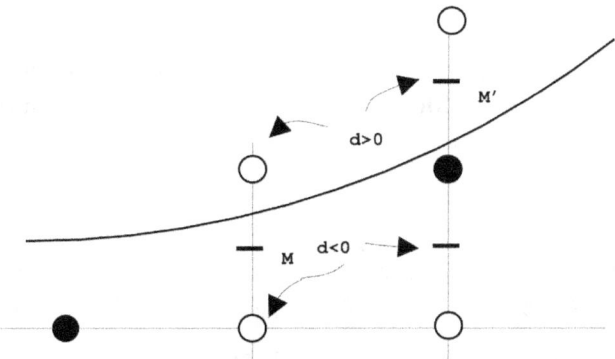

Figure 4.18: The midpoint algorithm for circle drawing

4.7.2 Circle drawing

Circles can be drawn with a similar algorithm. We observe that, because of 8-fold symmetry, we can limit the algorithm to the part of a circle from $x = 0$ to $x = y$. The midpoint argument is now slightly more complicated. The function for the circle is

$$F(x, y) = x^2 + y^2 - R^2,$$

and the decision value in the midpoint M is

$$d = F(x_p + 1, y_p + 1/2) = x^2 + 2x + y^2 + y + 5/4.$$

The two cases to consider are similar to before:

$d < 0$: M lies in the circle, so we take $y_{p+1} = y_p$;

$d \geq 0$: M lies outside the circle, so we take $y_{p+1} = y_p + 1$.

To update the decision value we get the two cases

$$\begin{aligned} d' &= F(x_{p+1} + 1, y_{p+1} + 1/2) = \\ d < 0: &= x^2 + 4x + y^2 + y + 4\,1/4 &= d + 2x + 3 \\ d \geq 0: &= x^2 + 4x + y^2 + 3y + 6\,1/4 &= d + 2(x+y) + 5 \end{aligned}$$

> **Exercise 45.** Why is there no need to consider bigger increments of y_p in the circle drawing algorithm? After all, a circle has curvature so the slope increases.

The circle algorithm can be further improved by observing that the quantities $2x$ and $2y$ can themselves easily by constructed by updating. This removes the need for any multiplication.

Victor Eijkhout

4.7.3 Cubics

Suppose we have a cubic function $f(t) = at^3 + bt^2 + ct + d$. Instead of evaluating this polynomial directly, using Horner's rule, we compute the value $f(t + \delta)$ by updating:
$$f(t + \delta) = f(t) + \Delta f(t).$$
We find
$$\begin{aligned}\Delta f(t) &= f(t+\delta) - f(t) \\ &= a(3t^2\delta + 3t\delta^2 + \delta^3) + b(2t\delta + \delta^2) + c\delta \\ &= 3a\delta t^2 + (3a\delta^2 + 2b\delta)t + a\delta^3 + b\delta^2 + c\delta\end{aligned}$$
This still leaves us with a quadratic function to evaluate, so we define
$$\begin{aligned}\Delta^2 f(t) &= \Delta f(t+\delta) - \Delta f(t) \\ &= 3a\delta(2t\delta + \delta^2) + (3a\delta^2 + 3b\delta)\delta \\ &= 6a\delta^2 t + 6a\delta^3 + 2b\delta^2\end{aligned}$$
Finally, we derive $\Delta^3 f(t) = \Delta^2 f(t+\delta) - \Delta^2 f(t) = 6a\delta^2$. Taken all together, we can now compute $f_{n+1} \equiv f((n+1)\delta)$ by initializing
$$\Delta^3 f_0 = 6a\delta^2, \quad \Delta^2 f_0 = 6a\delta^3 + 2b\delta^2, \quad \Delta f_0 = a\delta^3 + b\delta^2 + c\delta$$
and computing by update
$$f_{n+1} = f_n + \Delta f_n, \quad \Delta f_{n+1} = \Delta f_n + \Delta^2 f_n, \quad \Delta^2 f_{n+1} = \Delta^2 f_n + \Delta^3 f_0$$
The advantage of this algorithm is its low operation count, and the fact that it works fully by integer operations.

4.8 Rasterizing type

Typefaces can be described by curves, but several aspects to them make it necessary to do more than just rendering these curves, when rasterizing them. Part of the problem is that characters in a font are relatively small, and satisfy all sorts of constraints that both may be hard to satisfy (especially at low resolution), and are immediately noticed when rendered incorrectly.

Such problems result from using too simple algorithms for converting the character outlines to rasters. For instance, an obvious algorithm is

>A pixel is turned on if its center is within the curve.

Now consider the case where a curve with large radius exceeds location $y = n + 1/2$ for only one x. This results in the 'pimple' on top of the 'e' in figure 4.20. On the other hand, if such a curve stays just under such a halfpoint, we get a long plateau, as in the left side curve of the 'e'.

4.8. RASTERIZING TYPE

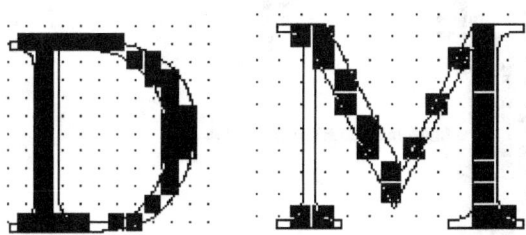

Figure 4.19: Problems in rasterizing type, and resulting illegible output

4.8.1 Scaled fonts

These rasterizing problems are largely due to the facts that

- Characters are scalable, so the relations between top/bottom or left/right are not always mapped the same way to a pixel grid;
- Even if characters are used at the same size, they need to be displayed on various kinds of rasters (printer, screen);
- Characters can be placed in any horizontal or vertical location, so relations to pixel boundaries are also flexible.

The conversion process goes more or less as follows[3]:

- Character outlines are based on coordinates on some grid, often expressed as fixed point, or other scheme with a finite mesh size.
- The character is scaled to the raster on which it will be rendered.
- The result is rounded to the raster, in figure 4.21 this puts the left and right sides on pixel boundaries; note that other vertical parts of the character are not necessarily pixel-aligned.
- The scaled and rounded outline is then rasterized by turning a set of pixels on.

We see that in both final steps, rounding to the raster, and switching on pixels, we can have unwanted effects.

4.8.2 Pixelation

Above we said that pixels are switched on if their center falls within the curve. There are two problems with this:

---

3. Much of this discussion is based on the definition of TrueType fonts.

Victor Eijkhout

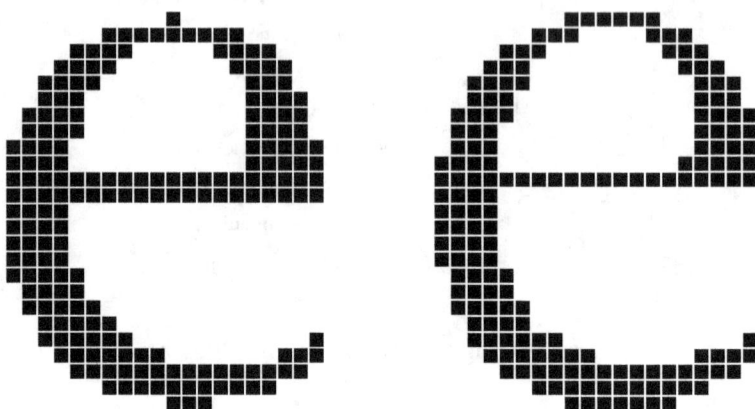

Figure 4.20: A bad and a good way of rendering a Times Roman 'e' at low resolution

- Sometimes not enough pixels are turned on to render the shape accurately, and
- Deciding whether a pixel is within the shape is not trivial to begin with. For instance, letters such as 'o' or 'p' have an inner region that should not be filled. In another example, sometimes it is convenient to describe a shape as non-disjoint union of other shapes; see figure 4.22

The second problem can be solved a number of ways. We could for instance look at a scan line, and switch to on/off mode every time we cross a curve boundary. This approach does not work for intersecting curves.

Better solutions are based on looking at the so-called 'winding number'. This number counts, for a given point in the plane, how often a curve winds around the point. If this is zero, the point is outside the curve, otherwise it is inside it.

That implementing winding number rules is not trivial can be seen from two screen shots of Acrobat Reader version 4; figure 4.24.

4.8.3 Font hinting / instructing

To prevent some of the problems indicated above, characters in a font file consist of more than just the outline description. Additionally, each character can have a short program in a language defined by the font file format. Such a program can enforce that certain distances in the font as exact multiples of pixel distances.

For instance, the letter 'O' in figure 4.25 has the following constraints

4.9. ANTI-ALIASING 179

Figure 4.21: Scaled and rasterized character outline

1. A certain amount of white space buffering the character; distance 3 is the 'transport';
2. The width of the band
5,6 Visual under and overshoot.
7 The height of the band

Distances 5 and 6 are over and undershoot: a letter with curved top/bottom like 'O' would seem too small if it stayed between the baseline and the cap height. To compensate for that, the letter is made slightly higher and deeper. However, for small sizes and low resolutions, this compensation needs to be switched off, since it would look too drastic.

4.8.4 Dropouts

In certain cases, pixels can not be switched on that are necessary for continuity of the figure drawn. Figure 4.26 shows a case where a connecting bit is too thin to hit the centers of any pixels. To cover such cases, the renderer usually has an algorithm that detects when a scan line enters and leaves a contour without setting any pixels. It will then set, for instance, the left pixel.

4.9 Anti-aliasing

In the algorithms so far, the decision was between switching a pixel on or off. There are a few problems with this. For instance, for certain slopes the rendered curve can have a very 'jagged' look. Also, a curve at slope 1 will have the same number of pixels on as a curve at slope 0, but on a path that is longer by $\sqrt{2}$. Thus, it may look lighter or thinner.

Victor Eijkhout

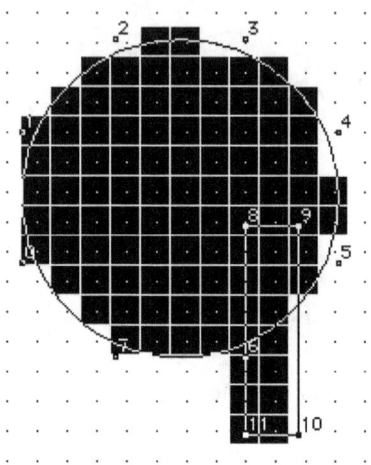

Figure 4.22: A shape consisting of overlapping contours

If the display supports a range of values ('grayscale'), we can try to use this and find a better visual rendering. First we will look at an example, then briefly consider the general theory of this phenomenon.

4.9.1 Raster graphics with larger bitdepths

In the algorithms above, pixels close to a line or other curve were switched on. If the display supports it, we can compute a measurement of proximity of the pixel to the line, and set a brightness based on that. There are various ways to implement this. For instance, one could consider the line to have an area, and to compute the intersection area of the line and the pixel box. Here we will use a 'filter function'. The support of this function will be larger than the pixel box.

We will modify the midpoint method for line drawing so that in each column three pixels will be nonzero, with an intensity based on the Euclidean distance to the line. Let v be the (signed) vertical distance from the midpoint to the line, and D the euclidean distance, then $D = vdx/\sqrt{dx^2 + dy^2}$. The denominator we can compute once and for all at the start of the algorithm, but a simple way of computing vdx is needed.

Consider the case where $d < 0$, in which case we choose $y_{p+1} = y_p$. Now we have
$$0 = F(x_p+1, y_p+v) = F(x_p+1, y_p) + 2bv \Rightarrow 2vdx = F(x_p+1, y_p),$$
and
$$d = F(M) = F(x_p+1, y_p+1/2) = F(x_p+1, y_p) + b$$
so $2vdx = d+dx$. Likewise, if $d \geq 0$, $2vdx = d-dx$. Since we know how to update d cheaply, we can now iteratively compute D.

4.9. ANTI-ALIASING

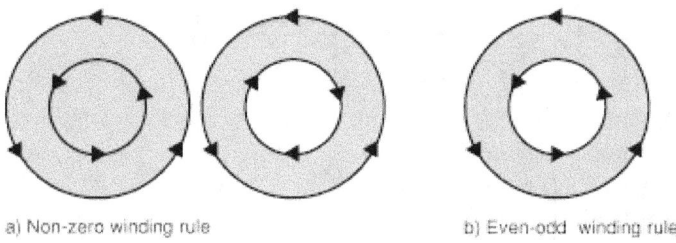

Figure 4.23: The effects of different winding number rules

For the top and bottom point, $D = 2(1-v)dx/\sqrt{\ldots}$ and $D = 2(1+v)/\sqrt{\ldots}$, respectively.

4.9.2 The general idea

Smoothing out a picture with grayscales is usually called 'anti-aliasing'. To see why, consider how the parts of a graphics system fit together. After we derive a curve or other two-dimensional object (this could be a projected surface) to display, the exact

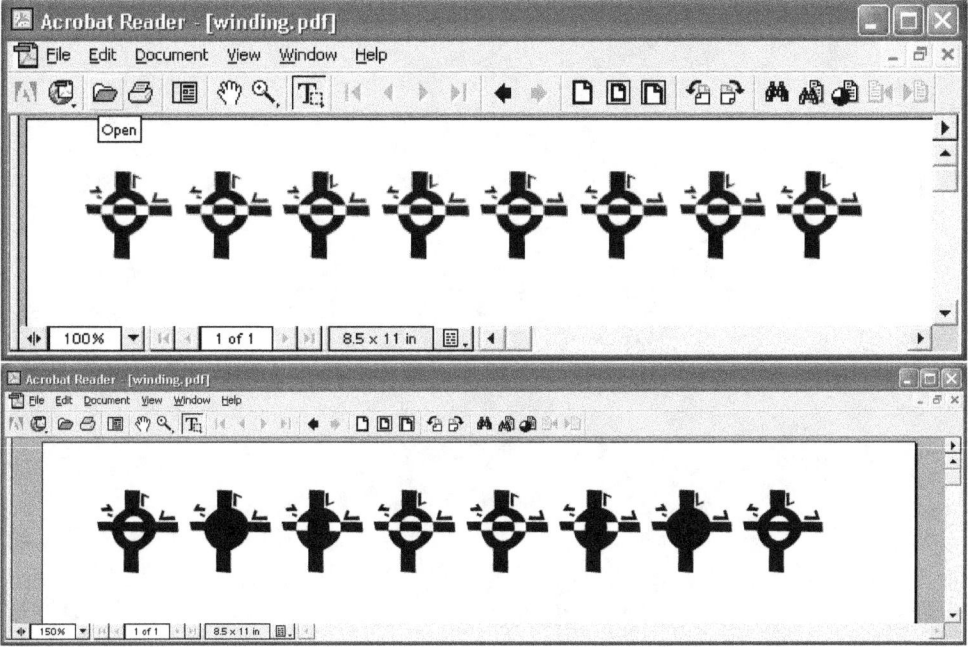

Figure 4.24: Acrobat 4 rendering of a complicated figure at different magnifications

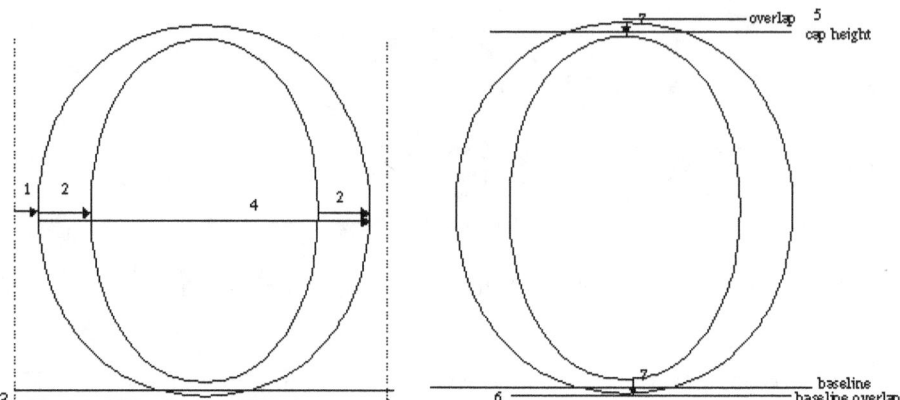

Figure 4.25: Constraints on the letter 'O'

values are sampled according to the pixel resolution. By computing a Fourier transform of these samples, we get an impression of the visual 'frequencies' in the picture.

If, instead of simply switching on pixels based on the sampled curve, we compute pixel values so that sampling them reproduces the frequency spectrum, we get a picture that looks closer to the intended one.

4.9. ANTI-ALIASING

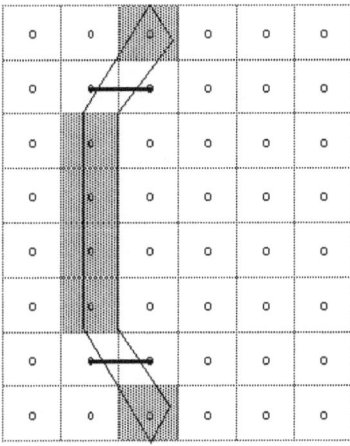

Figure 4.26: A case of 'dropout': missing pixels give a disconnected curve

Projects for this chapter.

Project 4.1. Bezier curves can also be used for graphics problems such as enlarging a bitmat or projecting text on a waving flag. Consult http://www.tinaja.com/cubic01.asp and report on the techniques used.

Project 4.2. (very mathematical) Explain elliptical integrals and how they are used to compute the length of a Bezier curve. Explain approximations. Same resource as the previous project.

Project 4.3. (very mathematical) Study the theory of NURBS (Non-Uniform Rational B-Splines); what are their capabilities and limitations? Start at http://devworld.apple.com/dev/techsupport/develop/issue25/schneider.html for an introduction.

Project 4.4. Investigate perception issues in font design or display technology. Start by browsing through Rubinstein's book.

Victor Eijkhout

Chapter 5

TeX's macro language – unfinished chapter

The programming language of TeX is rather idiosyncratic. One notable feature is the difference between expanded and executed commands. The expansion mechanism is very powerful: it is in fact possible to implement lambda calculus in it.

Handouts and further reading for this chapter

The inspiration for this chapter was the article about lists by Alan Jeffrey [8].

# Lambda calculus in TeX.

5.1 Logic with TeX

5.1.1 Truth values, operators

We start by defining a couple of simple tools.

```
\def\Ignore#1{}
\def\Identity#1{#1}
\def\First#1#2{#1}
\def\Second#1#2{#2}
```

For example:

```
Taking first argument:
input  : \First {first}{second}
output : first
Taking second argument:
input  : \Second {first}{second}
output : second
```

We define truth values:

```
\let\True=\First
\let\False=\Second
```

and logical operators:

```
\def\And#1#2{#1{#2}\False}
\def\Or#1#2{#1\True{#2}}
\def\Twiddle#1#2#3{#1{#3}{#2}}
\let\Not=\Twiddle
```

Explanation: And x y is y if x is true, false is x is false. Since True and False are defined as taking the first and second component, that gives the definition of And as above. Likewise Or.

To test logical expressions, we attach TF to them before evaluting; that was \True TF will print T, and \False TF will print F.

Let us test the truth values and operators:

5.1. LOGIC WITH TeX

True takes first of TF:
```
input : \True
output : T
```
False takes second of TF:
```
input : \False
output : F
```
Not true is false:
```
input : \Not \True
output : F
```
And truth table TrueTrue:
```
input : \And \True \True
output : T
```
And truth table TrueFalse:
```
input : \And \True \False
output : F
```
And truth table FalseTrue:
```
input : \And \False \True
output : F
```
And truth table FalseFalse:
```
input : \And \False \False
output : F
```
Or truth table TrueTrue:
```
input : \Or \True \True
output : T
```
Or truth table TrueFalse:
```
input : \Or \True \False
output : T
```
Or truth table FalseTrue:
```
input : \Or \False \True
output : T
```
Or truth table FalseFalse:
```
input : \Or \False \False
output : F
```

5.1.2 Conditionals

Some more setup. We introduce conditionals
```
\def\gobblefalse\else\gobbletrue\fi#1#2{\fi#1}
\def\gobbletrue\fi#1#2{\fi#2}
\def\TeXIf#1#2{#1#2 \gobblefalse\else\gobbletrue\fi}
\def\IfIsPositive{\TeXIf{\ifnum0<}}
```
with the syntax
```
\TeXIf <test> <arg>
```
We test this:
```
Numerical test:
input : \IfIsPositive {3}
output : T
Numerical test:
input : \IfIsPositive {-2}
output : F
```

5.1.3 Lists

A list is defined as a construct with a head, which is an element, and a tail, which is another list. We will denote the empty list by `Nil`.

Victor Eijkhout

```
\let\Nil=\False
```

We implement a list as an operator with two arguments:

- If the list is not empty, the first argument is applied to the head, and the tail is evaluated;
- If the list is empty, the second argument is evaluated.

In other words

$$L\,a_1\,a_2 = \begin{cases} a_2 & \text{if } L = () \\ a_1(x)\,Y & \text{if } L = (x, Y) \end{cases}$$

In the explanation so far, we only know the empty list `Nil`. Other lists are formed by taking an element as head, and another list as tail. This operator is called `Cons`, and its result is a list. Since a list is a two argument operator, we have to make `Cons` itself a four argument operator:

```
% \Cons <head> <tail> <arg1> <arg2>
\def\Cons#1#2#3#4{#3{#1}{#2}}
```

Since `Cons#1#2` is a list, applied to `#3#4` it should expand to the second clause of the list definition, meaning it applies the first argument (`#3`) to the head (`#1`), and evaluates the tail (`#2`).

The following definitions are typical for list operations: since a list is an operator, applying an operation to a list means applying the list to some other objects.

```
\def\Error{{ERROR}}
\def\Head#1{#1\First\Error}
\def\Tail#1{#1\Second\Error}
```

Let us take some heads and tails of lists. As a convenient shorthand, a singleton is a list with an empty tail:

```
\def\Singleton#1{\Cons{#1}\Nil}
```

Head of a singleton:
```
input  : \Head {\Singleton \True }
output : T
```
Head of a tail of a 2-elt list:
```
input  : \Head {\Tail {\Cons \True {\Singleton
    \False }}}
output : F
```

We can also do arithmetic tests on list elements:

Test list content:
```
input  : \IfIsPositive {\Head {\Singleton {3}}}
output : T
```

5.1. LOGIC WITH TeX

Test list content:
```
input : \IfIsPositive {\Head {\Tail {\Cons
    {3}{\Singleton {-4}}}}}
output : F
```
Exercise 46.
Write a function `\IsNil` and test with
```
\test{Detect NIL}{\IsNil\Nil}
\test{Detect non-NIL}{\IsNil{\Singleton\Nil}}
```

5.1.3.1 A list visualization tool

If we are going to be working with lists, it will be a good idea to have a way to visualize them. The following macros print a '1' for each list element.
```
\def\Transcribe#1{#1\TranscribeHT\gobbletwo}
\def\TranscribeHT#1#2{1\Transcribe{#2}}
```

5.1.3.2 List operations

Here are some functions for manipulating lists. We want a mechanism that takes a function f, an initial argument e, and a list X, so that

$$\text{Apply} f\, e\, X \Rightarrow f\, x_1\, (f\, x_2\, (\ldots (f\, x_n\, e)\ldots))$$

```
% #1=function #2=initial arg #3=list
\def\ListApply#1#2#3{#3{\ListApplyp{#1}{#2}}{#2}}
\def\ListApplyp#1#2#3#4{#1{#3}{\ListApply{#1}{#2}{#4}}}
```
This can for instance be used to append two lists:
```
\def\Cat#1#2{\ListApply\Cons{#2}{#1}}
```
For example:
```
Cat two lists:
input : \Transcribe {\Cat {\Singleton \Nil }{\Cons
    \Nil {\Singleton \Nil }}}
output : 111
```
From now on the `\Transcribe` macro will be implicitly assumed; it is no longer displayed in the examples.

5.1.4 Numbers

We can define integers in terms of lists: zero is the empty list, and to add one to a number is to `Cons` it with an empty list as head element. In other words,

$$n + 1 \equiv (0, n).$$

This defines the 'successor' function on the integers.

```
\let\Zero\Nil
\def\AddOne#1{\Cons\Nil{#1}}
```

Examples:

> Transcribe zero:
> ```
> input  : \Zero
> output :
> ```
> Transcribe one:
> ```
> input  : \AddOne \Zero
> output : 1
> ```
> Transcribe three:
> ```
> input  : \AddOne {\AddOne {\AddOne \Zero }}
> output : 111
> ```

Writing this many \AddOnes get tiring after a while, so here is a useful macro:

```
\newtoks\dtoks\newcount\nn
\def\ndef#1#2{\nn=#2 \dtoks={\Zero}\nndef#1}
\def\nndef#1{
  \ifnum\nn=0 \edef\tmp{\def\noexpand#1{\the\dtoks}}\tmp
  \else \edef\tmp{\dtoks={\noexpand\AddOne{\the\dtoks}}}\tmp
       \advance\nn by -1 \nndef#1
  \fi}
```

which allows us to write

```
\ndef\One1 \ndef\Two2 \ndef\Three3 \ndef\Four4 \ndef\Five5
\ndef\Seven7\ndef\Six6
```

et cetera.

It is somewhat surprising that, even though the only thing we can do is compose lists, the predecessor function is just as computable as the successor:

```
\def\SubOne#1{#1\Second\Error}
```

> Predecessor of two:
> ```
> input  : \SubOne {\AddOne {\AddOne \Zero }}
> output : 1
> ```

(If we had used \Ignore instead of \Second a subtle TEXnicality would come into play: the list tail would be inserted as {#2}, rather than #2, and you would see an Unexpected } error message.)

Some simple arithmetic: we test if a number is odd or even.

```
\def\IsEven#1{#1\IsOddp\True}
```

5.1. LOGIC WITH TEX

```
\def\IsOddp#1#2{\IsOdd{#2}}
\def\IsOdd#1{#1\IsEvenp\False}
\def\IsEvenp#1#2{\IsEven{#2}}
```

Zero even?:
`input : \IsEven \Zero`
`output : T`
Zero odd?:
`input : \IsOdd \Zero`
`output : F`
Test even:
`input : \IsEven {\AddOne`
`   {\AddOne {\AddOne \Zero`
`   }}}`
`output : F`
Test odd:
`input : \IsOdd {\AddOne`
`   {\AddOne {\AddOne \Zero`
`   }}}`

`output : T`
Test even:
`input : \IsEven {\AddOne`
`   {\AddOne {\AddOne`
`   {\AddOne {\Zero }}}}}`
`output : T`
Test odd:
`input : \IsOdd {\AddOne`
`   {\AddOne {\AddOne`
`   {\AddOne {\Zero }}}}}`
`output : F`

Exercise 47. Write a test `\IsOne` that tests if a number is one.

Zero:
`input : \IsOne \Zero`
`output : F`
One:
`input : \IsOne \One`
`output : T`
Two:
`input : \IsOne \Two`
`output : F`

5.1.4.1 Arithmetic: add, multiply

Above, we introduced list concatenation with `\Cat`. This is enough to do addition. To save typing we will make macros `\Three` and such that stand for the usual string of `\AddOne` compositions:

`\let\Add=\Cat`

Adding numbers:
`input : \Add {\Three }{\Five }`
`output : 11111111`

Instead of adding two numbers we can add a whole bunch

`\def\AddTogether{\ListApply\Add\Zero}`

For example:

```
Adding a list of numbers:
input : \AddTogether {\Cons \Two {\Singleton
    \Three }}
output : 11111
Adding a list of numbers:
input : \AddTogether {\Cons \Two {\Cons \Three
    {\Singleton \Three }}}
output : 11111111
```

This is one way to do multiplication: to evaluate 3×5 we make a list of 3 copies of the number 5.

```
\def\Copies#1#2{#1{\ConsCopy{#2}}\Nil}
\def\ConsCopy#1#2#3{\Cons{#1}{\Copies{#3}{#1}}}
\def\Mult#1#2{\AddTogether{\Copies{#1}{#2}}}
```

Explanation:

- If #1 of `\Copies` is empty, then `Nil`.
- Else, `\ConsCopy` of #2 and the head and tail of #1.
- The tail is one less than the original number, so `\ConsCopy` makes that many copies, and conses the list to it.

For example:

```
Multiplication:
input : \Mult {\Three }{\Five }
output : 111111111111111
```

However, it is more elegant to define multiplication recursively.

```
\def\MultiplyBy#1#2{%
  \IsOne{#1}{#2}{\Add{#2}{\MultiplyBy{\SubOne{#1}}{#2}}}}
```

```
Multiply by one:
input : \MultiplyBy \One \Five
output : 11111
Multiply bigger:
input : \MultiplyBy \Three \Five
output : 111111111111111
```

5.1. LOGIC WITH TeX

5.1.4.2 More arithmetic: subtract, divide

The recursive definition of subtraction is

$$m - n = \begin{cases} m & \text{if } n = 0 \\ (m-1) - (n-1) & \text{otherwise} \end{cases}$$

Exercise 48. Implement a function \Sub that can subtract two numbers. Example:

```
Subtraction:
input  : \Sub \Three \Five
output : 11
```

5.1.4.3 Continuing the recursion

The same mechanism we used for defining multiplication from addition can be used to define taking powers:

```
\def\ToThePower#1#2{%
  \IsOne{#1}{#2}{%
    \MultiplyBy{#2}{\ToThePower{\SubOne{#1}}{#2}}}}
```

```
Power taking:
input  : \ToThePower {\Two }{\Three }
output : 111111111
```

5.1.4.4 Testing

Some arithmetic tests. Greater than: if

$$X = (x, X'), \quad Y = (y, Y')$$

then $Y > X$ is false if $Y \equiv 0$:

```
\def\GreaterThan#1#2{#2{\GreaterEqualp{#1}}\False}
```

Otherwise, compare X with $Y' = Y - 1$: $Y > X \Leftrightarrow Y' \geq X$; this is true if $X \equiv 0$:

```
\def\GreaterEqualp#1#2#3{\GreaterEqual{#1}{#3}}
\def\GreaterEqual#1#2{#1{\LessThanp{#2}}\True}
```

Otherwise, compare $X' = X - 1$ with $Y' = Y - 1$:

```
\def\LessThanp#1#2#3{\GreaterThan{#3}{#1}}
```

Greater (true result):
```
input  : \GreaterThan \Two
           \Five
output : T
```

Greater (false result):
```
input  : \GreaterThan \Three
           \Two
output : F
```

Greater (equal case):
```
input : \GreaterThan \Two
   \Two
output : F
```
Greater than zero:
```
input : \GreaterThan \Two
   \Zero
output : F
```
Greater than zero:
```
input : \GreaterThan \Zero
   \Two
output : T
```

Instead of just printing 'true' or 'false', we can use the test to select a number or action:

Use true result:
```
input : \GreaterThan \Two \Five \Three \One
output : 111
```
Use false result:
```
input : \GreaterThan \Three \Two \Three \One
output : 1
```

Let's check if the predicate can be used with arithmetic.

$3 < (5 - 1)$:
```
input : \GreaterThan \Three {\Sub \One \Five }
output : T
```
$3 < (5 - 4)$:
```
input : \GreaterThan \Three {\Sub \Four \Five }
output : F
```

Equality:
```
\def\Equal#1#2{#2{\Equalp{#1}}{\IsZero{#1}}}
\def\Equalp#1#2#3{#1{\Equalx{#3}}{\IsOne{#2}}}
\def\Equalx#1#2#3{\Equal{#1}{#3}}
```

Equality, true:
```
input : \Equal \Five \Five
output : T
```
Equality, true:
```
input : \Equal \Four \Four
output : T
```
Equality, false:
```
input : \Equal \Five \Four
output : F
```
Equality, false:
```
input : \Equal \Four \Five
output : F
```

$(1 + 3) \equiv 5$: false:
```
input : \Equal {\Add \One
   \Three }\Five
output : F
```
$(2 + 3) \equiv (7 - 2)$: true:
```
input : \Equal {\Add \Two
   \Three }{\Sub \Two
   \Seven }
output : T
```

5.1. LOGIC WITH TeX

Fun application:
```
\def\Mod#1#2{%
  \Equal{#1}{#2}\Zero
    {\GreaterThan{#1}{#2}%
      {\Mod{#1}{\Sub{#1}{#2}}}%
      {#2}%
    }}
```
$\mathrm{Mod}(27,4) = 3$:
input : \Mod \Four \TwentySeven
output : 111
$\mathrm{Mod}(6,3) = 0$:
input : \Mod \Three \Six
output :

With the modulo operation we can compute greatest common divisors:
```
\def\GCD#1#2{%
  \Equal{#1}{#2}%
    {#1}%
    {\GreaterThan{#1}{#2}%                  % #2>#1
      {\IsOne{#1}\One
        {\GCD{\Sub{#1}{#2}}{#1}}}%          % then take GCD(#2-#1,#1)
      {\IsOne{#2}\One
        {\GCD{\Sub{#2}{#1}}{#2}}}}}         % else GCD(#1-#2,#2)
```
GCD(27,4)=1:
input : \GCD \TwentySeven \Four
output : 1
GCD(27,3)=3:
input : \GCD \TwentySeven \Three
output : 111

and we can search for multiples:
```
\def\DividesBy#1#2{\IsZero{\Mod{#1}{#2}}}
\def\NotDividesBy#1#2{\GreaterThan\Zero{\Mod{#1}{#2}}}
\def\FirstDividesByStarting#1#2{%
  \DividesBy{#1}{#2}{#2}{\FirstDividesByFrom{#1}{#2}}}
\def\FirstDividesByFrom#1#2{\FirstDividesByStarting{#1}{\AddOne{#2}}}
```
$5|25$:
input : \DividesBy \Five \TwentyFive
output : T

5 ∤ 27:
```
input  : \DividesBy \Five \TwentySeven
output : F
```
5 ∤ 27:
```
input  : \NotDividesBy \Five \TwentySeven
output : T
```
$10 = \min\{i : i \geq 7 \wedge 5|i\}$:
```
input  : \FirstDividesByFrom \Five \Seven
output : 1111111111
```

5.1.5 Infinite lists

So far, we have dealt with lists that are finite, built up from an empty list. However, we can use infinite lists too.

```
\def\Stream#1{\Cons{#1}{\Stream{#1}}}
```
Infinite objects:
```
input  : \Head {\Tail {\Stream 3}}
output : 3
```
Infinite objects:
```
input  : \Head {\Tail {\Tail {\Tail {\Tail {\Tail
         {\Stream 3}}}}}}
output : 3
```

Even though the list is infinite, we can easily handle it in finite time, because it is never constructed further than we ask for it. This is called 'lazy evaluation'.

We can get more interesting infinite lists by applying successive powers of an operator to the list elements. Here is the definition of the integers by applying the `AddOne` operator a number of times to zero:

```
% \StreamOp <operator> <initial value>
\def\StreamOp#1#2{\Cons{#2}{\StreamOp{#1}{#1{#2}}}}
\def\Integers{\StreamOp\AddOne\Zero}
\def\PositiveIntegers{\Tail\Integers}
\def\TwoOrMore{\Tail\PositiveIntegers}
```

Again, the `Integers` object is only formed as far as we need it:

Integers:
```
input  : \Head {\Tail {\Integers }}
output : 1
```
Integers:
```
input  : \Head {\Tail {\Tail {\Tail {\Tail {\Tail
         {\Integers }}}}}}
```

5.1. LOGIC WITH TEX

```
             output : 11111
```
Let us see if we can do interesting things with lists. We want to make a list out of everything that satisfies some condition.

```
\def\ConsIf#1#2#3{#1{#2}{\Cons{#2}{#3}}{#3}}
\def\Doubles{\ListApply{\ConsIf{\DividesBy\Two}}\Nil\PositiveIntegers}
\def\AllSatisfy#1{\ListApply{\ConsIf{#1}}\Nil\PositiveIntegers}
\def\FirstSatisfy#1{\Head{\AllSatisfy{#1}}}
```
third multiple of two:
```
             input  : \Head {\Tail {\Tail \Doubles }}
             output : 111111
             old enough to drink:
             input  : \FirstSatisfy {\GreaterThan \TwentyOne }
             output : 111111111111111111111
```
We add the list in which we test as a parameter:
```
\def\AllSatisfyIn#1#2{\ListApply{\ConsIf{#1}}\Nil{#2}}
\def\FirstSatisfyIn#1#2{\Head{\AllSatisfyIn{#1}{#2}}}
```
```
             input  : \FirstSatisfyIn {\NotDividesBy
                 {\FirstSatisfyIn {\NotDividesBy \Two
                 }\TwoOrMore }} {\AllSatisfyIn {\NotDividesBy
                 \Two }\TwoOrMore }
             output : 11111
```
And now we can repeat this:
```
\def\FilteredList#1{\AllSatisfyIn{\NotDividesBy{\Head{#1}}}{\Tail{#1}}}
\def\NthPrime#1{\Head{\PrimesFromNth{#1}}}
\def\PrimesFromNth#1{\IsOne{#1}\TwoOrMore
  {\FilteredList{\PrimesFromNth{\SubOne{#1}}}}}
```
Third prime; spelled out:
```
             input  : \Head {\FilteredList {\FilteredList
                 \TwoOrMore }}
             output : 11111
             Fifth prime:
             input  : \NthPrime \Four
             output : 1111111
```
However, this code is horrendously inefficient. To get the 7th prime you can go make a cup of coffee, one or two more and you can go pick the beans yourself.

```
%\def\FilteredList#1{\AllSatisfyIn{\NotDividesBy{\Head{#1}}}{\Tail{#1}}}
\def\xFilteredList#1#2{\AllSatisfyIn{\NotDividesBy{#1}}{#2}}
\def\FilteredList#1{\xFilteredList{\Head{#1}}{\Tail{#1}}}
```

Victor Eijkhout

Fifth prime:
```
input  : \NthPrime \Five
output : 11111111111
```

Chapter 6

Character encoding

This chapter is about how to interpret the characters in an input file – no there ain't such a thing as a plain text file – and how the printed characters are encoded in a font.

Handouts and further reading for this chapter

There is very little printed material on this topic. A good introduction is `http://www.joelonsoftware.com/articles/Unicode.html`; after that, `http://www.cs.tut.fi/~jkorpela/chars.html` is a good tutorial for general issues, and `http://en.wikipedia.org/wiki/Unicode` for Unicode.

For the technical details on Unicode consult `http://www.unicode.org/`. An introduction to ISO 8859: `http://www.wordiq.com/definition/ISO_8859`.

Input file encoding.

6.1 History and context

6.1.1 One-byte character sets; Ascii

Somewhere in the depths of prehistory, people got to agree on a standard for character codes under 127, ASCII. Unlike another encoding scheme, EBCDIC, it has a few nice properties.

- All letters are consecutive, making a test 'is this a letter' easy to perform.
- Uppercase and lowercase letters are at a distance of 32.
- The first 31 codes, everything below the space character, as well as position 127, are 'unprintable', and can be used for such purposes as terminal cursor control.
- Unprintable codes are accessible through the control modifier (for this reason they are also called 'control codes'), which zeros bits 2 and 3: hit `Ctrl-[` to get `Esc`[1].

The ISO 646 standard codified 7-bit ASCII, but it left certain character positions (or 'code points') open for national variation. For instance, British usage put a pound sign (£) in the position of the dollar. The ASCII character set was originally accepted as ANSI X3.4 in 1968.

20	21	22	23	24	25	26	27	28	29	2A	2B	2C	2D	2E	2F
	!	"	#	$	%	&	'	(	)	*	+	,	-	.	/
30	31	32	33	34	35	36	37	38	39	3A	3B	3C	3D	3E	3F
0	1	2	3	4	5	6	7	8	9	:	;	<	=	>	?
40	41	42	43	44	45	46	47	48	49	4A	4B	4C	4D	4E	4F
@	A	B	C	D	E	F	G	H	I	J	K	L	M	N	O
50	51	52	53	54	55	56	57	58	59	5A	5B	5C	5D	5E	5F
P	Q	R	S	T	U	V	W	X	Y	Z	[	\	]	^	_
60	61	62	63	64	65	66	67	68	69	6A	6B	6C	6D	6E	6F
`	a	b	c	d	e	f	g	h	i	j	k	l	m	n	o
70	71	72	73	74	75	76	77	78	79	7A	7B	7C	7D	7E	
p	q	r	s	t	u	v	w	x	y	z	{	|	}	~	

6.1.2 Code pages

This left the codes with the high bit set ('extended ASCII') undefined, and different manufacturers of computer equipment came up with their own way of filling them in. These standards were called 'code pages', and IBM gave a standard numbering to

---

1. The way key presses generate characters is typically controlled in software. This mapping from keyboard scan codes to 7 or 8-bit characters is called a 'keyboard', and can be changed dynamically in most operating systems.

them. For instance, code page 437 is the MS-DOS code page with accented characters for most European languages, 862 is DOS in Israel, 737 is DOS for Greeks.

Here is cp473:

	01 ☺	02 ☻	03 ♥	04 ♦	05 ♣	06 ♠	07 •	08 ◘	09 ○	0A ◙	0B ♂	0C ♀	0D ♪	0E ♫	0F ☼
10 ►	11 ◄	12 ↕	13 ‼	14 ¶	15 §	16 ▬	17 ↨	18 ↑	19 ↓	1A →	1B ←	1C ∟	1D ↔	1E ▲	1F ▼
20	21 !	22 "	23 #	24 $	25 %	26 &	27 '	28 (	29)	2A *	2B +	2C ,	2D -	2E .	2F /
30 0	31 1	32 2	33 3	34 4	35 5	36 6	37 7	38 8	39 9	3A :	3B ;	3C <	3D =	3E >	3F ?
40 @	41 A	42 B	43 C	44 D	45 E	46 F	47 G	48 H	49 I	4A J	4B K	4C L	4D M	4E N	4F O
50 P	51 Q	52 R	53 S	54 T	55 U	56 V	57 W	58 X	59 Y	5A Z	5B [	5C \	5D]	5E ^	5F _
60 `	61 a	62 b	63 c	64 d	65 e	66 f	67 g	68 h	69 i	6A j	6B k	6C l	6D m	6E n	6F o
70 p	71 q	72 r	73 s	74 t	75 u	76 v	77 w	78 x	79 y	7A z	7B {	7C |	7D }	7E ~	
80 Ç	81 ü	82 é	83 â	84 ä	85 à	86 å	87 ç	88 ê	89 ë	8A è	8B ï	8C î	8D ì	8E Ä	8F Å
90 É	91 æ	92 Æ	93 ô	94 ö	95 ò	96 û	97 ù	98 ÿ	99 Ö	9A Ü	9B ¢	9C £	9D ¥	9E ₧	9F ƒ
A0 á	A1 í	A2 ó	A3 ú	A4 ñ	A5 Ñ	A6 ª	A7 º	A8 ¿	A9 ⌐	AA ¬	AB ½	AC ¼	AD ¡	AE «	AF »
B0 ░	B1 ▒	B2 ▓	B3 │	B4 ┤	B5 ╡	B6 ╢	B7 ╖	B8 ╕	B9 ╣	BA ║	BB ╗	BC ╝	BD ╜	BE ╛	BF ┐
C0 └	C1 ┴	C2 ┬	C3 ├	C4 ─	C5 ┼	C6 ╞	C7 ╟	C8 ╚	C9 ╔	CA ╩	CB ╦	CC ╠	CD ═	CE ╬	CF ╧
D0 ╨	D1 ╤	D2 ╥	D3 ╙	D4 ╘	D5 ╒	D6 ╓	D7 ╫	D8 ╪	D9 ┘	DA ┌	DB █	DC ▄	DD ▌	DE ▐	DF ▀
E0 α	E1 ß	E2 Γ	E3 π	E4 Σ	E5 σ	E6 µ	E7 τ	E8 Φ	E9 Θ	EA Ω	EB δ	EC ∞	ED φ	EE ε	EF ∩
F0 ≡	F1 ±	F2 ≥	F3 ≤	F4 ⌠	F5 ⌡	F6 ÷	F7 ≈	F8 °	F9 ∙	FA ·	FB √	FC ⁿ	FD ²	FE ■	FF

MacRoman:

80 Ä	81 Å	82 Ç	83 É	84 Ñ	85 Ö	86 Ü	87 á	88 à	89 â	8A ä	8B ã	8C å	8D ç	8E é	8F è
90 ê	91 ë	92 í	93 ì	94 î	95 ï	96 ñ	97 ó	98 ò	99 ô	9A ö	9B õ	9C ú	9D ù	9E û	9F ü
A0 †	A1 °	A2 ¢	A3 £	A4 §	A5 •	A6 ¶	A7 ß	A8 ®	A9 ©	AA ™	AB ´	AC ¨	AD ≠	AE Æ	AF Ø
B0 ∞	B1 ±	B2 ≤	B3 ≥	B4 ¥	B5 µ	B6 ∂	B7 ∑	B8 ∏	B9 π	BA ∫	BB ª	BC º	BD Ω	BE æ	BF ø
C0 ¿	C1 ¡	C2 ¬	C3 √	C4 ƒ	C5 ≈	C6 ∆	C7 «	C8 »	C9 …	CA	CB À	CC Ã	CD Õ	CE Œ	CF œ
D0 –	D1 —	D2 “	D3 ”	D4 ‘	D5 ’	D6 ÷	D7 ◊	D8 ÿ	D9 Ÿ	DA ⁄	DB ¤	DC ‹	DD ›	DE ﬁ	DF ﬂ
E0 ‡	E1 ·	E2 ‚	E3 „	E4 ‰	E5 Â	E6 Ê	E7 Á	E8 Ë	E9 È	EA Í	EB Î	EC Ï	ED Ì	EE Ó	EF Ô
F0 ♥	F1 Ò	F2 Ú	F3 Û	F4 Ù	F5 ı	F6 ˆ	F7 ˜	F8 ¯	F9 ˘	FA ˙	FB ˚	FC ¸	FD ˝	FE ˛	FF ˇ

and Microsoft cp1252:

80 €		82 ‚	83 ƒ	84 „	85 …	86 †	87 ‡	88 ˆ	89 ‰	8A Š	8B ‹	8C Œ		8E Ž	
	91 ‘	92 ’	93 “	94 ”	95 •	96 –	97 —	98 ˜	99 ™	9A š	9B ›	9C œ		9E ž	9F Ÿ
A0	A1 ¡	A2 ¢	A3 £	A4 ¤	A5 ¥	A6 ¦	A7 §	A8 ¨	A9 ©	AA ª	AB «	AC ¬	AD -	AE ®	AF ¯
B0 °	B1 ±	B2 ²	B3 ³	B4 ´	B5 µ	B6 ¶	B7 ·	B8 ¸	B9 ¹	BA º	BB »	BC ¼	BD ½	BE ¾	BF ¿
C0 À	C1 Á	C2 Â	C3 Ã	C4 Ä	C5 Å	C6 Æ	C7 Ç	C8 È	C9 É	CA Ê	CB Ë	CC Ì	CD Í	CE Î	CF Ï
D0 Ð	D1 Ñ	D2 Ò	D3 Ó	D4 Ô	D5 Õ	D6 Ö	D7 ×	D8 Ø	D9 Ù	DA Ú	DB Û	DC Ü	DD Ý	DE Þ	DF ß
E0 à	E1 á	E2 â	E3 ã	E4 ä	E5 å	E6 æ	E7 ç	E8 è	E9 é	EA ê	EB ë	EC ì	ED í	EE î	EF ï
F0 ð	F1 ñ	F2 ò	F3 ó	F4 ô	F5 õ	F6 ö	F7 ÷	F8 ø	F9 ù	FA ú	FB û	FC ü	FD ý	FE þ	FF ÿ

More code pages are displayed on `http://aspell.net/charsets/codepages`.

`html`. These diagrams can be generated from Unicode mapping tables, which look like

```
=20     U+0020      SPACE
=21     U+0021      EXCLAMATION MARK
=22     U+0022      QUOTATION MARK
...
=A3     U+00A3      POUND SIGN
=A4     U+20AC      EURO SIGN
=A5     U+00A5      YEN SIGN
...
```

The international variants were standardized as ISO 646-DE (German), 646-DK (Danish), et cetera. Originally, the dollar sign could still be replaced by the currency symbol, but after a 1991 revision the dollar is now the only possibility.

6.1.3 ISO 8859

The different code pages were ultimately standardized as ISO 8859, with such popular code pages as 8859-1 ('Latin 1') for western European,

8859-2 for eastern, and 8859-5 for Cyrillic.

These ISO standards explicitly left the first 32 extended positions undefined. Microsoft code page 1252 uses ISO 8859-1.

More useful information about ASCII: `http://jimprice.com/jim-asc.htm`. History of ASCII out of telegraph codes: `http://www.wps.com/projects/codes/index.html`. A history, paying attention to multilingual use: `http://tronweb.super-nova.co.jp/characcodehist.html` History as written by the father of ASCII: Bob Bemer `http://www.bobbemer.com/HISTORY.HTM`.

A good inventory of ISO 8859, Latin-1: `http://www.cs.tut.fi/~jkorpela/latin1/index.html`, with a discussion by logical grouping: `http://www.cs.tut.fi/~jkorpela/latin1/4.html`.

6.1.4 DBCS

Since certain Asian alphabets do not fit in 256 positions, a system called the 'Double Byte Character Set' was invented where some characters were stored in one, others in two bytes. This is very messy, since you can not simply write `s++` or `s--` to traverse a string. Instead you have to use functions from some library that understands these encodings. This system is now only of historical interest.

6.2 Unicode

The systems above functioned quite well as long as you stuck to one language or writing system. Poor dictionary makers. More or less simultaneously two efforts started that aimed to incorporate all the world's character sets in one standard: Unicode standard (originally 2-byte), and ISO 10646 (oringally 4-byte). Unicode then was extended, so that it has all numbers up to `10FFFF`, which is slightly over a million.

6.2.1 ISO 10646 and Unicode

Two international standards organizations, the Unicode Consortium and ISO/IEC JTC1/SC2, started designing a universal standard that was to be a superset of all existing character sets. These standards are now synchronized. Unicode has elements that are not in 10646, but they are compatible where it concerns straight character encoding.

ISO 10646 defines UCS, the 'Universal Character Set'. This is in essence a table of official names and code numbers for characters. Unicode adds to this rules for hyphenation, bi-directional writing, and more.

The full Unicode list of code points can be found, broken down by blocks, online at `http://www.fileformat.info/info/unicode/index.htm`, or downloadable at `http://www.unicode.org/charts/`.

6.2.2 BMP and earlier standards

Characters in Unicode are mostly denoted hexadecimally as U+wxyz, for instance U+0041 is 'Latin Capital Letter A'. The range U+0000–U+007F (0–127) is identical to US-ASCII (ISO 646 IRV), and U+0000–U+00FF (0–255) is identical to Latin 1 (ISO 8859-1).

The original 2-byte subset is now called 'BMP' for Basic Multilingual Plane.

From http://www.hyperdictionary.com/:

BMP (Basic Multilingual Plane) The first plane defined in Unicode/ISO 10646, designed to include all scripts in active modern use. The BMP currently includes the Latin, Greek, Cyrillic, Devangari, hiragana, katakana, and Cherokee scripts, among others, and a large body of mathematical, APL-related, and other miscellaneous characters. Most of the Han ideographs in current use are present in the BMP, but due to the large number of ideographs, many were placed in the Supplementary Ideographic Plane.

SIP (Supplementary Ideographic Plane) The third plane (plane 2) defined in Unicode/ISO 10646, designed to hold all the ideographs descended from Chinese writing (mainly found in Vietnamese, Korean, Japanese and Chinese) that aren't found in the Basic Multilingual Plane. The BMP was supposed to hold all ideographs in modern use; unfortunately, many Chinese dialects (like Cantonese and Hong Kong Chinese) were overlooked; to write these, characters from the SIP are necessary. This is one reason even non-academic software must support characters outside the BMP.

6.2.3 Unicode encodings

Unicode is basically a numbered list of characters. When they are used in a file, their numbers can be encoded in a number of ways. To name the obvious example: if only the first 128 positions are used, the long Unicode code point can be truncated to just one byte. Here are a few encodings:

UCS-2 Obsolete: this was the original 'native' two-byte encoding before Unicode was extended.

UTF-32 Little used: this is a four-byte encoding. (UTF stands for 'UCS Transformation Format'.)

UTF-16 This is the BMP.

UTF-8 A one-byte scheme; details below.

UTF-7 Another one-byte scheme, but now the high bit is always off. Certain byte values act as 'escape', so that higher values can be encoded. Like UTF-1 and SCSU, this encoding is only of historical interest.

6.2. UNICODE

There is an important practical reason for UTF-8. Encodings such as UCS-2 are wasteful of space, if only traditional ASCII is needed. Furthermore, they would break software that is expecting to walk through a file with `s++` and such. Also, they would introduce many zero bytes in a file, which would play havoc with Unix software that uses null-termination for strings. Then there would be the problem of whether two bytes are stored in low-endian or high-endian order. For this reason it was suggested to store `FE FF` or `FF FE` at the beginning of each file as the 'Unicode Byte Order Mark'. Of course this plays havoc with files such as shell scripts which expect to find `#!` at the beginning of the file.

6.2.4 UTF-8

UTF-8 is an encoding where the positions up to 127 are encoded 'as such'; higher numbers are encoded in groups of 2 to 6 bytes. (UTF-8 is standardized as RFC 3629.) In a multi-byte group, the first byte is in the range 0xC0–0xFD (192–252). The next up to 5 bytes are in the range 0x80–0xBF (128–191, bit pattern starting with `10`). Note that `8 = 1000` and `B = 1011`, so the highest two bits are always `10`, leaving six bits for encoding).

U-00000000 - U-0000007F	7 bits	0xxxxxxx		
U-00000080 - U-000007FF	$11 = 5 + 6$	110xxxxx	10xxxxxx	
U-00000800 - U-0000FFFF	$16 = 4 + 2 \times 6$	1110xxxx	10xxxxxx	10xxxxxx
U-00010000 - U-001FFFFF	$21 = 3 + 3 \times 6$	11110xxx	10xxxxxx (3 times)	
U-00200000 - U-03FFFFFF	$26 = 2 + 4 \times 6$	111110xx	10xxxxxx (4 times)	
U-04000000 - U-7FFFFFFF	$31 = 1 + 5 \times 6$	1111110x	10xxxxxx (5 times)	

All bites in a multi-byte sequence have their high bit set.

> **Exercise 49.** Show that a UTF-8 parser will not miss more than two characters if a byte becomes damaged (any number of bits arbitrarily changed).

IETF documents such as RFC 2277 require support for this encoding in internet software. Here is a good introduction to UTF-8 use in Unix: `http://www.cl.cam.ac.uk/~mgk25/unicode.html`. The history of it: `http://www.cl.cam.ac.uk/~mgk25/ucs/utf-8-history.txt`.

6.2.5 Unicode tidbits

6.2.5.1 Line breaking

See `http://www.cs.tut.fi/~jkorpela/unicode/linebr.html` and `http://www.unicode.org/reports/tr14/`

Victor Eijkhout

6.2.5.2 Bi-directional writing

Most scripts are left-to-right, but Arabic and Hebrew run right-to-left. Characters in a file are stored in 'logical order', and usually it is clear in which direction to render them, even if they are used mixed. Letters have a 'strong' directionality: unless overridden, they will be displayed in their natural direction. The first letter of a paragraph with strong direction determines the main direction of that paragraph.

أوروبا, برمجيات الحاسوب + انترنيت :

تصبح عالميا مع يونيكود

تسجّل الآن لحضور المؤتمر الدولي العاشر ليونيكود, الذي سيعقد في 10-12 آذار 1997 بمدينة ماينتس ألمانيا. وسيجمع المؤتمر بين خبراء من كافة قطاعات الصناعة على الشبكة العالمية انترنيت ويونيكود, حيث ستتم على الصعيدين الدولي والمحلي على حد سواء مناقشة سبل استخدام يونكود في النظم القائمة وفيما يخص التطبيقات الحاسوبية, الخطوط تصميم النصوص والحوسبة متعددة اللغات.

عندما يريد العالم أن يتكلّم فهو يتحدّث بلغة يونيكود.

However, when differently directional texts are embedded, some explicit help is needed. The problem arises with letters that have only weak directionality. The following is a sketch of a problematic case.

> Memory: he said "I NEED WATER!", and expired.
> Display: he said "RETAW DEEN I!", and expired.

If the exclamation mark is to be part of the Arabic quotation, then the user can select the text 'I NEED WATER!' and explicitly mark it as embedded Arabic (`<RLE>` is Right-Left Embedding; `<PDF>` Pop Directional Format), which produces the following result:

> Memory: he said "`<RLE>`I NEED WATER!`<PDF>`", and expired.
> Display: he said "!RETAW DEEN I", and expired.

A simpler method of doing this is to place a Right Directional Mark `<RLM>` after the exclamation mark. Since the exclamation mark is now not on a directional boundary, this produces the correct result.

> Memory: he said "I NEED WATER!`<RLM>`", and expired.
> Display: he said "!RETAW DEEN I", and expired.

For the full definition, see `http://www.unicode.org/reports/tr9/`.

6.2.6 Unicode and oriental languages

'Han unification' is the Unicode strategy of saving space in the oriental languages (traditional Chinese, simplified Chinese, Japanese, Korean: 'CJK') by recognizing common characters. This idea is not uncontroversial; see `http://en.wikipedia.org/wiki/Han_unification`.

6.3 More about character sets and encodings

6.3.1 Character sets

Informally, the term 'character set' (also 'character code' or 'code') used to mean something like 'a table of bytes, each with a character shape'. With only the English alphabet to deal with that is a good enough definition. These days, much more general cases are handled, mapping one octet into several characters, or several octets into one character. The definition has changed accordingly:

> A '*charset* is a method of converting a sequence of octets into a sequence of characters. This conversion may also optionally produce additional control information such as directionality indicators.

(From RFC 2978) A conversion the other way may not exist, since different octet combinations may map to the same character. Another complicating factor is the possibility of switching between character sets; for instance, ISO 2022-JP is the standard ASCII character set, but the escape sequence `ESC $ @` switches to JIS X 0208-1978.

6.3.2 From character to encoding in four easy steps

To disentangle the concepts behind encoding, we need to introduce a couple of levels:

ACR Abstract Character Repertoire: the set of characters to be encoded; for example, some alphabet or symbol set. This is an unordered set of characters, which can be fixed (the contents of ISO 8859-1), or open (the contents of Unicode).

CCS Coded Character Set: a mapping from an abstract character repertoire to a set of nonnegative integers. This is what is meant by 'encoding', 'character set definition', or 'code page'; the integer assigned to a character is its 'code point'.

There used to be a drive towards unambiguous abstract character names across repertoires and encodings, but Unicode ended this, as it provides (or aims to provide) more or less a complete list of every character on earth.

CEF Character Encoding Form: a mapping from a set of nonnegative integers that are elements of a CCS to a set of sequences of particular code units. A 'code unit' is an integer of a specific binary width, for instance 8 or 16 bits. A CEF then maps the code points of a coded character set into sequences of code point, and these sequences can be of different lengths inside one code page. For instance
- ASCII uses a single 7-bit unit
- UCS-2 uses a single 16-bit unit
- DBCS uses two 8-bit units
- UTF-8 uses one to four 8-bit units.

- UTF-16 uses a mix of one and two 16-bit code units.

CES Character Encoding Scheme: a reversible transformation from a set of sequences of code units (from one or more CEFs to a serialized sequence of bytes. In cases such as ASCII and UTF-8 this mapping is trivial. With UCS-2 there is a single 'byte order mark', after which the code units are trivially mapped to bytes. On the other hand, ISO 2022, which uses escape sequences to switch between different encodings, is a complicated CES.

Additionally, there are the concepts of

CM Character Map: a mapping from sequences of members of an abstract character repertoire to serialized sequences of bytes bridging all four levels in a single operation. These maps are what gets assigned MIBenum values by IANA; see section 6.3.3.

TES Transfer Encoding Syntax: a reversible transform of encoded data. This data may or may not contain textual data. Examples of a TES are base64, uuencode, and quoted-printable, which all transform a byte stream to avoid certain values.

6.3.3 A bootstrapping problem

In order to know how to interpret a file, you need to know what character set it uses. This problem also occurs in MIME mail encoding (section 6.3.5), which can use many character sets. Names and numbers for character sets are standardized by IANA: the Internet Assigned Names Authority (`http://www.iana.org/`). However, in what character set do you write this name down?

Fortunately, everyone agrees on (7-bit) ASCII, so that is what is used. A name can be up to 40 characters from us-ascii.

As an example, here is the iana definition of ASCII:

```
  name ANSI_X3.4-1968
reference RFC1345,KXS2
MIBenum 3
  source ECMA registry
  aliases iso-ir-6,ANSI_X3.4-1986,ISO_646.irv:1991,ASCII,ISO646-US,
       US-ASCII (preferred MIME name),us,IBM367,cp367,csASCII
```

The `MIBenum` (Management Information Base) is a number assigned by IANA[2]. The full list of character sets is at `http://www.iana.org/assignments/character-sets`, and RFC 3808 is a memo that describes the IANA Charset MIB.

---

2. Apparently these numbers derive from the Printer MIB, RFC 1759.

6.3. MORE ABOUT CHARACTER SETS AND ENCODINGS

6.3.4 Character codes in HTML

HTML can access unusual characters in several ways:

- With a decimal numerical code: `&#32;` is a space token. (HTML 4 supports hexadecimal codes.)
- With a vaguely symbolic name: `&copy;` is the copyright symbol. See `http://www.cs.tut.fi/~jkorpela/HTML3.2/latin1.html` for a list of symbolic names in Latin-1.
- The more interesting way is to use an encoding such as UTF-8 (section 6.2.3) for the file. For this it would be nice if the server could state that the file is
  `Content-type: text/html;charset=utf-8`
  but it is also all right if the file starts with
  `<META HTTP-EQUIV="Content-Type" CONTENT="text/html;charset=utf-8">`

```
Description                            Char Code         Entity name
======================================  ==== ==========  ==============
non-breaking space                             -->        -->
inverted exclamation                    ¡    &#161; --> ¡ &iexcl;   --> ¡
cent sign                               ¢    &#162; --> ¢ &cent;    --> ¢
pound sterling                          £    &#163; --> £ &pound;   --> £
general currency sign                   ¤    &#164; --> ¤ &curren;  --> ¤
yen sign                                ¥    &#165; --> ¥ &yen;     --> ¥
broken vertical bar                     ¦    &#166; --> ¦ &brvbar;  --> ¦
```

It is requirement that user agents can at least parse the `charset` parameter, which means they have to understand us-ascii.

Open this link in your browser, and additionally view the source: `http://www.unicode.org/unicode/iuc10/x-utf8.html`. How well does your software deal with it?

See also section 6.7.1.

6.3.5 Characters in email

6.3.6 FTP

FTP is a very old ARPA protocol. It knows 'binary' and 'text' mode, but the text mode is not well defined. Some ftp programs adjust line ends; others, such as `Fetch` on the Mac, actually do code page translation.

6.3.7 Character encodings in editors and programming languages

Software must be rewritten to use character encodings. Windows NT/2000/XP, including Visual Basic, uses UCS-2 as native string type. Strings are declared of type `wchar_t` instead of `char`, and the programmer uses `wcslen` instead of `strlen`, et cetera. A literal string is created as `L"Hello world"`.

6.4 Character issues in TeX / LaTeX

6.4.1 Diacritics

Original TeX is not very good at dealing with diacritics. They are implemented as things to put on top of characters, even when, as with the cedilla, they are under the letter. Furthermore, TeX can not hyphenate a word with accents, since the accent introduces a space in the word (technically: an explicit kern). Both problems were remedied to a large extent with the 'Cork font encoding', which contains most accented letters as single characters. This means that accents are correctly placed by design, and also that the word can be hyphenated, since the kern has disappeared.

These fonts with accented characters became possible when TeX version 3 came out around 1990. This introduced full 8-bit compatibility, both in the input side and in the font addressing.

6.4.2 LaTeX input file access to fonts

If an input file for LaTeX is allowed to contain all 8-bit octets, we get all the problems of compatibility that plagued regular text files. This is solved by the package `inputenc`:

`\usepackage[code]{inputenc}`

where `codes` is `applemac`, `ansinew`, or various other code pages.

This package makes all unprintable ASCII characters, plus the codes over 127, into active characters. The definitions are then dynamically set depending on the code page that is loaded.

6.4.3 LaTeX output encoding

The `inputenc` package does not solve the whole problem of producing a certain font character from certain keyboard input. It only mapped a byte value to the TeX command for producing a character. To map such commands to actual code point in a font file, the TeX and LaTeX formats contain lines such as

`\chardef\i="10`

declaring that the dotless-i is at position 16. However, this position is a convention, and other people – type manufacturers – may put it somewhere else.

This is handled by the 'font encoding' mechanism. The various people working on the LaTeX font schemes have devised a number of standard font encodings. For instance, the `OT1` encoding corresponds to the original 128-character set. The `T1` encoding is a 256-character extension thereof, which includes most accented characters for Latin alphabet languages.

A font encoding is selected with

`\usepackage[T1]{fontenc}`

A font encoding definition contains lines such as

```
\DeclareTextSymbol{\AE}{OT1}{29}
\DeclareTextSymbol{\OE}{OT1}{30}
\DeclareTextSymbol{\O}{OT1}{31}
\DeclareTextSymbol{\ae}{OT1}{26}
\DeclareTextSymbol{\i}{OT1}{16}
```

6.4.4 Virtual fonts

Exercise 50. What does an `ALT` key do?

Exercise 51. What is EBCDIC? What is the basic idea?

Exercise 52. Find the Unicode definition. Can you find an example of a character that has two functions, but is not defined as two characters? Find two characters that are defined seperately for compatibility, but that are defined equivalent.

Exercise 53. ISO 8859 has the 'non-breaking space' at position `A0`. How does TeX handle the nbsp? How do TeX, HTML, Latin-1, MS Word, et cetera handle multiple spaces? Discuss the pros and cons.

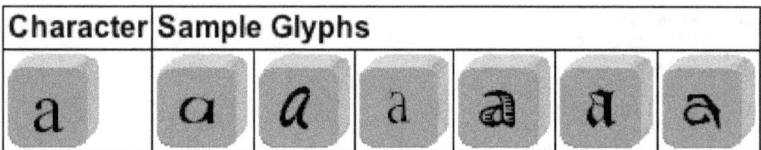

Figure 6.1: Different shapes of 'lowercase roman a'

Font encoding.

6.5 Basic terminology

Terminology of fonts and typefaces is quite confused these days. Traditionally, a typeface was a design, realized in number of fonts, that could be sorted in families, such as roman, and italic. A font would then be a style (medium weight bold italic) in a particular size.

Somewhat surprisingly, once you start throwing computers at this problem, even talking about characters becomes very subtle.

In Unicode, there are abstract characters and characters. They don't differ by much: an abstract character is a concept such as 'Latin lowercase a with accent grave', and a character is that concept plus a position in the Unicode table. The actually visible representation of a character is called a 'glyph'. According to ISO 9541, a glyph is 'A recognizable abstract graphic symbol which is independent of any specific design'.

6.5.1 The difference between glyphs and characters

Often, the mapping between character and glyph is clear: we all know what we mean by 'Uppercase Roman A'. However, there may be different glyph shapes that correspond to the same character.

An abstract character is defined as

> abstract character: a unit of information used for the organization, control, or representation of textual data.

This definition has some interesting consequences. Sometimes one glyph can correspond to more than one character, and the other way around.

For example, in Danish, the ligature 'æ' is an actual character. On the other hand, the ligature 'fl', which appears in English texts, is merely a typographical device to make

6.5. BASIC TERMINOLOGY

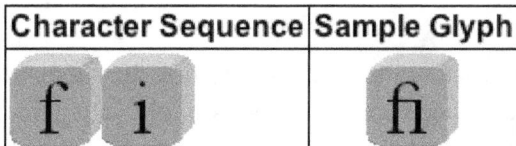

Figure 6.2: The f-i ligature

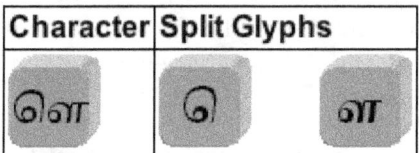

Figure 6.3: A split character in Tamil

the combination 'fl' look better, so one glyph corresponds to two characters.

The opposite case is rarer. In Tamil, a certain character is split, because it is positioned *around* other characters. It can then even happen that one of the split parts forms a ligature with adjacent characters.

A tricker question is how to handle accented letters: is 'é' one character or a combination of two? In math, is the relation in $a \neq b$ *one* symbol, or an overstrike of one over

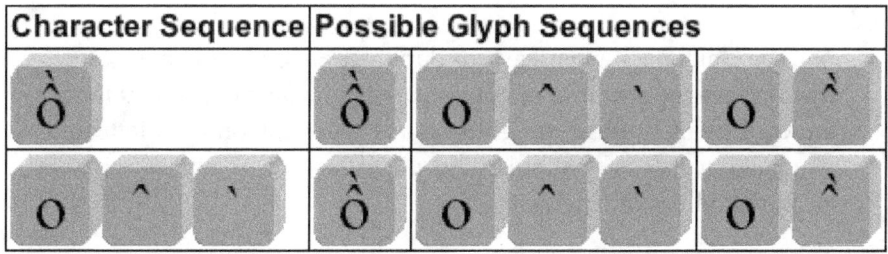

Figure 6.4: Different interpretations of an accented character glyph

another?

Another problem with ligatures is that a single glyph needs to be displayed, but two glyphs need to be stored to make searching for the string possible.

Victor Eijkhout

6.5.2 The identity of a character

Another problem in defining a character is whether two glyphs that look the same, or sometimes ever *are* the same, should be the same character. For example, uppercase Latin a, uppercase Greek α, and uppercase Cyrillic a, are all rendered 'A'. Still, in Unicode they are three distinct characters.

Similarly, in ASCII, there are no separate glyphs for minus, hyphen, and dash. In Unicode, these are three characters. Is the character 'superscript ^{2}' a separate glyph, or a typographical variant of the character 'digit 2'? The latter should be the logical solution, but for compatibility reasons with other standards it is defined as a separate glyph. There are quite a few of these 'compatibility characters.

Yet another example is the Greek letter Ω, which can be that letter, or the sign for electrical resistance in physics texts. Unicode defines them as two characters, but with identical glyphs.

A capital 'A' in Times Roman and in Helvetica are the same character, but what about italic?

All these matters are hard to settle objectively: everything is a matter of definition, or a judgement call. The official Unicode white paper on characters versus glyphs is http://www.unicode.org/reports/tr17/.

Here are some of the guidelines of the Unicode project:

- The Unicode Standard encodes characters, not glyphs.
- Characters have well-defined semantics.
- The Unicode Standard encodes plain text.
- And:
  > The Unicode Standard avoids duplicate encoding of characters by unifying them within scripts across languages; characters that are equivalent in form are given a single code. Common letters, punctuation marks, symbols, and diacritics are given one code each, regardless of language, [...]

6.5.3 Diacritics

Unicode, a bit like TeX, has two ways of dealing with diacritics. It has precomposed accented characters, but it can also compose accented characters by listing accents (yes, plural: transliterated Vietnamese regularly has two accents over a letter one relating to vowel quality, and one to tone) after the base symbol. This mechanism can also deal with languages such as Hangul (Korean) which have composite characters.

6.6 Æsthetics

6.6.1 Scaling versus Design sizes

Lots of attention is devoted to font scaling, with the implicit assumption that that is the way to get a font to display at different sizes. This is only true to an extent: a small version of a typeface was traditionally of a different design than the same typeface at larger sizes. With metal type, independent designs for the different sizes were of course the only way one could proceed at all, but with photo typesetters and computers the need went away, and with it the realization that independent designs are visually actually a Good Thing. Figure 6.5 shows the difference between a typeface set at its

Ten point type is different from magnified five-point type.

Figure 6.5: A typeface and a smaller version scaled up

'design size', and a scaled up smaller version of it.

Figure 6.6: Adobe's optical masters for a typeface

Adobe incorporated this idea in their Multiple Masters typefaces, which could interpolate between different designs. This technology seems to have been abandoned, but Adobe's Originals now have so-called 'Optical masters: four different designs of the same typeface, to be set at different sizes. Adobe labels their purposes as 'display', 'subhead', 'text', and 'caption' in decreasing design size; see figure 6.6.

Apple developed their own version of multiple design sizes in TrueType GX, released in 1994. The ideas in TrueType GX are incorporated in Apple Advanced Typography (AAT) in OS X, but there few AAT typefaces, and certainly very few non-Apple ones.

Victor Eijkhout

6.7 Font technologies

6.7.1 Unicode in fonts

It is unrealistic to expect any single font to support even a decent fraction of the Unicode character repertoire. However, TrueType and OpenType do support Unicode.

The few fonts that support (almost) the whole of Unicode are called 'pan-Unicode'. There are only a few of those. However, software these days is pretty sophisticated in gathering together symbols from disparate fonts. Some browsers do this, prompting the user for 'install on demand' of fonts if necessary.

6.7.2 Type 1 and TrueType

Type 1 ('Postscript fonts') was the outline font format developed by Adobe that was adopted by Apple in the mid 1980s. Since it was proprietary (Adobe had release the specifications for Type 3 fonts, but not Type 1), Apple and Microsoft later developed TrueType.

With Type 1 fonts, information is stored in two files, one for shape data and one for hinting and such. With TrueType, all information is in the one font file.

6.7.2.1 *Type1*

Adobe Type 1 fonts are stored in two common formats, .pfa (PostScript Font ASCII) and .pfb (PostScript Font Binary). These contain descriptions of the character shapes, with each character being generated by a small program that calls on other small programs to compute common parts of the characters in the font. In both cases, the character descriptions are encrypted.

Before such a font can be used, it must be rendered into dots in a bitmap, either by the PostScript interpreter, or by a specialized rendering engine, such as Adobe Type Manager, which is used to generate low-resolution screen fonts on Apple Macintosh and on Microsoft Windows systems.

The Type 1 outline files do not contain sufficient information for typesetting with the font, because they have only limited metric data, and nothing about kerning (position adjustments of particular adjacent characters) or ligatures (replacement of adjacent characters by a single character glyph, those for fi, ffi, fl, and ffl being most common in English typography).

This missing information is supplied in additional files, called .afm (Adobe Font Metric) files. These are ASCII files with a well-defined easy-to-parse structure. Some font vendors, such as Adobe, allow them to be freely distributed; others, such as Bitstream, consider them to be restricted by a font license which must be purchased.

6.7.2.2 TrueType ⇔ Type1 conversion

Beware! There is no such thing as a one-to-one reversible conversion. There are several problems:

The outlines are stored in different ways in both formats. In truetype, second-order Bezier curves are used, and in type 1, third-order Bezier curves are employed. One second order Bezier can be transformed into a third-order Bezier, but a third-order Bezier cannot be transformed into one, two or seventeen second-order Beziers–approximations are in order for that conversion. So, type 1 to truetype is problematic, right from the start. For truetype to type 1, there is a snake in the grass, in the form of integer grid rounding (see below).

Both formats require all control points to be integers (whole numbers), falling in a grid. Truetype uses a 2048x2048 grid, type 1 typically a 1000x1000 grid. For the truetype to type 1 direction, one could divide all grid values by two, but then what? Should 183.5 become 183 or 184? The type 1 to truetype direction is easier, at least from this point of view, as we could multiply each grid coordinate by two, so no rounding loss would be involved. However, in the truetype to type 1 direction, the rounding causes additional problems for the new control points needed for the perfect third-order Bezier outlines mentioned above.

Placing ink on paper: the formats have different rules for placing ink on paper in case of outlines that are nested or intersecting. These differences are not caught by many conversion programs. In most cases, the user should not worry about this—only rarely do we have overlapping outlines (I was forced once to have them, for other reasons).

Complexity of the outlines: truetype permits more complex outlines, with more control points. For example, I am sure you have all seen fonts made from scans of pictures of faces of people. Typically, these outlines are beyond the type 1 limit, so this restriction makes the truetype to type 1 conversion impossible for ultra complex fonts.

Encoding: truetype can work with a huge number of glyphs. There are truetype fonts for Chinese and Japanese, for example. In type 1, the number of active glyphs is limited to 256. Again, for most Latin fonts, this is a non-issue.

The remarks about grid rounding also apply to all metrics, the bounding boxes, the character widths, the character spacing, the kerning, and so forth.

Finally, there is the hinting. This is handled very differently in both formats, with truetype being more sophisticated this time. So, in truetype to type 1 conversions of professionally (hand-hinted) fonts, a loss will occur. Luckily, 99% of the truetype fonts do not make use of the fancy hinting possibilities of truetype, and so, one is often safe.

All this to tell people to steer away like the plague from format conversions. And a

Victor Eijkhout

plea to the font software community to develop one final format. My recommendation: get rid of truetype, tinker with the type 1 format (well, tinker a lot). More about that ideal format elsewhere.

6.7.2.3 Downsampling bitmaps

In principle, given adequate resolution, the screen preview quality of documents set in bitmap fonts, and set in outline fonts, should be comparable, since the outline fonts have to be rasterized dynamically anyway for use on a printer or a display screen.

Sadly, this is not the case with versions of Adobe Acrobat Reader, acroread, and Exchange, acroexch (version 5.x or earlier); they do a poor job of downsampling high-resolution bitmap fonts to low-resolution screen fonts. This is particularly inexcusable, inasmuch as the co-founder, and CEO, of Adobe Systems, is the author of one of the earliest publications on the use of gray levels for font display: [John E. Warnock, The display of characters using gray level sample arrays, Computer Graphics, 14 (3), 302–307, July, 1980.]

6.7.3 FreeType

FreeType is an Open Source implementation of TrueType. Unfortunately this runs into patent problems, since Apple has patented some of the hinting mechanism. Recently FreeType has acquired an automatic hinting engine.

6.7.4 OpenType

OpenType is a standard developed by Adobe and Microsoft. It combines bitmap, outline, and metric information in a single cross-platform file. It has Unicode support, and can use 'Optical Masters' (section 6.6.1) multiple designs. It knows about the distinction between code points and glyphs, so applications can render a character differently based on context.

6.8 Font handling in TEX and LATEX

TEX has fairly sophisticated font handling, in the sense that it knows a lot about the characters in a font. However, its handling of typefaces and relations between fonts is primitive. LATEX has a good mechanism for that.

6.8. FONT HANDLING IN TEX AND LATEX

6.8.1 TEX font handling

Font outlines can be stored in any number of ways; TEX is only concerned with the 'font metrics', which are stored in a 'tfm file'. These files contain

- Global information about the font: the \fontdimen parameters, which describe the spacing of the font, but also the x-height, and the slant-per-point, which describes the angle of italic and slanted fonts.
- Dimensions and italic corrections of the characters.
- Ligature and kerning programs.

We will look at these in slightly more detail.

6.8.1.1 Font dimensions

The tfm file specifies the natural amount of space, with stretch and shrink for a font, but also a few properties related to the size and shape of letters. For instance, it contains the x-height, which is the height of characters without ascenders and descenders. This is, for instance, used for accents: TEX assumes that accents are at the right height for characters as high as an 'x': for any others the accent is raised or lowered.

The 'slant per point' parameters is also for use in accents: it determines the horizontal offset of a character.

6.8.1.2 Character dimensions

The height, width, and depth of a character is used to determine the size of the enclosing boxes of words. A non-trivial character dimension is the 'italic correction'. A tall italic character will protrude from its bounding box (which apparently does not always bound). The italic correction can be added to a subsequent space.

'TEX has' versus 'TEX has'

6.8.1.3 Ligatures and kerning

The tfm file contains information that certain sequences of characters can be replaced by another character. The intended use of this is to replace sequences such as fi or fl by 'fi' or 'fl'.

Kerning is the horizontal spacing that can bring characters closer in certain combinations. Compare

'Von' versus 'Von'

Kerning programs are in the tfm file, not accessible to the user.

6.8.2 Font selection in LaTeX

Font selection in LaTeX (and TeX) was rather crude in the early versions. Commands such as `\bf` and `\it` switched to boldface and italic respectively, but could not be combined to give bold italic. The New Font Selection Scheme improved that situation considerably.

With NFSS, it becomes possible to make orthogonal combinations of the font family (roman, sans serif), series (medium, bold), and shape (upright, italic, small caps). A quick switch back to the main document font is `\textnormal` or `\normalfont`.

6.8.2.1 Font families

It is not necessary for a typeface to have both serifed and serifless (sans serif) shapes. Often, therefore, these shapes are taken from different, but visually compatible typefaces, for instance combining Times New Roman with Helvetica. This is the combination that results from

`\usepackage{times}`

Loading the package `lucidabr` instead, gives Lucida Bright and Lucida Sans.

The available font families are

roman using the command `\textrm` and the declaration `\rmfamily`.
sans serif using the command `\textsf` and the declaration `\sffamily`.
typewriter type using the command `\texttt` and the declaration `\ttfamily`. Typewriter type is usually a monospaced font – all characters of the same width – and is useful for writing about LaTeX or for giving code samples.

6.8.2.2 Font series: width and weight

The difference between normal and medium width, or normal and bold weight, can be indicated with font series commands:

medium width/weight using the command `\textmd` and the declaration `\mdseries`.
bold using the command `\textbf` and the declaration `\bfseries`.

6.8.2.3 Font shape

The final parameter with which to classify fonts is their shape.

upright This is the default shape, explicitly available through `\textup` or `\upshape`.
italic and slanted These are often the same; they are available through `\textit`, `\textsl`, and `\itshape`, `\slshape`.
small caps Here text is set through large and small capital letters; this shape is available through `\textsc` and `\scshape`.

Input and output encoding in LaTeX.

6.9 The `fontenc` package

Traditionally, in TeX accented characters were handled with control characters, such as in \' e. However, many keyboards – and this should be understood in a software sense – are able to generate accented characters, and other non-latin characters, directly. Typically, this uses octets with the high bit set.

As we have seen, the interpretation of these octets is not clear. In the absense of some Unicode encoding, the best we can say is that it depends on the code page that was used. This dependency could be solved by having the TeX software know, on installation, what code page the system is using. While this may be feasible for one system, if the input files are moved to a different system, they are no longer interpreted correctly. For this purpose the `inputenc` package was developed.

An input encoding can be stated at the load of the package:

```
\usepackage[cp1252]{inputenc}
```

or input encodings can be set and switched later:

```
\inputencoding{latin1}
```

With this, a (part of a) file can be written on one machine, using some code page, and still be formatted correctly on another machine, which natively has a different code page.

These code pages are all conventions for the interpretation of singly octets. The `inputenc` package also has limited support for UTF-8, which is a variable length (up to four octets) encoding of Unicode.

Projects for this chapter.

Project 6.1. What is the problem with 'Han unification'? (section 6.2.6) Discuss history, philology, politics, and whatever may be appropriate.

Project 6.2. How do characters get into a file in the first place? Discuss keyboard scan codes and such. How do modifier keys work? How can an OS switch between different keyboard layouts? What do APIs for different input methods look like?

Project 6.3. Dig into history (find the archives of `alt.folklore.computers`!) and write a history of character encoding, focusing on the pre-ascii years. Describe design decisions made in various prehistoric computer architectures. Discuss.

Chapter 7

Software engineering

In the course of writing TeX and Metafont, Knuth developed some interesting ideas about software engineering. We will put those in the context of other writings on the subject. One of the by-products of TeX is the Web system for 'literate programming'. We will take a look at that, as well as at the general idea of markup.

Handouts and further reading for this chapter

Knuth wrote a history of the TeX project in [10], reprinted in 'Literate Programming', which is on reserve in the library, *QA76.6.K644 1992*.

One of the classics of software engineering is Frederick Brooks' 'The Mythical Man-Month' [6].

For software engineering research, consult the following journals:
- Software practice and experience
- Journal of systems and software
- ACM Transactions on Software Engineering and Methodology
- IEEE Transactions on Reliability

Some of these the library has available online.

Literate programming.

7.1 The Web system

7.2 Knuth's philosophy of program development

7.2.1 The Trip and Trap tests

Software engineering. (Quotes by Knuth in this chapter taken from [10].)

7.3 Extremely brief history of TeX

Knuth wrote a first report on TeX in early 1977, and left it to graduate students Frank Liang and Michael Plass to implement it over the summer. Starting from their prototype, he then spent the rest of 1977 and early 1978 implementing TeX and producing fonts with the first version of METAFONT.

TeX was used by Knuth himself in mid 1978 to typeset volume 2 of The Art of Computer Programming; it was in general use by August of 1978. By early 1979, Knuth had written a system called Doc that was the precursor of WEB, and that produced both documentation and a portable Pascal version of the source; the original program was written in Sail.

In 1980 Knuth decided to rewrite TeX and METAFONT. He started on this in 1981, and finished, including producing the five volumes of *Computer and Typesetting*, in 1985.

7.4 TeX's development

7.4.1 Knuth's ideas

Inspecting the work of his students, Knuth found that they had had to make many design decisions, despite his earlier conviction to have produced 'a reasonably complete specification of a language for typesetting'.

> The designer of a new kind of system must participate fully in the implementation.

Debugging happened in about 18 days in March 1978. Knuth contrasts that with 41 days for writing the program, making debugging about 30% of the total time, as opposed to 70% in his earlier experience. The whole code at that time was under 5000 statements. The rewritten TeX82 runs to about 14 000 statements, in 1400 modules of WEB.

He considered this his first non-trivial program written using the structured programming methodology of Dijkstra, Hoare, Dahl, and others. Because of the confidence this gave him in the correctness of the program, he did not test TeX until both the whole program and the fonts were in place. 'I did not have to prepare dummy versions of non-existent modules while testing modules that were already written'.

By mid 1979, Knuth was using TeX, and was improving TeX 'at a regular rate of about one enhancement for every six pages typed'.

Victor Eijkhout

> Thus, the initial testing of a program should be done by the designer/implementor.

Triggered by a challenge of John McCarthy, Knuth wrote a manual, which forced him to think about TeX as a whole, and which led to further improvements in the system.

> The designer should also write the first user manual.

'If I had not participated fully in all these activities, literally hundreds of improvements would never have been made, because I would never have thought of them or perceived why they were important.'

Knuth remarks that testing a compiler by using it on a large, real, input typically leaves many statements and cases unexecuted. He therefore proposes the 'torture test' approach. This consists of writing input that is as far-fetched as possible, so that it will explore many subtle interactions between parts of the compiler. He claims to have spent 200 hours writing and maintaining the 'trip test'; there is a similar 'trap test' for METAFONT.

7.4.2 Context

Software engineering is not an exact science. Therefore, some of Knuth's ideas can be fit in accepted practices, others are counter. In this section we will mention some schools of thought in software engineering, and see how Knuth's development of TeX fits in it.

7.4.2.1 Team work

The upshot of the development of TeX seems to be that software development is a one-man affair. However, in industry, programming teams exist. Is the distinction between TeX and commercial products then that between academic and real-world?

Knuth's ideas are actually not that unusual. Programming productivity is not simply expressible as the product of people and time, witness the book 'The Mythical man-Month'. However, some software projects are too big, even for one *really* clever designer / programmer / tester / manual writer.

Dividing programming work is tricky, because of the interdependence of the parts. The further you divide, the harder coordination becomes, and the greater the danger of conflicts.

Harlan Mills proposed that software should be written by groups, where each group works like a surgical team: one chief surgeon who does all the real work, with a team to assist in the more mundane tasks. Specifically:

7.4. TEX'S DEVELOPMENT 227

- The Chief Programmer designs the software, codes it, tests, it, and writes the documentation.
- The Co-Pilot is the Chief Programmer's alter ego. He knows all the code but writes none of it. He thinks about the design and discusses it with the Chief Programmer, and is therefore insurance against disaster.
- The Administrator takes care of the mundane aspects of a programming project. This can be a part-time position, shared between teams.
- The Editor oversees production of documentation.
- Two Secretaries, one each for the Administrator and Editor.
- The Program Clerk is responsible for keeping records of all code and the test runs with their inputs. This post is also necessary because all coding and testing will be matter of public record.
- The Toolsmith maintains the utilities used by the other team members.
- The Tester writes the test cases.
- The Language Lawyer investigates different constructs that can realize the Chief Programmer's algorithms.

With such teams of 10 people, coordination problems are divided by 10. For the overall design there will be a system architect, or a small number of such people.

Recently, a development methodology name 'Extreme Programming' has become popular. One aspect of this is pair programming: two programmers share one screen, one keyboard. The advantage of this is that all code is immediately reviewed and discussed.

7.4.2.2 Top-down and bottom-up

Knuth clearly favours the top-down approach that was proposed by Nicklaus Wirth in 'Program Development by Stepwise Refinement' [20], and by Harlan Mills, who pioneered it at IBM. The advantage of top-down programming is that the design of the system is set from the beginning. The disadvantage is that it is hard to change the design, and testing that shows inadequacies can only start relatively late in the development process.

Bottom-up programming starts from implementing the basic blocks of a code. The advantage is that they can immediately be tested; the disadvantage is that the design is in danger of becoming more ad hoc.

An interesting form of bottom-up programming is 'test-driven development'. Here, first a test is written for a unit (a 'unit test'), then the code. At all times, all tests need to be passed. Rewriting code, usually to simplify it, with preservation of functionality as defined by the tests, is known as 'refactoring'.

Victor Eijkhout

7.4.2.3 Program correctness

The Trip test is an example of 'regression testing': after every change to the code, a batch of tests is run to make sure that previous bugs do not reappear. This idea dates back to Brooks; it is an essential part of Extreme Programming.

However, the Trip test only does regression testing of the whole code. TDD uses both Unit tests and Integration tests. A unit is a specific piece of code that can easily be tested since it has a clear interface. In testing a unit, the code structure can be used to design the tests. Integration testing is usually done as Black Box testing: only the functionality of an assemblage of units is known and tested, rather than the internal structure. One way of doing integration testing is by 'equivalence partitioning': the input space is divided into classes such that within each classes the input are equivalent in their behaviour. Generating these classes, however, is heuristic, and it is possible to overlook cases.

On the opposite side of the testing spectrum is program proving. However, as Knuth wrote in a memo to Peter van Emde Boas: 'Beware of bugs in the above code; I have only proved it correct, not tried it.'

Markup.

7.5 History

The idea of markup has been invented several times. The ideas can be traced by to William Tunnicliffe, chairman of the Graphic Communications Association (GCA) Composition Committee, who presented a talk on the separation of information content of documents from their format in 1967. He called this 'generic coding'. Simultaneously, a New York book designer named Stanley Rice was publishing articles about "Standardized Editorial Structures", parameterized style macros based on the structural elements of publications.

7.5.1 Development of markup systems

Probably the first software incorporating these ideas comes out of IBM. Charles Goldfarb recounts (http://www.sgmlsource.com/history/roots.htm) how in 1969 he invented GML with Ed Mosher and Ray Lorie. They were tackling the problem of having a document storage system, an editor, and a document printing system talk to each other, and found that each was using different 'procedural markup' for its own purposes. Gradually the idea grew to use markup for a logical description of the document. The project was called 'Integrated Text Processing', and the first prototype 'Integrated Textual Information Management Experiment': InTIME.

GML was officially published in 1973, and by 1980 an extension, SGML, was under development. This was published in 1986 as ISO 8879. Actually, SGML is a standard for defining markup languages, rather than a language itself. Markup languages are defined in SGML through 'Document Type Definitions' (DTDs).

The most famous application of SGML is HTML. However, HTML quickly began violating the separation of function and presentation that was the core idea of markup languages. A renewed attempt was made to introduce a system for markup languages that truly defined content, not form, and this led to the 'eXtensible Markup Language'. XHTML is a realization of HTML as an XML 'schema'. While SGML made some attempts at readability (and saving keystrokes for poor overworked typists), XML is aimed primarily at being generated and understood by software, not by humans.

Another well-known application of SGML is 'DocBook'. However, this has also been defined as an XML DTD[1], and this seems to be the current definition. DocBook is

---

1. XML has both DTDs, which are SGML-like, and Schemas, which themselves XML. Schemas are the more powerful mechanism, but also newer, so there are established DTDs that may not be redefined as Schemas. Furthermore, Schemas are more complicated to transmit and parse.

a good illustration of the separation of content and presentation: there are XSL style sheets that render DocBook files as Pdf, Rtf, HTML, or man pages.

7.5.2 Typesetting with markup

In the early 1970s, nroff/troff was written at Bell Labs, at first in PDP assembler and targetting a specific photo typesetter for producing Unix documentation. Later it was recoded in C, with device independent output. Various tasks such as tables and equations were hard in nroff/troff, so preprocessors existed: eqn for formulas, tbl for tables, and refer for bibliographies.

Brian Reid's thesis of 1980 descibed a markup system called Scribe. Scribe source files can be compiled to several target languages. For instance, recent versions Scribe can compile to LaTeX, HTML, or man pages.

Projects for this chapter.

Project 7.1. Do a literature study of code/documentation development. Here are some places to start:
   POD Plain Old Documentation; used for Perl. http://www.perl.com/pub/a/tchrist/litprog.html
   JavaDoc http://java.sun.com/j2se/javadoc/
   Doxygen http://www.stack.nl/~dimitri/doxygen/
   Fitnesse http://fitnesse.org/
   Leo http://webpages.charter.net/edreamleo/front.html
   What schools of thought are there about developing medium size codes such as TeX? How does Knuth's philosophy relate to the others?

Project 7.2. Compare the TeX "way" to MS Word, PageMaker, FrameMaker, Lout, Griff, previewLaTeX.

Project 7.3. TeX has been criticized for its arcane programming language. Would a more traditional programming language work for the purpose of producing text output? Compare TeX to other systems, in particular lout, http://www.pytex.org/, ant http://www-mgi.informatik.rwth-aachen.de/~blume/Download.html and write an essay on the possible approaches. Design a system of your own.

Project 7.4. TeX and HTML were designed primarily with output in mind. Later systems (XML, DocBook) were designed so that output would be possible, but to formalize the structure of a document better. However, XML is impossible to write by hand. What would be a way out? Give your thoughts about a better markup system, conversion between one tool and another, et cetera.

Project 7.5. Several improvements on TeX and LaTeX have been developed or are under development. Investigate NTS, LaTeX3, Context, Lollipop TeX describe their methodologies, and evaluate relative merits.

Project 7.6. Knuth has pretty liberal ideas about publishing software; somewhat against the spirit of the times. Report on software patents, the difference between patents and copyright, the state of affairs in the world. Read http://swpat.ffii.org/gasnu/knuth/index.en.html

Project 7.7. Knuth devised the 'torture test' approach to program correctness. Report on various schools of thought on this topic. Where does Knuth's approach stand?

Victor Eijkhout

Bibliography

[1] Richard E. Bellman and Stuart E. Dreyfus. *Applied Dynamic Programming*. Princeton University Press, 1962.

[2] Carl de Boor. *A Practical Guide to Splines, Revised Edition*. Springer-Verlag, New York, Berlin, Heidelberg, 2001.

[3] V. Eijkhout. An indentation scheme. *TUGboat*, 11:613–616.

[4] V. Eijkhout. A paragraph skip scheme. *TUGboat*, 11:616–619.

[5] V. Eijkhout and A. Lenstra. The document style designer as a separate entity. *TUGboat*, 12:31–34, 1991.

[6] jr Frederick P. Brooks. *The Mythical Man-Month, essays on software engineering*. Addison-Wesley, 1995. Aniversary edition; originally published in 1975.

[7] Michael R. Garey and David S. Johnson. *Computers and Intractibility, a guide to the theory of NP-completeness*. W.H. Freeman and company, San Francisco, 1979.

[8] A. Jeffrey. Lists in TeX's mouth. *TUGboat*, 11:237–245, 1990.

[9] D.E. Knuth. *Digital Typography*.

[10] D.E. Knuth. The errors of TeX. *Software Practice and Experience*, 19:607–681.

[11] D.E. Knuth. *TeX: the Program*. Addison-Wesley, 1986.

[12] D.E. Knuth. *The TeX book*. Addison-Wesley, reprinted with corrections 1989.

[13] D.E. Knuth and M.F. Plass. Breaking paragraphs into lines. *Software practice and experience*, 11:1119–1184, 1981.

[14] Donald E. Knuth. *The Art of Computer Programming, Volume 3, Sorting and Searching*. Addison Wesley Longman, 1998. Second edition.

[15] Helmut Kopka and Patrick W. Daly. *A Guide to LaTeX*. Addison-Wesley, first published 1992.

[16] L. Lamport. *LaTeX, a Document Preparation System*. Addison-Wesley, 1986.

[17] Frank Mittelbach, Michel Goossens, Johannes Braams, David Carlisle, and Chris Rowley. *The LaTeX Companion, 2nd edition*. Addison-Wesley, 2004.

[18] Michael F. Plass. *Optimal Pagination Techniques for Automatic Typesetting Systems*. PhD thesis, 1981. also Xerox technical report ISL-81-1.

[19] Richard Rubinstein. *Digital Typography*. Addison-Wesley, 1988.

[20] Niklaus Wirth. Program development by stepwise refinement. *Comm. ACM*, 14:221–227, 1971.

www.ingramcontent.com/pod-product-compliance
Lightning Source LLC
Chambersburg PA
CBHW080908170526
45158CB00008B/2034